HOMES & GARDENS

THE *Complete Curtain* BOOK

HOMES & GARDENS

THE *Complete Curtain* BOOK

A Comprehensive Guide to Styles and Projects, Techniques and Fabrics

Isabella Forbes

conran
OCTOPUS

For William and Celia

First published in 1993 by Conran Octopus Limited
a part of Octopus Publishing Group
2–4 Heron Quays
London E14 4JP
www.conran-octopus.co.uk

This paperback edition published in 2000

The measurements in this book are approximate. The conversion of measurements from metric to Imperial are approximate.

The publishers have made every effort to ensure that all instructions given in this book are accurate, but they cannot accept liability for any resulting loss or damage, whether direct or consequential and howsoever arising.

Art editor: Ruth Prentice
Design Assistant: Gail Jones
Picture Researcher: Jessica Walton
In-house editor: Denny Hemming
Copy editor: Sarah Widdicombe
Editorial assistant: Jane Chapman
Production: Jill Macey

Illustrator: Cherrill Paris

British Library Cataloguing-in-Publication Data
A catalogue record for this book is available from the British Library

ISBN 1-84091-060-7

DTP Ruth Prentice
Printed in China

First steps

Inspiration

Fabrics

Contents

Projects

Fitting

introduction

CURTAIN-MAKING IS A SKILL THAT ONCE ACQUIRED GIVES LASTING PLEASURE. And many are now discovering that to produce a simple, elegant curtain need take no more than a little deftness and a mastery of basic techniques. With perseverance, the amateur can often aspire to match the handiwork of the professional. Many effects are easy to achieve, others intricate and testing. This book aims to provide a comprehensive guide. It takes the reader through the entire process of curtain-making from inspiration to the final fitting. It sets out all the options from the humble roller blind to elaborate confections of swags and tails, explaining how each is selected, measured, made and fitted.

The opening section, First Steps, gives practical tips on what is most appropriate to the different styles of window, and looks at how particular circumstances may determine the reader's choice of treatment. Does a period home, for example, dictate a particular style and how can curtains best be used to combat draughts? In the inspirational section that follows, the book looks at how others have dealt with particular rooms, offering ideas for the reader to borrow or adapt. A third section provides an illustrated inventory of fabrics with advice on how each is best displayed. Then comes the strictly practical: precisely how to make and fit 35 different permutations of curtain, pelmet, blind and trimmings. A breakdown of the techniques used in measuring, hanging and fitting comes in section five, accompanied by extensive diagrams to illustrate the main sewing techniques used. Advice on the care and maintenance of curtains and blinds follows. The book closes with an appendix of sources listing suppliers and craftsmen, books and magazines, houses or museums where the interested reader can find useful information or seek inspiration.

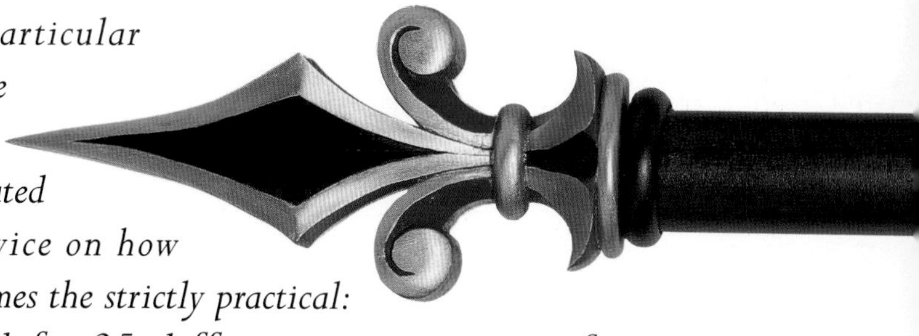

Time spent in preparation is never wasted. To start with the right practical and stylistic considerations is to avoid costly mistakes and make certain of a successful outcome every time

first steps

It is important to set about a project in the right spirit and armed with the knowledge of what's really practical. For example, will a style date quickly, will a treatment insulate the room or mask too much of the window? Will too much or too little light penetrate the curtain or blind? Does the design accord with the period of the house or the rest of the decoration? What are suitable combinations of colour and pattern, fabric and trimming? Will certain colours and fabrics fade in the sunlight? Quite as important are the different window shapes, each of which suggests a number of different solutions – sash, dormer or picture, bow, bay or skylight; when to use a pelmet, a lambrequin or a blind? Familiarity with all the appropriate options leads to treatments that are both imaginative and efficient. For a happy outcome such considerations must be made before the first selvedge is snipped or the first needle threaded.

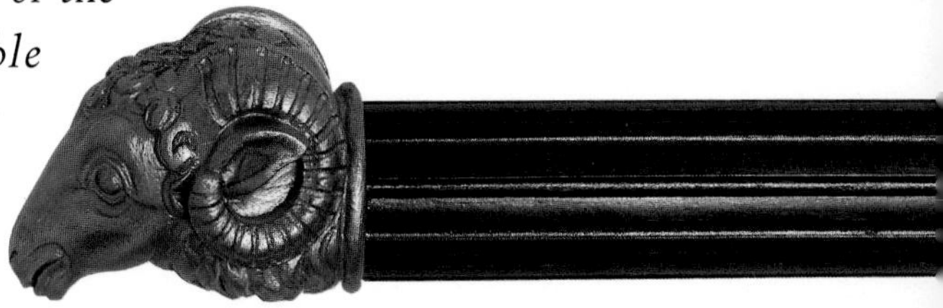

Curtain schemes should be sympathetic to their surroundings in general and window shapes in particular. Here, the formality of swags and tails is altogether appropriate for an elegant Regency terrace.

Practical Considerations

A French window, opening inwards, needs curtains that will not obstruct. Here a double solution is found: for decoration the area around the window is swathed in a length of cloth – making use of a convenient pipe that runs along the top of the opening. In contrast to the busy floral drapes a pair of plain lace curtains is gathered and fixed to the window itself, wrapped around the 'curtains' in a form of tieback to open and close in tandem with the window. (RIGHT)

Time spent in contemplation is never wasted when planning new decoration schemes. Most people have to live with their curtains or blinds for years ahead. A few basic guidelines will ensure that the best choices are made.

STYLE AND FASHION

Style is a principal consideration, achieved by a subtle balance between fashion, period, personal taste and practicalities.

To a greater or lesser extent we are all the victims of fashion and a lack of funds to realise each passing craze is, in the long run, a boon. The pendulum of fashion is never still. All styles will eventually date and, in time, will find their way into the fashion dustbin. Your own preferences will last longer.

PERIOD

Decorative style and architectural period are inextricably linked whether decorating a country cottage or a Georgian terrace. It is dangerous to pronounce on the wisdom of mixing periods – this must always be a matter of judgement. The lover of Victoriana, living in a red-brick Victorian terrace, might swag the windows in heavy, velvet drapes. But others might strip away the dark wallpaper and plush, paint the walls in pale shades of honey and cream and dress the windows in the simplest calico or muslin. Equally, a judicious use of grandiose effects can turn a featureless modern flat into a palace.

To make a success of any arrangement requires panache and consistency: swags and tails hang uncomfortably at cottage windows and frilly chintzes are inappropriate among streamlined modern furniture.

ROOMS

Is the room to be curtained a day or evening room? Does it matter if sunlight is excluded during the day – or is it more important to achieve a grand effect at night? Think carefully about the special characteristics of each room and its use before making any decision.

Sitting rooms, used during the day, particularly east- or north-facing, can ill afford any loss of light from deep drapes at the window. By contrast, heavy curtains in dark fabrics will come into their own in a dining room or formal drawing room, used mainly at night.

Consider, too, the problem of heat loss. A draught is often more noticeable when sitting still and interlining is therefore particularly valuable in a living or dining room.

A bedroom should be cosy at night and look fresh on waking in the morning.

Bathrooms require a treatment that is unaffected by steam, can be removed for cleaning and will draw out of the way of splashes.

Kitchens, too, need treatments that are easily taken down for cleaning and will not retain cooking smells. Steam from saucepans and kettles should discourage the use of interlining or buckram.

LIGHT

Before starting on any project consider how much light will be excluded. Mock up the scheme in paper or hang sheets at the window. Only then reach a decision.

HEAT

Curtains can play a vital part in keeping a room warm or cool according to the season. Interlined curtains retain heat and exclude draughts.

PRIVACY AND OUTLOOK

Nets are not the only means of blocking the public's gaze – curtains and blinds in translucent fabrics are an alternative. Deeply draped curtains, perhaps on a fixed heading, will leave only a small part of the window exposed. Consider, too, a window box filled with geraniums.

COLOUR

Although colour is a highly subjective and complex issue, some basic principles should be observed.

A cold, north- or east-facing room should be treated kindly with warm, muted colours and soft textures. West- or south-facing rooms can bear the colder blues and greys. All but the most confident should keep colour schemes simple and pale, starting with two basic colours – for example, cream and white, blue and yellow, pink and green. Follow a consistent approach without violent changes of mood from one room to another. Vivid colours should be treated with circumspection.

Golden rules when choosing fabrics:

1. Never buy on the basis of a tiny sample; borrow or buy a large piece and look at it in situ.
2. Inspect the fabric in natural light.
3. Never think of the window in isolation but as part of the decorative scheme.

FADING

At a sunny window avoid fabrics that tend to fade or rot. Silks, bright colours and coloured linings are vulnerable.

CLEANING AND MAINTENANCE

Expert cleaning is a very expensive business. If your curtains need frequent cleaning, avoid elaborate treatments and pale fabrics.

Shapes and Sizes

Elegantly draped curtains with the most formal of swags and tails adorn a classic bay window. On this large scale such a treatment is well adapted – the deep swags lend warmth and grandeur, each one balanced by its own set of curtains. An extra set of curtains has been made to cover the wall beyond the windows, lending greater emphasis to the space. What can be a cold expanse of glass has been turned into a haven of comfort in which to sit and read by the light of a graceful column-lamp. (RIGHT)

BAY WINDOWS

A bay window can be the vehicle for elaborate treatments, usually with floor-length curtains.

Curtains

A curtain track must be bent around the window. For the best results a corded track should be measured, bent and fitted professionally. There are DIY bendable tracks available, but these can cause problems as the curtains run unwillingly around the angled corners.

It is possible to screw the track to the window's architrave but it is then visible and can be unsightly. For a more satisfactory solution, suspend it from a pelmet board. The track can then be hidden by a pelmet, valance or covered fascia.

There are two ways of treating the three panels of a bay window – a pair of curtains can be hung at each section and draped back with tiebacks (see illustration) or one pair of wide curtains can be drawn back to either side, leaving the window free.

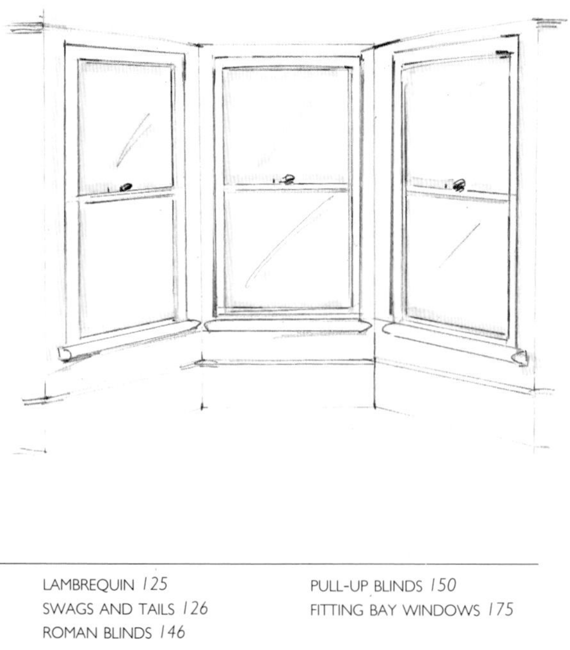

DORMER WINDOWS 27
DOOR CURTAIN 33
INTERLINED CURTAINS 94
LAMBREQUIN 125
SWAGS AND TAILS 126
ROMAN BLINDS 146
PULL-UP BLINDS 150
FITTING BAY WINDOWS 175

Blinds

Roman or pull-up blinds work well on bay windows. The fittings are much simpler than those for curtains, radiators or window seats will pose no problems and cording can be carried across the top of the window, to be operated by a single cord.

Roman blinds are economical with fabric. They can be painted or stencilled, and any fabric design is shown to best effect.

Pull-up blinds can be excellent vehicles for trimmings – cording, rosettes or bows, for example.

BOW WINDOWS

A continuous curve requires a curtain track to be bent and pelmet board cut to fit the shape. Often an inexpensive plastic DIY track is bent to the curve and fixed to the architrave, remaining visible. This will save money but does little to enhance a pair of curtains. A better solution is to use either professional fitters or the furnishings department of a large department store to measure, bend and fit a tailored track and pelmet board. Like the bay window, the board can carry a pelmet, valance, or a band of covered buckram.

The scale of a bow window suggests the use of floor-length curtains. Blinds are usually inadvisable as the curve of the window is not well adapted to the flat fixing needed.

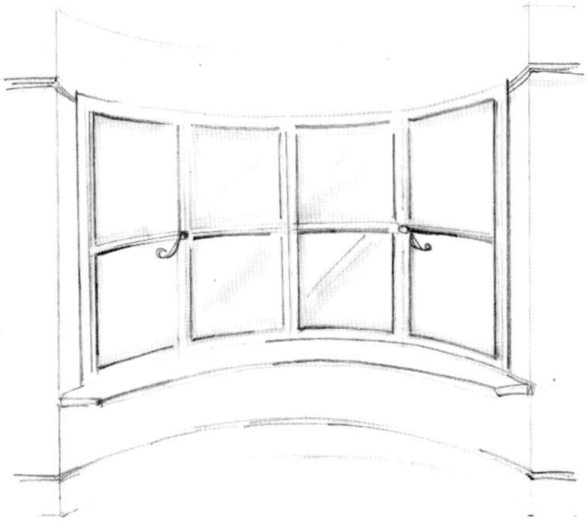

SKYLIGHT/VELUX

Set at an angle, curtains or blinds for skylights or Velux windows must be specially adapted to allow for the slope. Often the window tilts as it opens and should not be obstructed.

A pole with rings can be fitted above the window using rod sockets. The base of short curtains can then be gathered onto another pole fitted below the window. Long curtains can be pinned back to the wall behind a similarly positioned pole or rod.

It is often sensible to order special blinds from the window manufacturers – these are efficient, if lacking decorative scope.

For functional purposes a roller blind is most appropriate. When pulled down, it can be held against the wall by cup hooks inserted below the window ledge.

DORMER WINDOWS

Dormer windows can present problems, having little surrounding space to accommodate curtains or blinds. Being small windows, set into attic roofs, any loss of light is particularly serious.

One solution is to gather curtains onto a hinged pole that swings back against the reveal. Alternatively, the outer edge of curtains hung outside the reveal can be cut at an angle and pinned back against the wall using battens screwed into the sloping ceiling. The edge of the curtain is attached to the side edge of the batten using touch-and-close fastening or tacks.

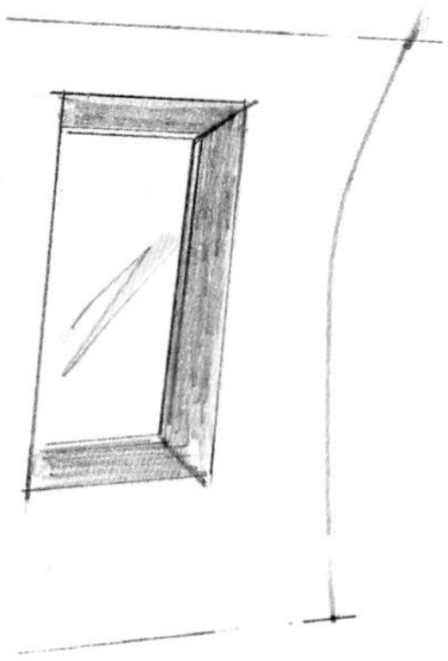

Skylight/Velux

Dormer

In a deeply recessed window, without the need for curtains, a tiny lace valance adds a graceful note to the rough cast walls of an ancient dwelling. From time immemorial little pieces of handmade lace have adorned just such a nook or cranny. (RIGHT)

If there is no need to exclude light, a filmy valance of lace or cotton will decorate the window and soften the outline without interfering with the sunlight.

A lambrequin provides decorative scope and makes a small window more important. It can either be used alone or with a roller blind.

If there is any space above the window, a roller, or even Roman, blind can be fitted.

SMALL WINDOWS

Two approaches to small windows:

1. Small-scale: for a solution that is in scale with the window, achieving a 'cottagey' feel, try sill-length, gathered curtains or a simple lace valance.

Use blinds inside the reveal if they can stack, or roll, back above the window. Blinds hung outside the reveal are more flexible but they can look strangely detached if the window is deeply recessed.

2. Large-scale: try to disguise the modest nature of the window by surrounding it with a pelmet and full-length curtains. In this way the window can be made to appear higher and wider, deceiving the onlooker. Care should be taken, however, to avoid excessive contrast between window and curtain treatment.

Wide or voluminous blinds may make the window appear large when lowered but, in their raised position, the window is revealed as out of scale.

What was once a modest cottage window is transformed into a major decorative focus with the use of a gilded pelmet and full-length curtains. The pelmet has been raised to mask as little light as possible and the curtains draw well back to either side for the same reason. Good judgement is needed to juxtapose such a grand treatment with a rustic setting.

Two contrasting solutions to the same shape of window. In the first the clean lines of tall, arched windows are complemented by black curtains pinned back to reveal their white linings. The starkness of the design is in keeping with the room's bold, modern feel – the black tab headings cut across the arches, which remain as architectural features. (RIGHT) *In the second a pair of pull-up blinds, cut in the conventional way to follow the window's curved top, use the yielding texture of gathered white muslin to soften, without masking, the garden view beyond.* (BELOW RIGHT)

ARCHED WINDOWS

The usual approach is to use fixed-headed curtains, cut to follow the line of the arch, and either tied back or operated by Italian stringing. The curtains hang from screw eyes inserted around the curved architrave.

A variation on this treatment is to use pull-up blinds cut to the shape of the window (see illustration). They will mask light and will not pull up beyond the beginning of the arch's curve.

For curtains which pull back clear of the window, use a pole, either above the window or

cutting across below the semi-circular top. Blinds, too, can be hung from a straight fixing but will also cause the arch to be lost or the window to be chopped into two.

TALL WINDOWS

A tall and narrow window will look gaunt without a little visual trickery. A pelmet or valance, combined with full-length curtains which pull well back to either side of the window, will make such a window appear wider.

Similarly, a pair of curtains with a fixed heading will drape back and frame the glazed section while extending well to either side and lending apparent substance to the window. To avoid revealing bare wall, drape the leading edges over tieback arms to either side of the reveal.

A charming use of drawn-thread work serves a practical purpose in diffusing the light falling onto a dressing table while visually breaking up the tall lines of a leaded window. (ABOVE LEFT) Contrastingly, short curtains inside the window reveal and vertically pleated blinds serve to emphasize the tallness and narrowness of the differing locations. (LEFT AND ABOVE)

A pair of checked curtains, hanging from a wooden pole, satisfy all the criteria for such a setting. The fresh cotton has just the right feel for a light and airy room, the lack of valance allows maximum daylight to penetrate and the curtains pull well back to avoid obstructing passage to the small garden beyond. Heavy interlining keeps out the heat of summer and the cold draughts of winter.

FRENCH DOORS

Some French doors open inwards and need a treatment that will not cause an obstruction. This calls for one of three possible solutions:

1. Curtains that pull back to either side, probably hung from a pole.
2. Curtains slotted onto one or two rods that are fixed to the glazed part of the doors.
3. Roller blinds, fixed over the glazed section of the doors. Roman or pull-up blinds, even if stacked above the door, will tend to get in the way, and are thus less efficient.

SASH WINDOWS

Sash windows are the best proportioned and most graceful of their kind and are correspondingly receptive to all forms of curtaining. The decorative moulding of the architrave sometimes make them objects of beauty in themselves, often served more than adequately by a set of contemporary shutters.

A sash window can use a pelmet, valance or blind either inside or outside the reveal. Curtains should be floor-length whenever possible with pelmets or valances in proportion.

Inspired by a multitude of Scandinavian sources, heart-shaped metal arms hold in place a simple swag of black-and-white cotton, lined in white. For a window without the practical need for curtains or blinds, such a solution lends interest and a softening touch – unostentatiously echoing the curves of the candelabra and the round wicker baskets that adorn the walls and ceiling of a country kitchen.

PICTURE WINDOWS

Often picture windows are installed to open up a pleasant view that should not then be blocked with curtaining. By night, however, the view turns to one of oppressive darkness which calls for some form of covering. The third consideration is one of traffic – the 'window' is actually a door, through which people must pass without obstruction and often there is no space to the side for a curtain to be drawn back.

The modern style of many picture windows – composed as they are of large sheets of glass with little surrounding decoration – sits unhappily with all but the sleekest curtains or blinds.

A hard upholstered pelmet, with a shaped lower edge and accompanied by a curtain, is one option. However, pelmets seem to call for symmetry and may look unbalanced without a pair of curtains beneath.

Perhaps more successfully, a single curtain – hung from a pole or from a covered board and fascia – can stack back to one side of the window, away from the opening side, during the day and can be drawn across at night.

Avoid pretty floral chintzes, ruffles or gathers – the contrast of styles may jar.

Roman blinds are often ideal in this context when there is room above the window in which to stack them. Their clean lines marry well with those of the window.

DOORS

There are generally two reasons for wishing to cover a door:

1. Draughts: these can be excluded by a single, heavy curtain, hung from a portière rod fixed to the door.

2. Light/privacy: a curtain, its top and base sewn to form slots, is gathered onto a rod fixed above and below the glazed section.

DIFFERENTLY-SIZED WINDOWS

Different sizes of curtain, side by side or in the same room, can look clumsy. Try to treat the windows similarly. Find a compromise solution that will work for both.

A glazed wall is masked by a voluminous loop of white cotton. (ABOVE) Three solutions to a lack of space around a window: blinds and a single curtain use unity of colour to disguise the lack of symmetry. (ABOVE RIGHT) Small curtains are positioned inside the reveal. (RIGHT) A pair of dormer rods carry curtains away from a window. (FAR RIGHT)

RADIATOR OR WINDOW SEAT

Floor-length curtains will block a radiator's heat and cannot be closed over a window seat. Sill-length curtains overcome this problem but are often visually inadequate – Roman or pull-up blinds are sometimes better suited to sill length. To achieve the effect of curtains with the practical advantages of blinds use full-length curtains, tied permanently back, with a set of roller or Roman blinds behind to pull down at night.

SHUTTERS

Never obstruct or remove shutters that belong in a house.

SHELVES OR WALL TO ONE SIDE OF THE WINDOW

Use either a single curtain hung from a pole and swept back to one side, or a blind – roller, Roman or pull-up.

INACCESSIBLE WINDOWS

A lambrequin or simple pelmet would be suitable as decoration.

More practical is a blind operated by cords hanging well below the window.

FROM HALL TO DRAWING ROOM, FROM CHILD'S BEDROOM TO CONSERVATORY, A ROOM-BY-ROOM STUDY OF HOW OTHERS HAVE CREATED THEIR OWN SCHEMES PROVIDES A RICH SOURCE OF INSPIRATION

inspiration

INSPIRATION IS THE STARTING POINT for any project. And the first step will often be the hardest. The choices are limitless – and so too is the scope for creativity. Spurs for the imagination abound from Sydney penthouses to Swedish farmhouses. But often the best approach will be the simplest and existing furnishings and decoration will help to clarify the options. Never be afraid to crib: see what others have done and adapt it to your own circumstances. Remember that simpler – and cheaper – variants will often work quite as well as the most extravagant. This chapter sets out some of the possibilities, from the humblest to the grandest, offering suggestions for every room in the house. It shows how a kaleidoscope of design and fabric, colour and pattern, shapes and settings can succeed. Use the treatments for inspiration, not as gospel truths. A personal flavour is a vital element in any scheme.

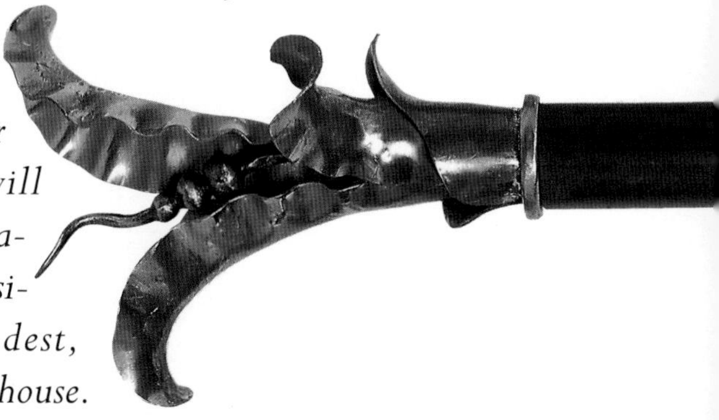

Tieback decorated with coquilles Saint Jacques. This imaginative effect is easily achieved, the hard sculpted ridges of the seashells serving as a foil to the soft drapes of the cream silk curtain.

Halls and Staircases

An interlined curtain, positioned across an opening, will stop draughts from the front door whistling through the rest of the house. These curtains are both functional and decorative, their jewel colours set off by golden walls and polished wooden floorboards.

DOORS *20*
INACCESSIBLE WINDOWS *21*
INTERLINED CURTAINS *94*
LAMBREQUINS *125*
BOWS *158*

First impressions of a house are often gained from the hall and stairway so effort and imagination here will not go unrewarded. It is not always essential to close curtains at night – and on staircases it is not always possible – so grand or theatrical effects need not be restricted by practicality. Thus windows can be dressed in a myriad of ways, from little lace pelmets to deep velvet drapes, from Moorish-inspired lambrequins to hand-painted pelmets.

Door curtains profit from well draped hems as an effective aid to insulation. Drawn back to one side along a wooden pole, this curtain mimics the warm colour of the studded front door and keeps out of the way of passing traffic. (ABOVE LEFT)

Practical considerations can be waived for a staircase window, where taffeta bows or an antique lambrequin can find a suitable setting. (LEFT AND ABOVE)

Living Rooms

An unusual combination of contrasting styles: white walls, plenty of space and a limited range of glorious colours allow this flamboyant scheme to work – the delicate gilded serpents and vivid fringed drapery vying for attention with wedding-cake cornice and bold abstract art. (BELOW)

Maximum effort and expense is generally laid out on a drawing room or sitting room. Whether comfort or elegance is the priority, these are the curtains or blinds that have to be lived with the longest; they deserve careful planning. Often the largest windows in the house are located in the living room which gives scope for the most interesting and formal treatments. Make sure the rest of the decorative scheme complements the window treatment: the furniture, walls and flooring should work together to form a satisfying whole, to be enjoyed for years to come.

INTERLINED CURTAINS *94*
PELMETS *125, 148*
SWAGS AND TAILS *126*
STENCILS *154*
BOWS *158*
FITTING POLES *168*
FITTING BAY WINDOWS *175*

The Regency fantasies of the Brighton Pavilion are the starting points for this oriental flight of fancy – gold and jade green drapes, with an exotic tasselled valance, and lilac walls unite in an explosion of exotic decoration. (LEFT)

To juxtapose ornamental Indian embroidery with a swagged valance turns convention on its head but produces a surprisingly successful result. Formal striped bows punctuate the swags, while elegantly draped curtains are supported by a set of Venetian blinds. The rich colours and shapes of the hand-sewn embroidery are highlighted in the sunlight, and the intricate leaves and flowers of the banner, each finished in a tiny bobble, are seen to full effect. (ABOVE)

Two pairs of interlined curtains are draped back to frame an enchanting garden view. Their simple gathered headings are decorated with central tassels and hung from handsome wooden poles, in keeping with the restrained elegance of the rest of the room. (RIGHT)

Basic stencilling turns a plain pelmet into a suitably chic companion to a pair of lustrous curtains. To paint such a pelmet is most rewarding while requiring little technical skill. Stencils can either be purchased ready-cut or cut out of special stencil paper; any colour can then be mixed and applied to a prepared surface. Here circular wreaths – taken from a pair of pillared lamp bases – adorn a flat wooden pelmet, their background the egg-yolk yellow of curtains and walls. (RIGHT)

Themes from the antique world – Corinthian capitals and chairs that seem to have been borrowed from ancient Rome – run through this sitting room. Its translucent curtains, suspended in loops on verdigris rings, take one back to the Neo-classical, while the modern upholstery acts as a reminder of its real contemporary origins. (BELOW)

The discipline needed to free a room of the usual clutter is turned to good use in this restrained curtain treatment. The draped poles are composed of single lengths of fabric, and are accompanied by curtains hung from hidden tracks fixed to the top of the windows. Deep, dense folds in the cream cloth, its toga-like pleats of unusual density – lend a necessary softness to the hard wooden floor and solid white walls. (LEFT)

Studies and Workrooms

Warm and cosy, book-lined studies are the right setting for rich dark colours and soft, yielding textures – tapestries and muted paisley prints, for example, will glow in the evening light. Daytime workrooms should, in contrast, inspire feelings of vigour and industry. A fresh and airy room, quiet and still, helps to envigorate the imagination. As a haven from the noise and commotion of the rest of the house, a study should contain all that gives inspiration and comfort. The window treatment should lend itself to happy contemplation, provide a suitable frame to the view and blot out the rest of the world when solitude is required.

A professional decorator soon tires of frills and excessive decoration. With its Italian-strung curtains, this designer's studio uses solid shapes and plain surfaces, in natural colours and textures. (ABOVE)

Plain curtains provide simple solutions to sunny windows. The first carries through the feeling of coolness and light from a terracotta-filled balcony; the second, with headings flapped forward in a casual frill, adorns tall, narrow windows. (RIGHT AND FAR RIGHT)

FRENCH PLEATS *97, 107*
PUFFED HEADING *99*
ITALIAN STRINGING *134*
FITTING POLES *168*

This window treatment – more of a hanging that might be found in a contemporary art gallery than a curtain in the traditional sense – is an example of function stripped to its barest minimum. Its part in the overall decorative scheme is vital, providing the principal soft surface and curving shape, in powerful contrast to the stark walls and solid furniture. Its scrolled, black border lends weight and decoration, contrasting with the translucent linen above and emphasizing the airy wastes of the room itself. The upper corners are sewn with large rings which suspend the curtain from hooks, set into the wall. The height of the hooks makes a rod, also sewn to the upper corner of the curtain, necessary for opening and closing.

Kitchens and Dining Rooms

A pair of striped Roman blinds is imaginatively hung from a row of cloak hooks, the cording mechanism operated through screw eyes fixed to the top of the window. (ABOVE)

Every effort is made to make a small kitchen appear light and airy. The blue-and-white checked curtain provides a note of cheerfulness and – when not in use – pulls back, out of the way of the sink. (RIGHT)

DOORS *20*
TRIMMINGS *76*
GOBLET HEADING *97*
TIED HEADING *100*
CABLE HEADING *102*
SERPENTINE VALANCE *114*
ATTACHED VALANCE *118*
PELMETS *125*
ITALIAN STRINGING *134*
ROMAN BLINDS *146*
PULL-UP BLINDS *150*
POLES *170*

In recent years kitchens have become an important feature of a house, no longer just the home of the sink and mop, but a room in which much time is spent, cooking, eating and sitting. Frequently the kitchen and dining room have merged and the curtains or blinds are the focus of quite elaborate schemes. Decorative possibilities know no bounds – from the simplest of checked curtains to theatrical stripes in pink and peppermint.

A glazed door makes full use of a delicate lace or voile. With casing slots top and bottom, the little curtain is drawn in at its waist, excluding the glances of passers-by and providing the room with an additional decorative touch. (ABOVE LEFT)

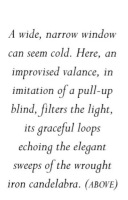

A wide, narrow window can seem cold. Here, an improvised valance, in imitation of a pull-up blind, filters the light, its graceful loops echoing the elegant sweeps of the wrought iron candelabra. (ABOVE)

What better use could be made of the small space above the kitchen sink than as a setting for ranks of Minton's most charming cups and saucers? A pleated pull-up blind provides the ideal vehicle. (LEFT)

Italian-strung curtains pull back in the manner of a toy theatre, surmounted by a wooden cut-out pelmet of singular originality. The pleasure clearly taken in the design of such an arrangement gives the air of gaiety appropriate to a dining room. (ABOVE)

In a dining room set for Christmas dinner the greens and reds of the hand-painted walls and curtains provide a warm and intimate setting for the festivities. The small, leaded window is made to seem larger and grander with full-length curtains and serpentine valance hung with a heavy matching fringe. (LEFT)

In hot climates wooden shutters take on some of a curtain's normal functions, as the most effective means of excluding powerful heat and sunlight. Here, light striped curtains, inspired by the aquamarine blues of the Mediterranean, act as a foil to the hard quarry tiled floor, ready to drift in the cool morning breeze. Their attached valances, hung from simple iron poles, come into their own in the evening, when the room profits from any additional warmth or softness. (ABOVE)

A loop of striped silk, lined in caramel, decorates a window. The window itself is covered by a blind; the curtain is purely for adornment, its bold shape perfectly in keeping with the pure lines and natural colours of the floor and walls. The sweep of the curtain, in combination with the curly chairs upholstered in lipstick pink, bring the room to life. (RIGHT)

In some ways a kelim is better as a curtain than as a floorcovering. Heels cannot become trapped and its rich colours and patterns can be admired to the full. Here it is used as an ornamental feature, hung from a high pole and draped back, softening the view through to a potentially chilly conservatory. (RIGHT)

Exuding the ordered tranquillity of a modern cathedral, with its altar-like table and ecclesiastical candlesticks, this room uses curtaining more as an architectural feature than mere soft furnishing. Quilted fabric, hung in orderly folds, covers almost an entire wall – its unusual texture, zigzag rope cording and burnished steel pole providing a subtle combination of effects. Strong light from a side window enhances the dramatic effect, casting the folds into deep shadow. (RIGHT)

Bedrooms

In a bedroom where the pictures and furniture take one back two hundred years, antique shawls and the most delicate muslin curtains – a simplified interpretation of Regency style – seem at one with their surroundings. Practical roller blinds are hidden behind the improvised valances. (BELOW)

The bedroom is a haven of comfort and tranquillity. Curtains or blinds should exclude light and keep out draughts – light and warmth are two key elements in a successful bedroom – and the first and last sights of the day should give quiet pleasure and reassurance. No other window treatment will be used and viewed as much – waking every morning to a badly chosen design or collapsing track will be particularly annoying. The decorative possibilities are endless – yards of fancy chintzes or simple bordered blinds, for example – which might take inspiration from the bedspread or headboard, carpet or wallpaper.

The simplest of lined curtains, on a gathered heading, are made up in a candy-striped cotton. In a room full of objets d'art and other diversions they serve their useful purpose without ostentation. The vivid bands of yellow, green and red are given plenty of room to breathe and bring life to the plain walls and floor. (ABOVE)

Asymmetrical drapes across a curtain pole treat two, closely-spaced, windows as one and lend a suitably masculine atmosphere to this bedroom. With the help of Venetian blinds, the arrangement is both decorative and practical, allowing for the maximum entry or exclusion of light. By day the blinds can be adjusted to allow a discreet view of the outside world or can be drawn up and hidden behind the drapes. By night the blinds drop, their dark wooden slats harmonizing with the polished mahogany wardrobe and ancestral portrait. Two candlestick lamps lend added formality, framed by the blinds. (RIGHT)

TRIMMINGS 78
LINED CURTAINS 92
FRENCH PLEATS 97, 107
SLOTTED HEADING 104
SWAGS AND TAILS 126
REVERSE ROLLER BLIND 145
PULL-UP BLINDS 150
FITTING POLES 168

Nothing frames a garden view more prettily than a fresh, floral cotton, strewn with tulips in the colours of a bright spring morning. Here, a French-pleated valance, generously in proportion with the full-length curtains, is decorated with covered buttons and accompanied by a matching bedspread. The curtains are overlapped with the wall to either side of the window and the valance is hung well above the window space. In this way neither will serve to block daylight and the window is made to seem larger than it really is. (ABOVE)

The frame of a campaign bed stands in contrast to the silk folds of a pretty 18th-century pull-up curtain. Instead of falling to its historically-correct floor length, this contemporary version skims a radiator and window seat. (RIGHT)

A reverse roller blind, in a bright gingham check, is visible through the lightest of muslin curtains, edged in a bobble fringe, turning the tiny dressing room into a haven of tranquillity. (RIGHT)

A silk curtain is swept back in a grandiose gesture to one side of what is actually a modest-sized window. White, creams and honey colours make a restful background for the filtered morning sun. (BELOW)

Elaborately painted walls and coving preclude the need for anything more elaborate than the most virginal of curtains and draped valances. (ABOVE)

A room filled with visual interest and diversion – tented toy cupboards and flying acrobats – uses a tab heading for its yellow-and-white curtains. The white stripes appear to extend over the back of the pole and attach to the front with coordinating blue buttons. (RIGHT)

Blues and terracotta have always been used together as a happy balance of visual warmth and coolness – here, warm ironstone-coloured walls set off the cool blue and white stripes of the Roman blinds. With inward-opening windows the blinds pull up above the reveal to stay well out of the way of rampaging children and allow for a pair of divans to be placed end to end, discreetly providing extra accommodation by night and a generous-sized sofa by day. (RIGHT)

GATHERED HEADING *99, 107*
TAB HEADING *102*
PELMETS *125*
ROLLER BLIND *143*
ROMAN BLIND *146*

Children's Rooms

Our most vivid and lasting memories are acquired in childhood. A nursery curtain or wallpaper motif will often be remembered for life, and should aim to inspire happy memories. When a new baby is born the child's room becomes a focus for the parent's best decorating skills – stencilled bunnies hop around the ceiling, spotted muslin and floppy bows adorn the window. Whether it is the strictly conventional that appeals or the more unusual, a child's room should both reassure and amuse, developing and changing as the years pass.

In adult life nothing evokes childhood memories as strongly as the scent and sight of flowers. Glimpsed through the simple muslin-clad window of a small attic bedroom, the delicious scent of lilac is certain to leave a most lasting impression. White cane chairs and the sloping wooden ceiling add to the quiet atmosphere. (RIGHT)

Childhood fantasies are fuelled by legions of Noah's animals as they process across wall and blind in a coordinating frieze, wallpaper and fabric scheme. The roller blind has its wavy lower edge picked out in a contrasting colour while a cloud-shaped pelmet is adorned with fat blue polka dots. By way of visual relief the area below the dado rail is painted in a cool blue-green and a comfortable yellow armchair, prey to a thousand felt-pen marks, offers itself to a tired parent. (ABOVE)

Bathrooms

UNLINED CURTAINS *90*
ROMAN BLINDS *147*

While privacy and the steamy atmosphere are the twin considerations when planning a bathroom curtain or blind, there is still much scope for invention. The shapes and colours of shells or fishes might provide artistic inspiration; shining chrome taps and a gleaming enamel bath might call for a sleeker, monochrome treatment. Blinds are useful in bathrooms; they can be made up in a variety of ways that will let in light without a loss of privacy. Muslins and voiles, too – plain, patterned or fringed – come into their own in such settings.

An exotic garden and a room full of seashells call for the coolest and lightest of natural materials – here provided by caramel-coloured rattan blinds and floating muslin curtains with unusual frilled headings. Tolerant of a humid bathroom atmosphere, they will cater for the most modest bather, excluding the outside world when necessary. (LEFT)

The dramatic sweep of a double-layered curtain of checked cotton and printed voile lends a note of high drama to an otherwise ordinary bathroom. (ABOVE)

The best solution for any bathroom window is often a neat Roman blind. This one, its deckchair stripes in keeping with the clean white porcelain and scrubbed wooden floor, will pull clear of splashes and can be let down, partially or completely, to screen a bathing figure. Lined in a plain, translucent cotton, sunlight will still be able to penetrate. (LEFT)

Style and application: from the tartan of Queen Victoria's Balmoral to the delicate muslins of a Scandinavian interior, from the floral chintzes of the English drawing room to the printed silks of the French chateau

fabrics

From time immemorial fabrics have provided a rich inspiration and medium for designers and artists. Titian's sixteenth-century nudes are set against swags of lavish silks and damasks; the painter Raoul Dufy turned his vibrant palette to the design of printed cotton and, in the 1880s, the Arts and Crafts movement found expression in the patterns of William Morris. Unlike so much of fashion, taste has come full circle, traditions have endured and the French brocade and Indian chintzes of two hundred years ago can still be found – at a price. With toiles de Jouy, checked cottons and striped silks vying for attention, making the right choice can be a bewildering experience. Achieving a happy balance stylistically, while remaining aware of the practical implications of each type of cloth, is vitally important.

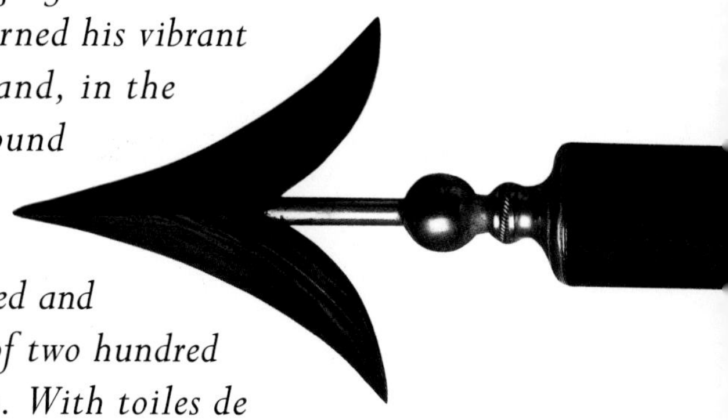

Silk brocades jostle heavy tassels; swirling paisley designs vie with twisted cords as trimmings are matched with materials in the pursuit of the perfect decorative scheme.

Cottons and Linen
Checks and stripes

Combinations of checks and stripes in natural materials are currently enjoying a considerable vogue. Such fabrics are inexpensive, easily cared for and can evoke either a sunny Swedish farmhouse or a wooden verandah in Cape Cod. Tickings and ginghams look perfect against polished floorboards or pale washed walls. Use checks and stripes in coordinating colours for treatments with simple, clean shapes to create a fresh, light, summery feel. By combining such patterns with plain cottons, successful schemes can be achieved with ease.

All fabrics cotton unless indicated

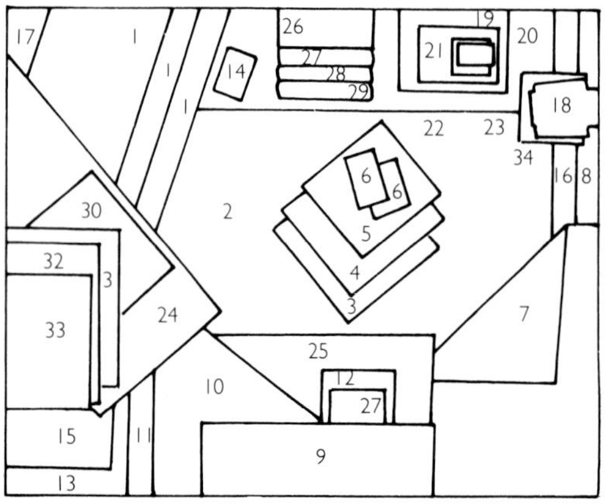

1. Glazed plain chintz 2. Woven check 3. Indian handwoven slub 4. Woven check 5. Indian handwoven slub 6. Handwoven solid rib 7. Indian handwoven slub 8. Woven check 9. Indian handwoven cotton 10. Glazed printed chintz 11-12. Indian handwoven slub 13-14. Plain weave 15. Colour woven cotton 16. Glazed plain chintz 17. Canvas 18. Handwoven cotton 19. Printed cotton 20. Indian handwoven slub 21. Handwoven rib 22-3. Indian plain rib 24. Handwoven slub 25. Indian handwoven slub 26. Herringbone weave 27-8. Colour woven cotton 29. Herringbone weave 30. Gingham 31. Herringbone weave 32. Gingham 33. Herringbone weave 34. Natural canvas

SMALL WINDOWS *15*
LINED CURTAINS *92*
GATHERED HEADING *99, 107*
TAB HEADING *102*
FITTING POLES *168*

Lined cotton curtains and a shallow gathered valance lend themselves well to this room, with its emphasis on natural wooden surfaces and pale colouring. To maximize the daylight the valance is less than the usual one fifth of the curtain length, and is set on the outside of the reveal to avoid interfering with the inward-opening windows. (RIGHT)

Sunlight filters through a pair of blue-checked gingham curtains, looped onto a brass pole with a tab heading. The freshness of gingham makes it a versatile fabric, perfect for a sunny cottage bedroom. (FAR LEFT)

Set against the fancy plaster cornice of a Parisian apartment or the chalky surface of a whitewashed wall, the earthy colours and soft finish of natural cottons and linens find their place. (LEFT AND RIGHT)

Cottons and Linen
Small-scale prints

The South of France has given us a taste for brightly-coloured Provençal cottons. The blues, yellows and pinks, inspired by the strong sunlight and flowers of the region, bring with them a feeling of spring. Gathered into simple treatments for small bedrooms, bathrooms and kitchens they can be hung from a plain brass pole or soften the line of a window in a simple gathered valance. Generally made from pure cotton, they are easily washed, regaining their brilliance and crispness every time.

Discretion is the key word when dealing with small-scale patterns. A tiny floral motif should be matched sympathetically with diminutive windows, using narrow edgings and delicate trimmings, with informal gathered headings taking precedence over formal pleats.

All fabrics cotton unless indicated

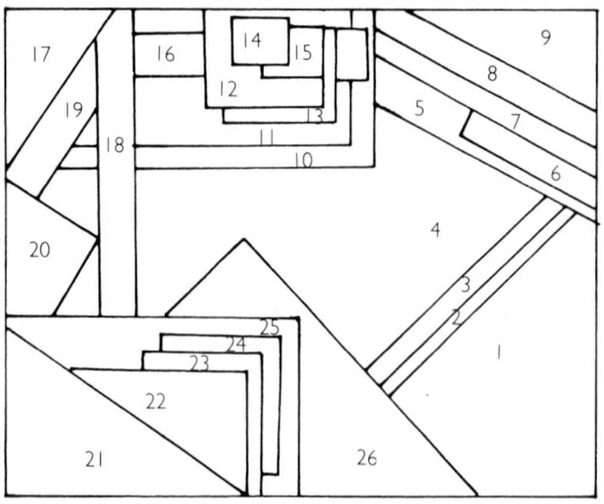

1.Provençal printed percale 2. Glazed plain chintz 3. Provençal printed percale 4. Printed linen 5. Glazed plain chintz 6-7. Printed cotton 8. Heavy printed cotton 9. Provençal printed percale 10. Glazed plain chintz 11. Printed cotton 12. Linen union 13. Provençal printed percale 14-18. Printed cotton 19-20. Provençal printed percale 21-3. Printed cotton 24-6. Provençal printed percale

GATHERED HEADING *99, 107*
GOBLET PLEATS *97*
CORDING *100*
PULL-UP BLIND *150*

Small prints can also be used on a large scale. The most formal of staircase windows becomes a major decorative focus with a floral chintz, suggestive of the leafy garden beyond, making the prettiest possible use of a constricted space. The narrow stripes of wallpaper and roller blind match the curtains in colour and scale, setting off the design to great effect. (BELOW)

White bedlinen and walls call for a curtain fabric that lends warmth and colour while retaining the freshness that is such a part of the room's ambience. (ABOVE)

Very small windows can cause problems when it comes to curtaining, particularly in a bedroom where light must be excluded. Here, a concoction of pattern and stripe echoes the bedlinen in a combination of valance and curtains. (LEFT)
A discreet blue and cream design is similarly at one with the whitewashed charm of a small kitchen. (ABOVE)

Cottons and Linen
Large-scale prints

Large-scale prints are at the heart of many successful schemes but should be approached with care. Set against a complementary plain or geometric fabric, such a design can act as the centre of the decorative scheme, with the wall colour, flooring and upholstery subsequently chosen to form a happy combination.

Floral designs usually have either a cream or a white background. Make sure the rest of the scheme is consistent – a white background set against cream will tend to make the one look stark and the other dirty. Against a bare white wall, a fresh pink and white design will be shown to effect while a smokey-blue linen will be lost.

Try to fit the scale of the design to the size of the treatment. Exceptionally large designs should be reserved for windows on the grand scale.

All fabrics cotton unless indicated

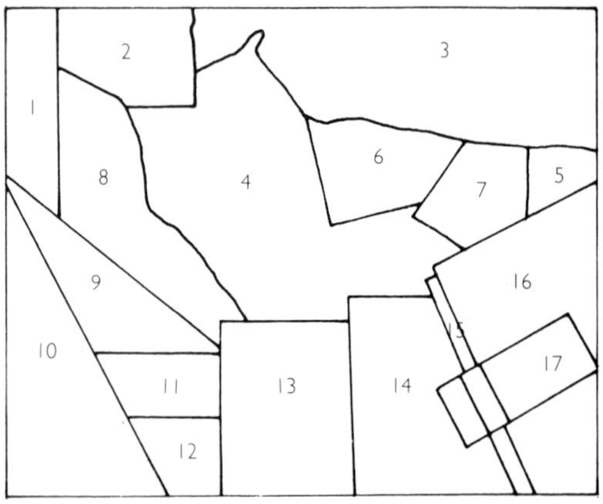

1. Glazed printed chintz 2. Printed linen union 3. Printed linen 4. Printed chintz 5. Printed linen union 6. Glazed printed chintz 7. Printed toile de Jouy 8. Printed linen 9. Glazed printed chintz 10. Printed linen 11-15. Glazed printed chintz 16. Printed linen 17. Glazed printed chintz

FRENCH DOORS *19*
TRIMMINGS *77, 182*
PELMETS *120*
SWAGS AND TAILS *126*
ROMAN BLINDS *146*
CONTRAST EDGE *161*
POLES *170*
DRESSING CURTAINS *177*

Even with a plethora of different fabrics, a strict palette and a balanced combination of designs are needed. Stripes and checks complement a floral chintz while peppermint fringe and banding draw the scheme tightly together. Bright, summery colours in natural fibres bring cheer to the cool rustic interior, with its hard tiled floor and distempered walls. (Below)

Two printed fabrics: one dressed with military precision, the other left to find its own gentle folds; each, in its own way, is well adapted to its surroundings. In a low-ceilinged cottage, linen curtains blend with the age of the house, the mellow background colour merging with the walls, while soft pinks lend warmth to a dark room. A bolder design would jar with the powerful presence of the Turkey rug, an insipid plain fabric would be too 'towny' and much less cosy. (Above)

In a city drawing room, on the other hand, where etiquette takes precedence over comfort, an elegant combination of serpentine pelmet and full-length curtains - covering an entire wall and made up in a vivid design - lends grandeur and height to what is, on closer inspection, a small and architecturally undistinguished room. By keeping to a limited range of well-matched colours and by a disciplined balance of the plain, patterned and geometric, combined with the most symmetrical of furniture placements, a happy result is achieved. (Right)

Matching wall coverings to curtains is a fine art. Here an unusual combination of Roman blind and swags in a muted printed linen (ABOVE) is set off against a coordinating wallcovering fabric. What could seem ostentatious made up in garish colours or fancy finishes is given grace by a unified and restrained choice of designs and colours. Another approach is to merge curtains and walls. Done with aplomb – the floral design lightened with a plentiful pale background colour – a grand effect is achieved. (BELOW)

Cottons and Linen
Modern prints

Over the last forty years or so textile design has moved from the mill into the art school, providing a choice between 'traditional' and 'modern'. Here the 'modern' ranges from the coffee bars of the fifties to the Habitat-inspired interiors of the sixties and seventies, from the Matisse-led fashions of the eighties to the classical revival of the early nineties with a short detour into Bloomsbury's Omega Workshops. Blocks of vivid colour wrestle with abstract images, the columns of antiquity with the palm trees of the South of France. Consistency is the key. In the airy spaces of a streamlined modern interior, matched to the stark shapes of contemporary furniture, show off strong colours against pale surfaces and combine hard and soft textures in a generous use of fabric, with simple headings and plain fittings.

All fabrics cotton unless indicated

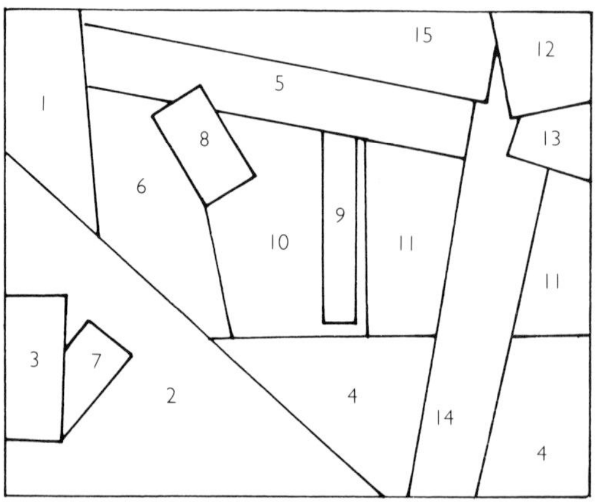

1. Printed sateen 2. Kashmiri embroidery on cotton 3. Printed stripe 4-5. Glazed printed chintz 6-9. Printed cotton 10. Sateen and brushed cotton 11-12. Glazed printed chintz 13-15. Printed cotton

UNPLEATED HEADING 99
CABLE HEADING 102
PELMETS 120
ROMAN BLINDS 146
PAINT EFFECTS 156
POLES 170

A revival of interest in classical engravings has spawned a whole new genre of fabric designs – here a composition of ruins and mythological figures is cleverly relieved by a bold stripe that intersects the pelmet and runs along the leading edges of the curtain. In this way the scenes can be viewed in detail, framed by the coordinating fabric. (RIGHT)

Stripes are very satisfying to the eye and in a sleek, modern interior they can be almost architectural in their effect, reminiscent of the layered marbles of an Italian cathedral. (RIGHT AND FAR RIGHT)

It is no longer taboo to use more than a single fabric at the window. A carefully balanced combination of cup and check, united by a simple colour scheme, works well in an airy modern bedroom (ABOVE), *while an Omega Workshop-inspired design is used with plain velvet in a more conventional manner, lending a contemporary feel to the urns and painted garlands of a drawing room.* (LEFT)

Sheer Fabrics
Voiles, lace and nets

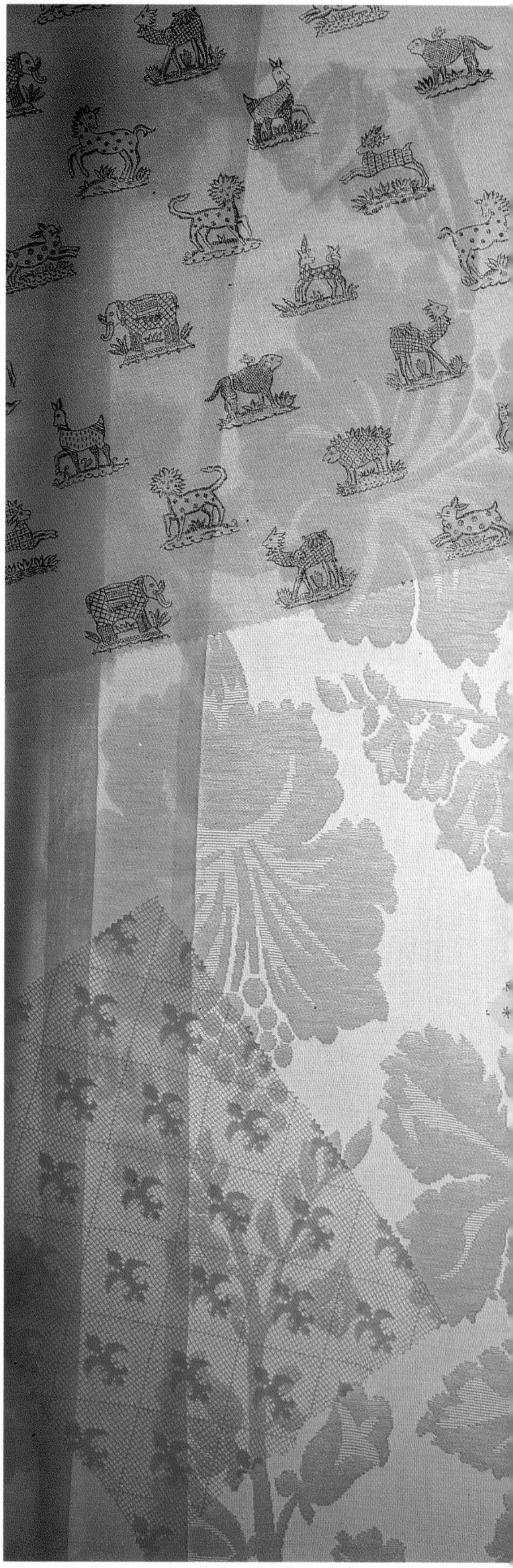

Translucent fabrics are no longer burdened with their reputation as barriers to a hostile world, hung on drooping lengths of plastic-coated wire, their hems a depth chart of yellow staining. They have lately come to be appreciated for the brightness and the airy elegance that they lend to a room. Patterns, woven or printed, are shown off to best advantage as the light penetrates, creating shadows that twist and turn in the curtain's shifting folds. Cottons and silks; muslin, lace or organza; embroidered, woven or printed; these fabrics are friends to the light and can find a home at the tiniest dormer window or festooned from the highest ceiling. The freshness given by featherlight fabrics – sometimes backed with a roller blind for night-time use – is inestimable.

All fabrics cotton unless indicated

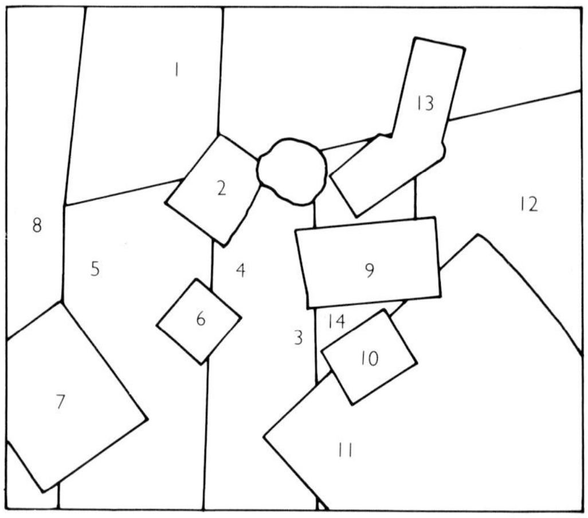

1. Voile 2. Silk organza 3. Spotted muslin 4. Self-woven check 5. Lace 6. Silk organza 7. Fine lace 8. Muslin 9. Cotton mix voile 10. Embroidered cotton 11. Embroidered cotton and silk sheer 12. Lace 13. Cotton and silk sheer 14. Muslin

GATHERED HEADING *99, 107*
TIEBACKS *138*
POLES *170*
PINCER RINGS *1, 171*

In a room already full of colour and interest a white lace curtain, hung from simple pincer rings, is a welcome relief. (BELOW) *Its purpose is to filter, not to exclude, the light that penetrates the window. In the same way the single muslin curtain, caught in at its waist, cuts out none of the brilliant sunlight that is such a feature of this all-white dining room.* (RIGHT)

Colour and pattern are by no means the only considerations when planning a scheme. A successful marriage of texture, shape and volume between wall, floor, furniture and furnishings requires an indefinable, instinctive sensitivity. A fear of straying from conventional, ready-made coordinations blunts the pleasure of putting together delicious combinations of mossy velvets and crisp linens, silks and delicate voiles and whitewashed walls. A Scandinavian dining room, all polished and painted wood, the honey-coloured floor fading to the palest dove-grey walls, is set off by featherlight muslin curtains. (FAR LEFT) In a similar combination of hard and soft, solid and translucent, the textures emphasized by the strictest range of vanilla and dusty-blue-grey with an improvised valance of knotted muslin, this country sitting room invites contemplation and tranquillity. (LEFT) In a third example, daylight is again used to highlight the glorious feel and colour of Indian saris, here used in a highly original - if not strictly practical - manner, permanently draped at a bedroom window. (ABOVE)

Silks and Damask

From time immemorial luxurious silks and damasks have been highly prized. The manufacture of such cloth dates back to ancient China, Egypt and Constantinople. France and Italy now lead the field, producing cloth of superb design and quality. However, cheaper equivalents can be found in many a high street store and there is much modest fun to be had from combining inky velvets and gleaming silks, and using a little fantasy to design exotic treatments. Plain silks can look sumptuous in almost any context, their lustrous finish acting as an excellent foil to dark stained poles and gilded or brass fittings. The traditional shapes found in damask designs often provide a useful dimension in the balance between floral, geometric and plain colours, finding a place in the most conventional or up-to-date decorative schemes.

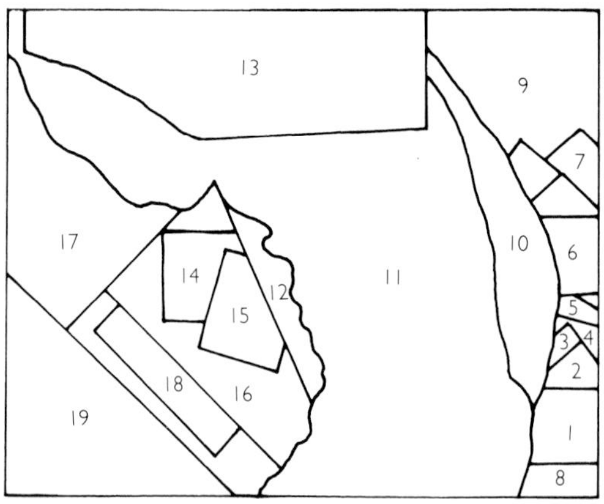

1. Embroidered viscose with satin finish 2-5. Plain silk 6-7. Printed silk 8. Moiré silk and embroidery 9. Embroidered damask 10. Plain velvet 11. Embroidered silk damask 12. Plain velvet 13. Embroidered silk 14-15. Printed silk 16. Silk damask 17. Colour woven silk 18 . Embroidered damask 19. Colour woven silk

TRIMMINGS *77*
UNLINED CURTAINS *90*
INTERLINED CURTAINS *94*
FRENCH PLEATS *97*
SWAGS AND TAILS *126*
FITTING POLES *168*

Early 19th-century France is powerfully evoked here. The furniture and furnishings are of a piece with the swagged curtains straight out of a Napoleonic upholsterer's manual, the blue silk decorated with the golden repeated motif so typical of the period. A gilded pole continues the theme, with the Emperor's laurel wreath as its central focus. (RIGHT)

Silks usually make the happiest of companions for tassels and fringing. A simple pair of lightly interlined curtains is given discreet importance with a pair of central tassels. The curtains' hems carry matching fringe reflecting the fabric's amber-coloured stripes (RIGHT). *The green taffeta of a pair of unlined curtains is lent a decorative touch with matching tassel tiebacks and fringing.* (FAR RIGHT)

Opulent damask, antique embroidery and a band of beaded velvet give a splendid feeling of opulence to surroundings as varied as a rustic French staircase and the muralled halls of an Italian palazzo. A flat blind is a novel use for a rich silk damask but its subdued colours complement the pitted plaster and Delft tiles. (ABOVE LEFT) *An embroidered banner* (LEFT) *has strayed far from its origins but is clearly much loved by its eclectic owner. In an interior full of objets trouvés its unusual position above a staircase seems quite appropriate. Finally, in a setting not short of visual interest, golden silk curtains, decorated with a pearl-encrusted bandana, add to the high theatricality of garlanded pomegranates and fantastic pilasters.* (ABOVE)

Velvets and Tapestry

Setting layers of richly coloured, densely woven fabrics together, unified by a basic colour palette of deep burgundy, forest green or midnight blue, can create an appealing style that spells warmth and comfort. The Victorians used such fabrics to great effect with deeply swagged velvet curtains and tartan covered walls. For an interpretation of the style, use velvet for heavy fringed curtains, drawn to each side with twisted rope, or try tapestry for a draught-excluding portière curtain over a doorway. A Gothic-shaped lambrequin or deep pelmet, decorated with fringes or cording, will help to create a soft, dark interior.

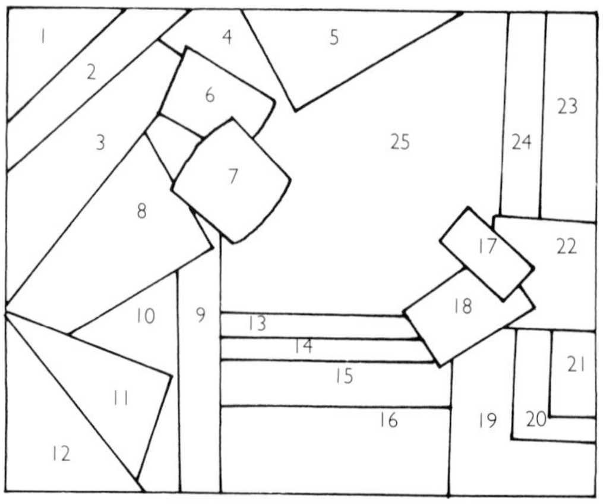

1. Wool and cotton bouclé 2. Cut and uncut velvet 3. Printed cotton velvet 4. Heavy mohair-mix velvet woven plush 5. Cotton damask 6-7. Crushed cross-dyed viscose velvet 8. Wool and cotton cut bouclé 9. Silk and cotton damask 10. Textured cotton velvet 11. Printed cotton 12. Silk-screen printed cotton 13. Heavy printed cotton 14. Jacquard 15. Wool and cotton bouclé 16. Cut and uncut bouclé 17. Smooth cotton velvet 18. Linen and cotton union 19. Classic colour-woven damask 20. Printed cotton 21. Finely woven wool plaid 22. Cotton and cupro cut velvet 23-5. Printed silk damask

TRIMMINGS *77*
SLOTTED HEADING *104*
SWAGS AND TAILS *126*
TIEBACKS *138*
PADDED EDGE *161*

In a room of masculine sobriety a paisley print of midnight blue and deep burgundy evokes a suitable atmosphere. (RIGHT) The Arts and Crafts movement favoured weighty cloths decorated in dense botanical prints. Here the greens and ambers of a William Morris tapestry look very much at home against polished wooden panelling. (BELOW)

The dense luxuriance of old-fashioned plush lends warmth of colour and cosiness of atmosphere, effectively insulating one part of a room from another. (ABOVE)

Crimson double-tasselled velvet drapes create a curvaceous outline that is echoed in the arabesques of the oriental wallpaper and the lines of the chaise longue, confirming the consistency of the designer's approach. (RIGHT)

A rich pattern is never shown to better effect than on full-length curtains – and here the excellent draping qualities of a woollen paisley provides a subtle contrast to bare boards and translucent undercurtains. (ABOVE)

Trimmings

Trimmings should not be underestimated. A good quality fringe can bring an air of luxury to the simplest cottons and calicos. Colour and scale are the main considerations – a heavy linen swag merits a thick bullion fringe, an unlined cotton curtain requires something lighter. Many companies produce ranges of colour-coordinated fabrics and trimmings, sparing the customer the long hunt for the perfect match – and trimmings can be dyed to match a fabric. Borders and fringes, braid and piping can be used to add sharp colour accents and add extra definition, while cords and tassels add movement. Textural contrast adds another dimension – for example, a soft cotton fringe throws the sheen of glazed chintz into relief. Trimmings can also effect proportions: a deep fringe along a pelmet will help to stress the horizontal, while a tassel at the centre point of draped curtains reduces height.

Soft linen fringe in a brindled black and white is a conventional finish to a generous serpentine valance, showing off the curved shape while supplying welcome monochrome relief in a room filled with pattern. (LEFT)

A white linen curtain, by contrast, uses an exotic beaded fringe as decoration, the light highlighting both fabric and coloured glass while passing breezes trigger a delicate tinkling sound. (RIGHT)

Border braid can be used to outline and define the shape of curtains and blinds and other decorative details. Used to pick out colours from the room scheme, trimmings can impart a sense of unity. (FAR RIGHT)

SERPENTINE VALANCE 114
PELMET 120
TIEBACKS 138
PULL-UP BLIND 150
ROSETTE 160

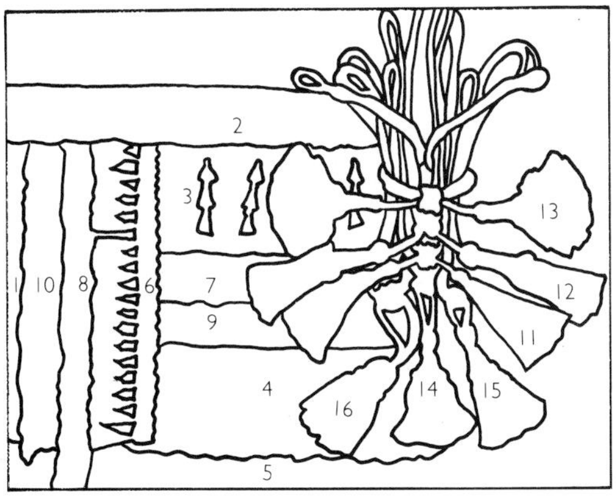

HEAVYWEIGHT TRIMMINGS
1. Viscose fan edging 2. Viscose tassel fringe 3-4. Light tassel fringe 5. Heavy tassel fringe 6. Tufted bullion fringe 7. Viscose and cotton gimp 8. Viscose and cotton narrow braid 9. Viscose and cotton broad braid 10. Viscose and cotton frayed fringe 11. Cotton tassel tieback 12. Cotton tassel tieback 13. Double tassel tieback 14. Cotton double tassel tieback 15. Viscose and cotton double tassel tieback 16. Single tassel tieback

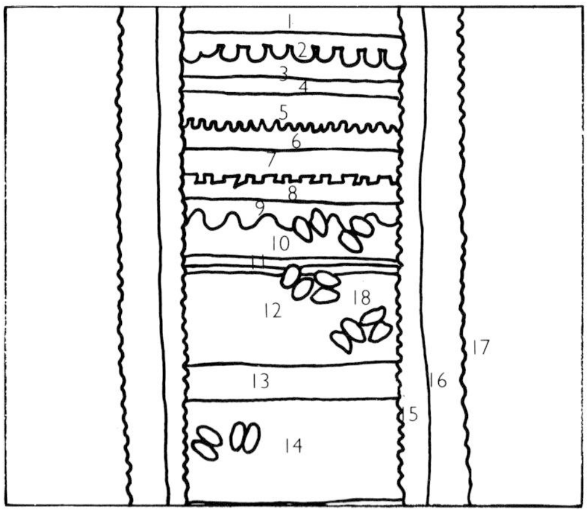

LIGHTWEIGHT TRIMMINGS
1. Linen and cotton bullion fringe 2. Cotton bobble fringe 3. Cotton fringe 4. Linen and cotton fringe 5. Linen and cotton seersucker braid 6. Linen and cotton long fringe 7. Linen fan edging 8. Narrow cotton braid 9. Small cotton fringe 10. Large cotton fringe 11. Cotton braid 12. Wide cotton braid 13. Small cotton fringe 14. Large cotton fringe 15. Wide cotton fringe 16. Small cotton bullion fringe 17. Scalloped cotton edging 18. Linen and cotton button tufts

Fringes and braids can take on a multitude of forms and uses, edging a tieback (ABOVE LEFT) or pinched into rosettes on a scalloped pelmet. (ABOVE RIGHT) In both cases the colours are coordinated, the textures softening hard outlines and adding interest to basic shapes.

Linen fringe finds a novel home along the top edge of a pull-up blind, where it echoes the stripey theme of wall and fabric. (LEFT)

Translucent cotton curtains are lent a decorative air with a two-colour bobble fringe. The simplicity of the curtain complements the jade green walls and patterned floor, and the fringe links the principal colours of the room while adding a delicate touch to the sweeping drapery. (LEFT)

Fabric Glossary

The enormous variety of fabrics now available for curtainmaking – from inexpensive cotton duck and linen union to luminous silks and damasks – offers all manner of decorative possibilities. But no matter how expertly constructed the window treatment, the wrong choice of fabric will mar the end result.

Practical considerations – as well as aesthetics – must be borne in mind. How will it drape? Will it crease? Will it fade in bright sunlight? Will washable fabrics shrink? Try to obtain a sample length to look at – a small swatch can be misleading. Always look at fabric in all lights and be sure to buy enough material; an extra length from new stock may show a noticeable colour variation.

Here is a selection of the most commonly used fabric types.

BASIC FIBRES

Cotton: The vast majority of furnishing fabrics are made of cotton or cotton mixtures. Its virtues are many but its principal charm is perhaps its versatility. Cotton can be dyed, printed or finished in a multitude of ways. It can be rendered colourfast, will withstand heat and light and yet remains inexpensive. One drawback, shared with all natural fabrics, is that it will tend to crush and will react to humidity.

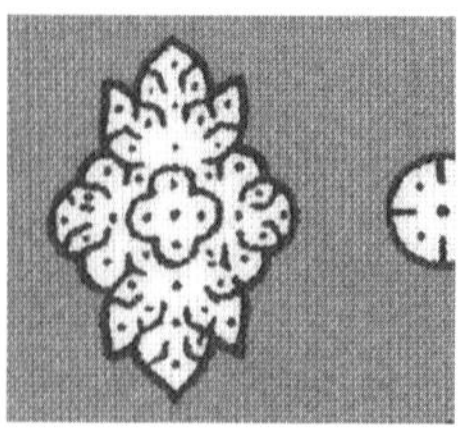

Silk: In its many different forms, silk dominates the market for luxury furnishing fabrics. So far, no artificial fibre can match its lustrous surface, its draping quality or its subtle response to light. However, it may rot faster than other fabrics when exposed to light. If necessary, silk curtains can be protected by a roller blind. Not all silk is expensive: simple, plain-coloured silks can come within even modest budgets. Take special care with the maintenance of silk curtains or blinds: they should always be dry cleaned. Silk will show water marks.

Linen: Linen is made from processed flax which lends the finished fabric unusual strength, so it is a good choice for curtains or blinds. Linen is not only slow to deteriorate and hard-wearing, it also drapes well to give graceful folds. It is no surprise that many leading fabric companies use linen for their designs.

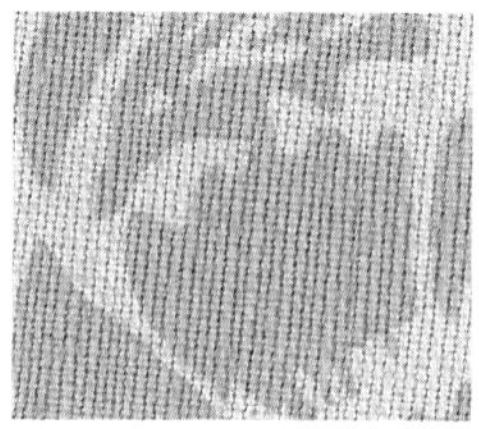

Wool: As a clothing fabric wool is unrivalled; as a furnishing fabric it has few uses. The only major exception is wool tartan, borrowed from the clothing industry for its colours and patterns.

MAN-MADE FIBRES

Acetate: Many convincing artificial silks are made from acetate. It has almost the same finish and draping qualities of real silk but is less prone to fade or rot.

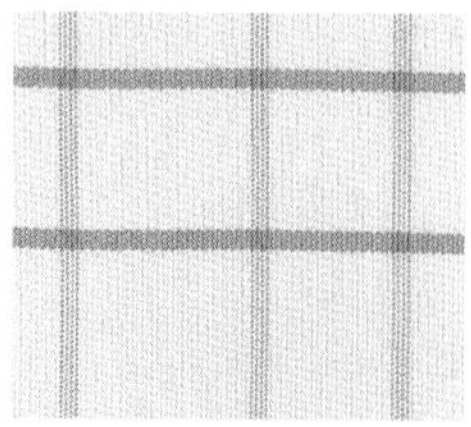

Viscose (rayon)
Viscose is the oldest man-made fibre, developed from coal waste around the turn of the century. It adds strength and lustre to cotton and silk fabrics. Its distinctive sheen is used to highlight patterns, particularly in damask.

GLOSSARY

Baize Dyed green or less commonly red, baize is a flannel-like cloth used for card tables and the linings of cutlery drawers. Its interesting colour and texture make it a handy fabric for improvised curtains or blinds. Baize fades in strong sunlight.

Batik Created by a distinctive dyeing process developed by the Javanese. Wax and other substances that resist dye are applied; after dyeing the wax is washed out to leave dramatic patterns.

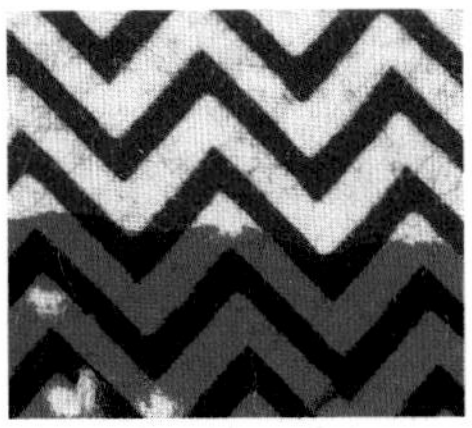

Broderie Anglaise A white cotton fabric, punched with flower-shaped holes and embroidered – useful for lightweight curtains or unlined blinds.

Brocade A fine fabric originally made of silk but now produced with man-made fibres. Traditionally patterned with floral and naturalistic motifs, the raised design is woven on a Jacquard loom and distinguished by long horizontal threads along the back.

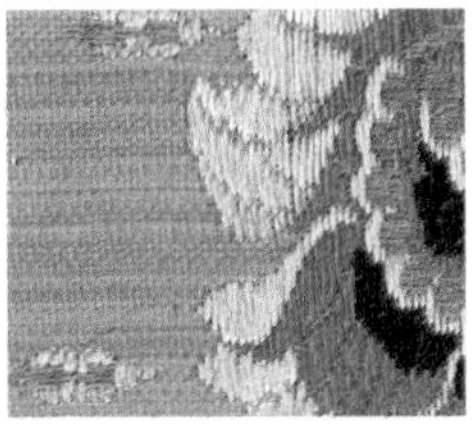

Butter muslin A cheap, loose woven cotton much in demand for translucent window curtains. In urban settings it will quickly lose its original whiteness and body and, although easily washed, muslin will shrink. This fabric also creases badly.

Cotton lawn A finely woven cotton, with a finish almost as smooth as silk.

Calico Plain-woven cream cotton, varying in weight. It can be painted or stencilled, bordered or used alone.

Canvas A heavy woven linen and cotton mix. See **cotton duck**.

Chintz Plain chintzes are used for contrast pipings, banding or even as the main fabric. Floral chintzes, inspired by painted Indian cloths, were block-printed and glazed with waxes and starch to brighten the colours. Gradually the designs developed into the lush floral patterns that are so closely identified with English style. Chintzes are made from cotton finished with a shiny glaze that is easily lost by crushing or cleaning.

Cotton duck A cream cotton varying in weight from 200-425g (7-15oz) per sq yd. Heavier varieties are hard to penetrate with a needle and so are ideal for no-sew curtains as they need no lining and the edges can be pinked and glued. Widths range from 91cm (36in) to 340cm (134in). As cotton duck is not a furnishing fabric, the edges may be wavy and need trimming.

Crewelwork An Indian-made cotton fabric decorated with wool chainstitch. It can be used to great effect as curtains or covers. The background is usually cream in colour.

Damask Cotton or silk damask is a highly traditional fabric, woven with large, abstract leaf and flower designs in contrasting matt and satin textures. It is made on a Jacquard loom, the warp and the weft usually in the same colour. Damask is also woven in wool and man-made mixtures. It is similar to brocade but is flatter and reversible.

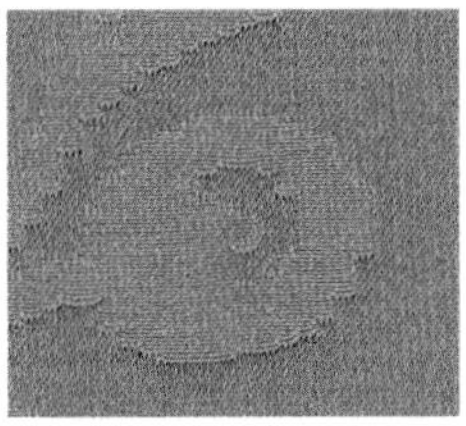

Dupion Used to describe forms of real or artificial silk. Both have a distinctive slubbed surface. Real silk dupion is generally imported from India; it is a lightweight fabric which, like other silks, tends to fade and rot. Artificial dupion is made of acetate and viscose.

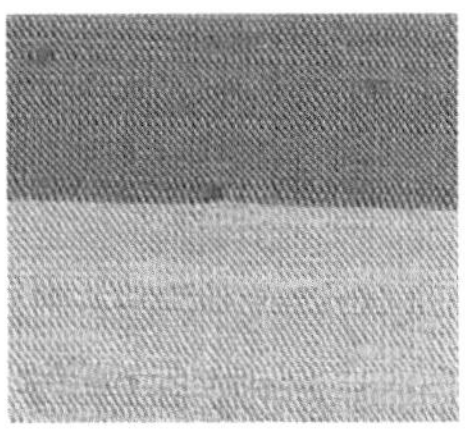

Gingham A checked cotton fabric which has recently found favour as a cheap and charming furnishing fabric. Gingham comes in a wide range of primary colours and check size. The best gingham is made of pure cotton.

Grosgrain A silk cloth recognized by the pronounced ribbed effect across its surface.

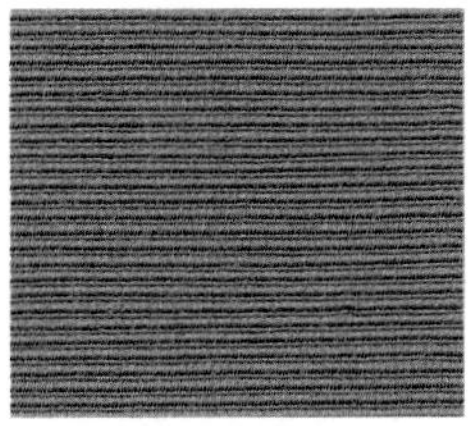

Holland Medium-weight cloth made from linen or cotton. The non-fraying edges can be trimmed to any size so it is ideal for roller blinds.

Ikat Chinese silk fabric tie-dyed to create softly outlined geometric patterns. It can also be made of cotton.

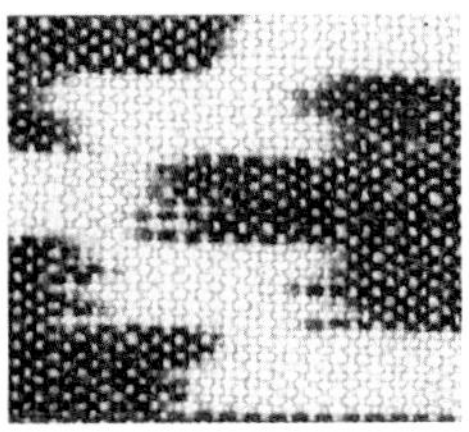

Lace An open work fabric, usually made of cotton, and a useful substitute for net. Lace designs are almost infinite, from the tiny repeated floral motif to large-scale designs of birds and animals.

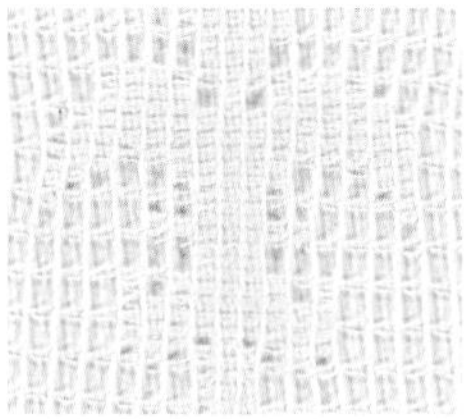

Linen union An inexpensive linen mixture, used alone or banded in a complementary fabric.

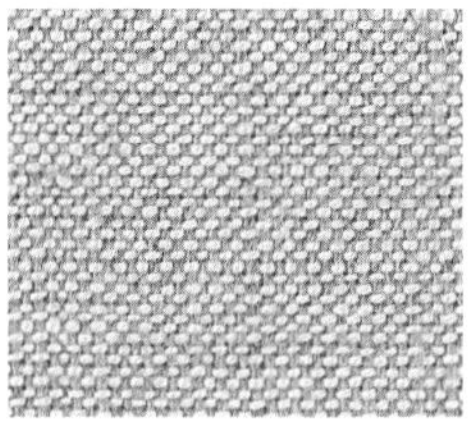

Madras cotton Brightly-coloured fabric, woven with a checked or striped design. Imported from India.

Moiré A watermark effect on silk, now a popular finish to man-made silk imitations. Water spills remove the finish permanently.

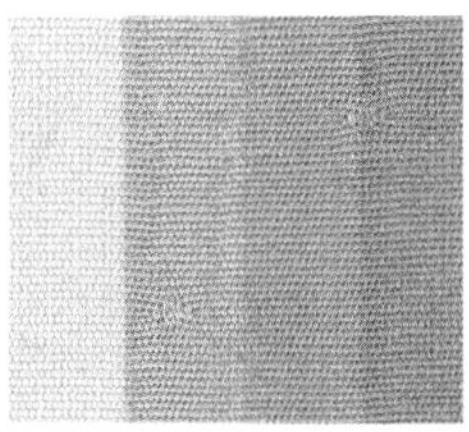

Muslin lawn A crisper and more finely woven version of butter muslin. It makes excellent translucent curtains.

Net An open-mesh fabric used to preserve privacy, often made from artificial fibres.

Paisley Fine woollen cloth printed with intricate scroll or pine designs. The colours and shapes have become a classic design motif.

Plush Old fashioned form of velvet, with deeper but sparser pile. Favoured by the Victorians for furnishing, it was traditionally made from wool or mohair and sometimes cotton. The modern equivalent is man-made.

Sateen A weave usually associated with cotton fabrics. The mercerized yarns used give the cloth a smooth, almost shiny, finish.

Shantung Unevenly textured wild silk, once made on handlooms in the Shantung province of China.

Spotted muslin Also called 'dotted Swiss', this type of muslin, with its pattern of dotted tufts, makes a charming curtain fabric.

Taffeta Fine, crisp silk with a finish that also gives it the name 'paper taffeta'. It has numerous man-made imitations. It should be treated with care as it creases badly.

Tapestry Now made on a Jacquard loom, woven tapestry was originally made in imitation of hand-sewn tapestries. It is a heavy fabric – too heavy to interline – and will make a good insulating curtain.

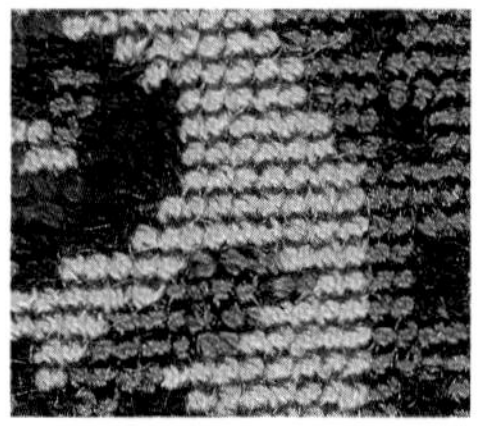

Tartan A woollen cloth woven with a particular checked pattern of specific colours, each belonging to one of the Highland clans of Scotland. Its rich, deep colours can be most effective in any interior and it has good insulating qualities.

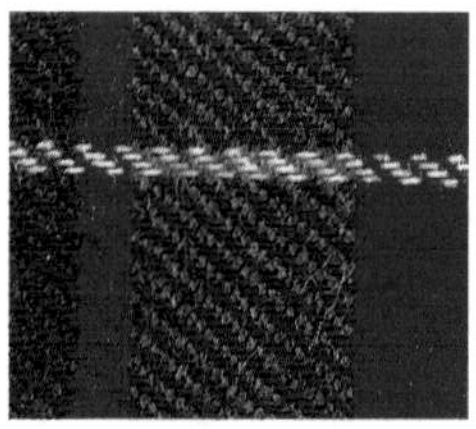

Ticking Originally used to cover mattresses, ticking is a striped cotton material. Traditional ticking is composed of narrow black and white stripes, but modern tickings come in a range of colours. White downproof ticking is intended for cushion pads but can also be made up into curtains and blinds.

Toile de Jouy A cotton or linen fabric printed with scenes of French pastoral life, traditionally in dark red on a cream background. First fashionable in the 18th century when it was produced in the French town of Jouy, it can now be found in numerous single colours on a plain background. A most effective furnishing fabric, but to be used in moderation.

Tussah silk A wild silk, originally Indian. Not easily dyed, it is typically a natural yellowy-brown colour.

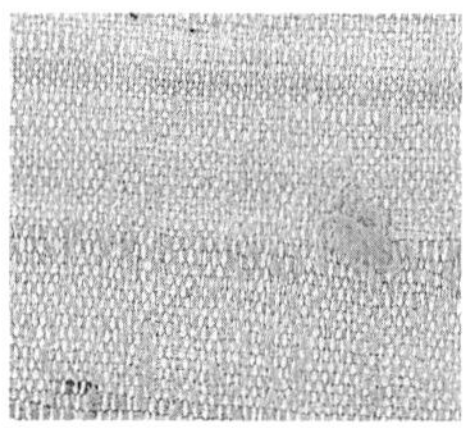

Velvet A cotton fabric (more rarely silk or wool) whose pile gives it a soft surface that absorbs light. Velvet curtains are luxurious but need careful handling when pressed. Gaufraged velvet has an impressed pattern. Brocade, or façonné, velvet has a pattern burnt out of the pile.

Voile A white translucent fabric, ideally of cotton, to be used behind curtains or as a window dressing in its own right.

LININGS

Cotton sateen
Lining comes in various qualities and prices. A more expensive lining will retain its body after cleaning and will help the curtains or blinds to hang well. Cheap lining has more dressing in the weave, which with age and cleaning leaves the fabric limp. Ivory, cream and white are the usual basic shades, although lining is now available in a wide range of colours and patterns. If the curtain is to be tied back in such a way as to show the lining, a coordinated colour or pattern should be used. Swags and tails, where the lining is visible, should also be lined in a coordinated design. Coloured linings are colourfast but will fade in a sunny window. With patterned linings care should be taken to ensure that the lining design will not show through to the right side of lightweight curtains.

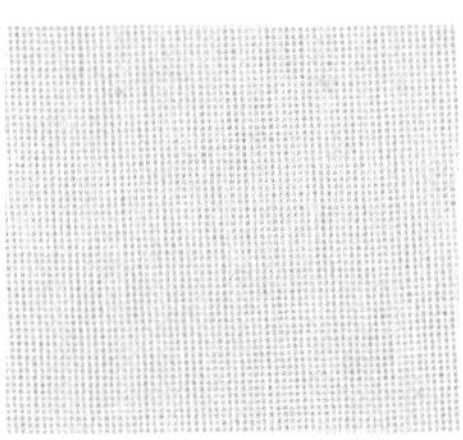

Milium (aluminium coated thermal)
Without adding much extra bulk this type of lining will help to exclude light, cold or heat. It can be used with curtains or, when bulk is particularly unwelcome, to line blinds. The aluminium coated surface faces inside the curtain or blind, while the visible side shows cream woven cotton.

Blackout A layer of opaque material is sandwiched between two layers of cotton fabric. In this way all light is excluded. Some blackout linings are heavy and difficult to penetrate with a needle, others are softer. Both will add to the weight but will also improve the draping qualities. Usually obtainable in cream or white.

INTERLININGS

Bump A heavy, blanket-like interlining, available bleached or unbleached, it is sewn into a curtain between the fabric and lining. Bleached bump is suitable for white curtains or backgrounds, unbleached for other fabrics when a cream cast will not matter. Lockstitch links the bump to the fabric and helps to create plump folds in the curtains. Bump has excellent thermal qualities – it excludes both cold and heat – and gives a luxurious look to curtains. It is often too heavy to use with silk or other light fabrics.

Domette A lighter interlining, for use inside blinds (to give a very slightly padded finish) and to interline silk or other lightweight curtains. Swags and tails are interlined using domette. Hard pelmets are given a soft finish with a layer of bump or domette. Like bump, it comes bleached or unbleached.

Synthetic Usually composed of 85% viscose and 15% polyester, synthetic interlinings are cheaper than the cotton equivalents but lack some of their qualities. They do not have the same softness or body and so will not drape as well. Cotton interlinings will adhere to the face fabric, synthetic will tend to repel other fabrics and thereby lose fullness. Light will tend to penetrate a synthetic interlining more than a cotton bump. However, being man-made, they do not have the weaving faults of cotton interlinings, nor is there the danger of shrinkage through humidity or cleaning. They are clean and easy to handle.

Wadding Wadding is a fluffy man-made fibre, sometimes used for padding leading edges.

BUCKRAMS

Fusible pelmet
An open-weave fabric, made from jute, then impregnated with glue. It is very stiff and is best cut with a heavy-duty craft knife. Used as the base of a hard pelmet, a hot iron will release the adhesive in the buckram. Available in 46cm (18in) or 90cm (36in) widths, it is turned on its side to avoid any joins along a pelmet.

Non-fusible pelmet
Made from jute, this material is not impregnated with glue but is double starched and two-ply. It is not easily cut with scissors so again use a heavy-duty craft knife. This buckram should be sewn in. It has the same uses as the fusible pelmet buckram but has the advantage of being more easily cleaned.

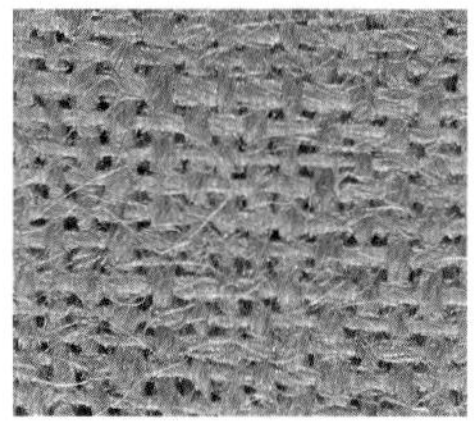

White tieback
A flexible buckram that will fold well when used in a tieback. It is made from cotton and is sewn in.

Fusible heading
This is a strip of white cotton impregnated with adhesive. It is used inside hand-pleated headings, giving the requisite stiffness without the visible machine stitching of a sewn-on heading tape. It comes in widths of 10cm (4in), 13cm (5in) or 15cm (6in).

THIRTY-FIVE PROJECTS, WITH DETAILED STEP-BY-STEP INSTRUCTIONS ON MAKING EVERY SORT OF CURTAIN, PELMET AND BLIND FROM MEASURING UP TO VARIATIONS ON A THEME

projects

IT IS NOT WITHOUT GOOD REASON that the upholsterer's apprentice took many years to master the basic skills of curtainmaking. Even today professional workrooms take great pride in the subtleties of curtainmaking, only fully mastered after long experience at the worktable. Although it is the custom for curtainmakers to swathe the intricacies of their art in mystery, with a thorough knowledge of the basic skills, the mysteries can be revealed and confidence gained to tackle ever more ambitious projects. A little practice and experimentation will reap dividends – whether interlining a curtain, trying out a handmade heading, designing your own pelmet or painting your own fabric patterns. It is vital that measurements are taken with exceptional care. Accurate measuring is just as important as every other aspect of the upholsterer's art and time spent in preparation is never wasted.

Green cotton banding snakes around the edge of a floral chintz curtain, its lively checked contrast lining providing an expert-looking finish.

Measuring
Curtains, Pelmets and Valances

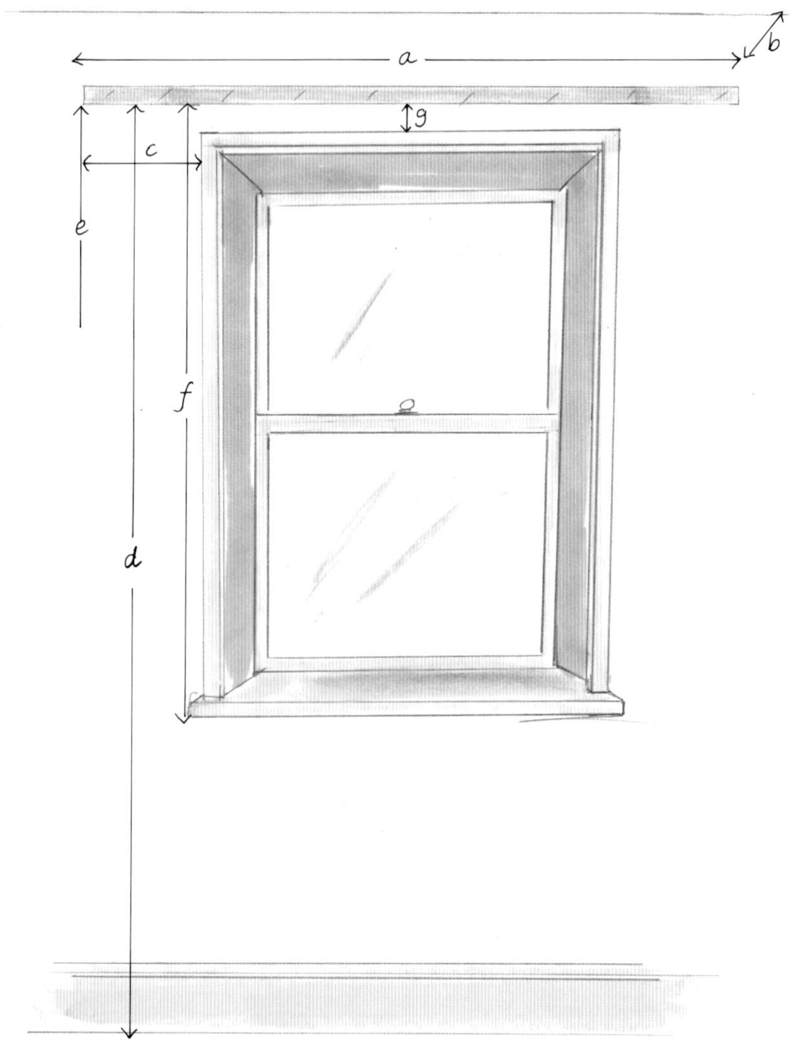

a: Finished width of curtain headings. Add 8cm for overlap
b: Returns: add to width if applicable
c: Housing space for curtains to stack back
d: Finished length to floor
e: Finished length of pelmet 20%-25% of (*d*)
f: Finished length of sill-length curtains
g: Space between pelmet board and window

Armed with accurate, detailed measurements any project can be tackled with confidence. There is no worse task than unpicking and remaking a lovingly-constructed curtain or blind just because a single digit was written down incorrectly. Keep your notes, sketches and Polaroid photographs handy – you will be surprised how often you will need to refer to them. Never stint on the time spent taking measurements – and it can be a time-consuming business – or underestimate the importance of the odd millimetre here or quarter inch there; they are all essential.

MEASURING FOR CURTAINS

First, decide on the length of your curtains. Floor-length is often preferable, particularly in a main room where they will emphasize the window, and are needed to balance pelmets or valances. Flamboyant arrangements can bear draped hems, but avoid them if no-one in the house is prepared to arrange the hems every time the curtains are opened or closed. Shorter, sill-length curtains – either to, or just below, the ledge – are suitable for more modest windows, often in kitchens and bathrooms where longer curtains would be impractical.

WIDTH

❑ Measure the length of the track, pole or pelmet board (*a*), allowing for any returns (*b*) and sufficient housing space (*c*) for the curtains to stack back. Allow 8cm (3in) for an overlap.

LENGTH

❑ Allow for a 12mm (½in) gap between the top of the curtain and the base of the pelmet board. For covered boards and fascia allow for the heading to run flush with the top of the pelmet board. Allow for the heading to cover an exposed track when the curtains are closed.

Floor-length curtains

❑ Grazing the floor (*d*): deduct 6mm (¼in) to allow for clearance.

CURTAINS, FLOOR-LENGTH *24*
CURTAINS, DRAPED HEM *13, 25*
CURTAINS, SILL-LENGTH *32, 42*
CURTAINS, FIXED HEAD *54*
VALANCE *108*
TIEBACKS *138*
SWAGS AND TAILS *128*
ROLLER BLIND *143*
ROMAN BLIND *146*
PULL-UP BLIND *150*

❑ Draped on the floor (*d*): add 5-10cm (2-4in) to the finished length.

Sill-length curtains

❑ To the windowsill (*f*): make the curtains to this length if the sill is too deep for the curtains to hang clear.

❑ If possible try to make the curtains to just below the windowsill.

Fixed-headed curtains

❑ Measure in the same way as pull-up blinds but allow for two curtains that overlap in the centre.

❑ The curtains will be hung either from screw eyes or touch-and-close fastening, run along the front edge of the pelmet board.

❑ The overlap should be held in place by a tack or small-headed nail. This is often hidden by a rosette or cording; or use a tack and work the head through the front layer of fabric.

Pelmet or valance

❑ The depth (e) should be 20-25% of the curtain length, although a serpentine pelmet or valance may drop much lower at the sides.

Track position

❑ The track will either hang alone and exposed – in which case it should be positioned just above the window, fixed to the wall or the architrave – or it will be screwed to the base of the pelmet board and hidden behind a covered fascia, valance or pelmet.

❑ Where appropriate, the distance between the pelmet board and track and the window (g) can be adjusted to alter the apparent height of the window. The higher the board and track, the taller the appearance of the window. Make sure not to position the board, track or pole too high: it will seem out of proportion and leaves a section of wall exposed. This is best disguised with a pelmet or valance. Otherwise keep the fittings in their usual place, just above the window.

MEASURING FOR TIEBACKS

❑ Tiebacks are needed when the curtains are to be draped back from a wholly or partially closed position.

❑ Measure around the curtain at the chosen height, ensuring that the tieback neither crushes the fabric nor hangs limply away from the leading edge of the curtain.

❑ Allow for piping if required.

❑ Depending on the fabric design, tiebacks can be cut on the straight or the cross grain. Make a template and experiment with the most economical use of fabric.

MEASURING FOR BLINDS

When measuring for blinds the main consideration is whether to hang them inside or outside the window reveal. The first option is often the neatest, particularly for Roman or roller blinds, but beware of blocking light or impeding the window itself. Blinds hung outside the reveal will

Points to remember

❑ Always measure once the fittings are in place.

❑ Make notes and sketches to help recall details. A Polaroid camera can be helpful in this respect.

❑ Use a 5m (16ft) retractable steel tape measure.

❑ Enlist help to hold the tape measure in position.

❑ Use a step ladder to reach the top of the window.

❑ It is vital to ensure that all measurements are correct before cutting into the fabric. Check every measurement twice.

❑ Make several finished-length measurements as floors can be uneven and windows out of true.

❑ Don't forget to add seam and turning allowances to all measurements.

❑ Allow for radiators, window seats and sills. Nothing should push against the back of the curtains or blind.

❑ If a picture rail obstructs the edges of a hard pelmet, make a template and shape the edges to fit.

❑ Don't forget to allow for contrasting fabrics, tiebacks and piping.

❑ Check the pattern repeat and take into account before calculating the fabric requirement (see page 89).

❑ For curtains hung from a track screwed to the pelmet board, measure the finished length from the base of the pelmet board. Then calculate the hook drop – this will depend on the different configurations of heading tape and curtain track. Allow 12mm (½in) clearance between the top edge of the curtain and the base of the board.

❑ For curtains hung from a pole measure from the base of the curtain ring.

❑ For fixed-headed curtains attached to the front and side edges of the pelmet board, measure from the top of the board and add a few centimetres for the top edge of the curtain to stand up above the board.

❑ For Roman blinds, measure the finished length from the top edge of the pelmet board, then add the depth of the touch-and-close fastening (2.5cm/1in is usually enough) – this will be run along the top of the board, just behind the front edge.

❑ For pull-up blinds measure from the top of the pelmet board and add a few centimetres for the heading to stand up above the board.

❑ Allow for turnings and hems at the top, bottom and sides. Different curtains and blinds require different dimensions so check the project instructions.

give greater flexibility as regards size and can also be used to make the window appear substantially larger.

WIDTH

❑ Pull-up blinds (*a*) : to extend along the front of the board and the returns.

❑ Roman blinds (*b*) : to cover the front edge of the board, not the returns.

❑ Roller blinds using either a side-winding or sprung-roller mechanism: these may be fixed either to the outside (*c*) or inside (*d*) of the window reveal. They may be side-, top- or face-fixed, depending on which is the best surface. The pin length (the overall length of the roller fitting) is 3.2cm (1¼in) less than the cloth width. If hung inside the reveal, allow for the pin length to be 6mm (¼in) less than the actual width of the reveal. In this way there is a 3mm (⅛in) gap between the end of the roller and the wall.

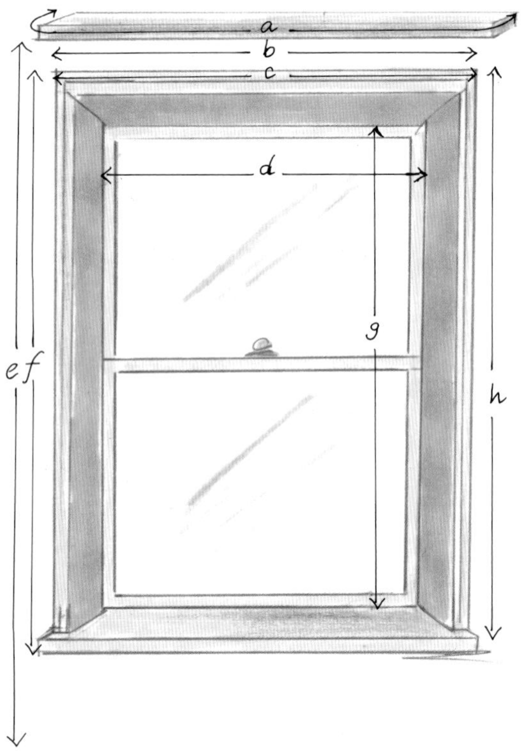

a: Pull-up blind: finished width
b: Roman blind: width
c: Roller blind outside reveal: width
d: Roller blind inside reveal: width
e: Pull-up blind: finished length
f: Roman blind: length to sill
g: Roller blind inside reveal: length
h: Roller blind outside reveal: length

LENGTH

❑ The hem of a pull-up blind should hang 20-30cm (8-12in) below the sill, so that the scallops along the lower edge are still visible when the blind is fully extended (e). A pull-up curtain should be made to graze the floor.

❑ A Roman blind (*f*) or roller blind (*g* and *h*) will hang to the sill, or slightly below if the sill does not protrude. Add 25-30cm (10-12in) to be left rolled up at the top of a roller blind, even when down.

CALCULATING FABRIC QUANTITY

❑ The flat width (hem measurement) of a pull-up blind is two to two and a half times the finished width (heading measurement).

❑ The flat width of a Roman or roller blind is the same as the measured width (see above) plus allowances for top, hem and side turnings. A Roman blind lining should be given extra length to allow for the pleated batten slots (see page 146).

MEASURING FOR SWAGS AND TAILS

Like other pelmets and valances, swags and tails hang from a pelmet board which, when accompanied by curtains, is fitted with a curtain track beneath.

❑ To work out the dimensions of a swag, hang a chain or piece of leadweight tape from either end of the pelmet board. Adjust to follow the lower curve of the finished swag (*a*).

❑ The distance along the top of the pelmet board represents the top edge of the swag (*b*).

❑ With (*a*) as the base edge and (*b*) as the top edge, and with a depth (*d*) two to two and a half times the pleated depth (c), cut out a template to the correct shape to assess fabric quantity. Allow for cutting the swag on the cross grain for plain fabrics. Fabrics with an obvious pattern or noticeable nap, which cannot be tilted to a 45° angle, must be cut on the straight grain.

❑ The inside edge of the tails should be the same depth as the swag (*c*).

❑ The outside edge should be half the length of the curtains (e).

❑ The width requirement for tails varies, depending on the type of tail. The best solution is to cut a (paper) template for the tail, pleat it up and work out the dimensions. The tail in the project (see page 129) requires seven times the finished width, plus the return, plus a 5cm (2in) flap to curl around the inner edge of the tail.

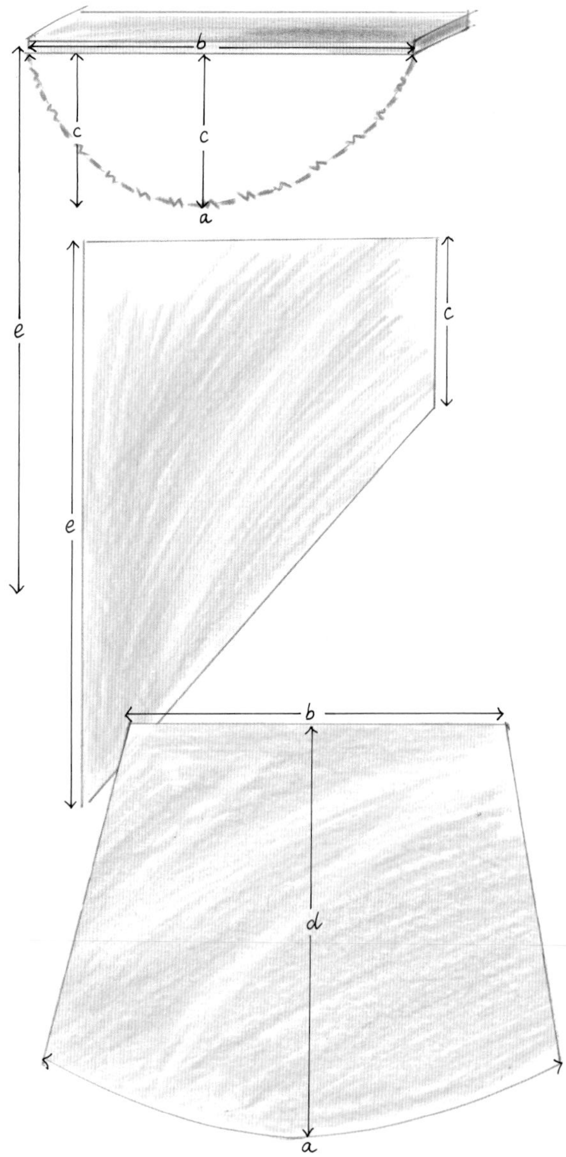

MATCHING PATTERNS

Patterned fabrics have what is known as a 'repeat'. This is the vertical distance between each section of repeated pattern. Establish the size of the repeat before buying or cutting the fabric.

❑ When the pattern is matched horizontally the sums involved in calculating fabric quantities are straightforward. Work out how many repeats will need to be cut to fit into the required cut length of fabric. For example, if a repeat is 61cm (24in) and the cut drop needs to be 2m (79in), four repeats (2.4m/96in) will need to be cut each time. It is necessary to cut more than is needed to avoid cutting a different part of the pattern with each drop. There will often be wastage, particularly with large repeats (**1** top).

❑ Less easy are the fabrics with a half drop repeat. When laid side by side the pattern does not match horizontally and the fabric has to be dropped by one half of a repeat so that the pattern abutting the selvedge coincides horizontally. One whole extra repeat should be added to the number of repeats calculated above as one half of a repeat will be lost at the top and bottom of joined lengths. Bear this in mind, too, when making a pair of curtains. The pattern should run across a pair of drawn curtains (**2** below).

❑ To overcome the need to cut off a whole repeat each time, it is possible to cut a section of pattern off the side of a drop. In this way, the next vertical section of pattern is exposed; this will match the adjoining drop without the need to raise or lower the fabric. Because of the loss of width this is not usually the best solution (**3** above).

❑ To match a pattern accurately, the use of ladderstitch is advisable (see page 179). Few patterns are printed in a perfect horizontal. Be prepared to follow the pattern in favour of the strict grain of the fabric. If the design is seriously out of true to such an extent that it is quite visibly squint, return the fabric (before cutting into it) to the supplier.

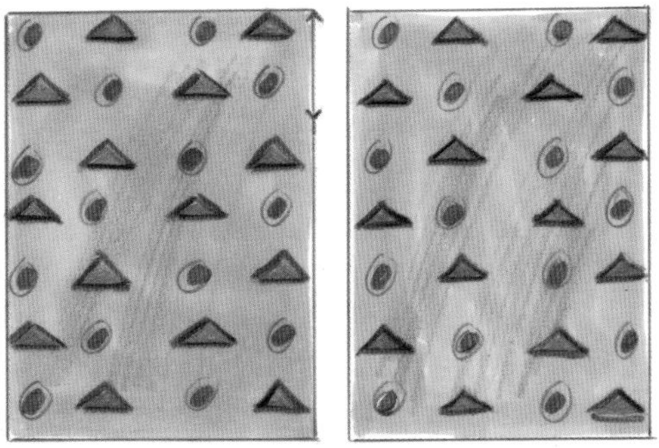

1

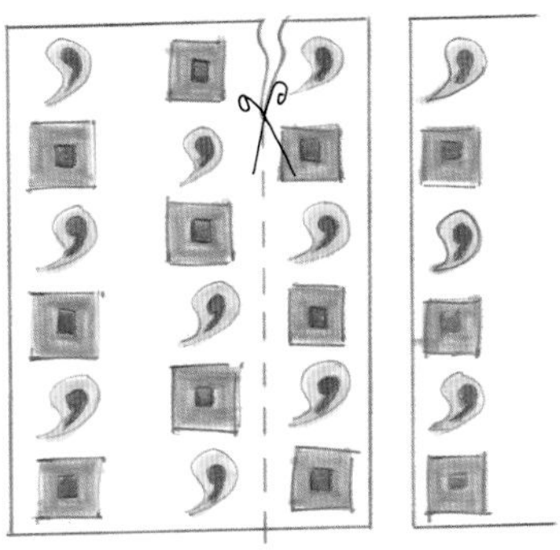

3

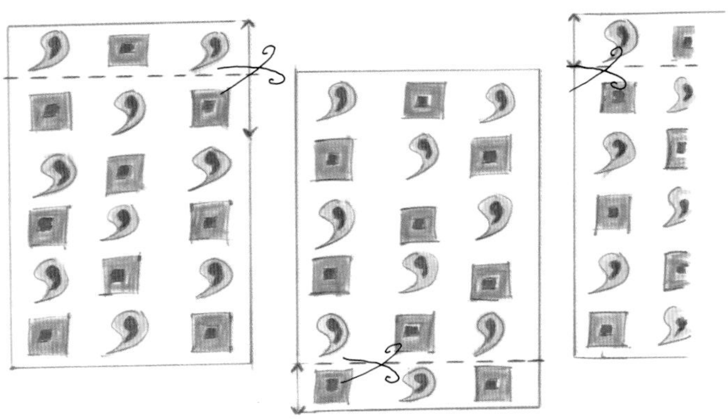

2

Before you start

❑ Before you start, check the whole length of fabric for flaws and quantity.

❑ Check all calculations and measure out the drops carefully before cutting.

❑ Cut a small piece of fabric across the top corner of each drop – then you will always know which is the top and which the bottom.

❑ As each drop is cut, fold it carefully and put it to one side, or roll it back on to the cardboard tube to avoid creasing or damaging glazes.

❑ Buy plenty of fabric in the first place. Different dye lots can vary markedly in colour.

❑ Buy lining and interlining in the same width as the face fabric: the seams will then coincide.

❑ Match thread carefully to the fabric for colour and fibre. Large projects will need more than a single reel.

❑ If weights are difficult to obtain, use coins.

❑ Make sure that the machine needle is sharp – blunt needles will pull threads. Keep a good stock of needles and pins.

❑ A soft pincushion and well-fitting thimble are important aids to good sewing.

❑ Have plenty of clear workspace, and keep threads and needles orderly. Much time can be wasted searching for lost scissors or pincushions.

❑ Tidy up at the end of each day. It is much easier to start with everything in its place.

❑ Make sure that a good light source illuminates the work.

❑ Sewing, perhaps while listening to books on tape or to the radio, can be a real pleasure.

❑ Keep hands clean.

❑ Avoid leaving cups of tea or coffee where they might be spilled.

❑ An extension lead is helpful for the iron and sewing machine.

❑ Beware of melting nylon carpets with the iron if you are working on the floor. Use a folded piece of cloth as protection.

❑ Avoid overfilling the steam iron – splashes can be disastrous.

Unlined Curtains

MATERIALS
- ❑ Face fabric
- ❑ Heading buckram (handmade heading)
- ❑ Heading tape (machine-stitched heading)
- ❑ Weights or leadweight tape (optional)

Unlined cotton curtains act as a gentle filter to bright sunlight. (BELOW)

Unlined curtains can provide a gentle, translucent finish to a window, softening – but not excluding – daylight. Like any other curtain, they can carry stiffened headings, pleated headings (French, pencil or gathered, either machine-stitched or handmade) and delicate trimmings – a bobble fringe, for example, looks at its best on a simple, white cotton curtain.

Making unlined curtains is an excellent project for those who are inexperienced in the art of curtainmaking, and the quick and effective results provide the encouragement needed to try something a little more challenging next time.

If the curtains are intended to be washed, it is advisable to pre-wash the fabric and use pre-shrunk heading tape. If this is likely to cause a loss of body or finish, leave a generous hem to be let down at a later date. Watch out for handmade headings: heading buckrams, particularly fusible, are difficult to wash or dryclean.

INSPIRATION *40, 70*
BUCKRAM (FABRICS) *83*
MEASURING *86*
MATCHING PATTERNS *89*
HEADING TAPES *107*
CUTTING OUT *178*
SLIPSTITCH *180*
FRENCH SEAMS *181*
FLAT-FELL SEAMS *181*
MITRING CORNERS *181*

MEASURING

❑ Width: the flat, unpleated width should be two and a half times the finished width. Add 5cm (2in) for side turnings.
❑ Length: add 10cm (4in) to the finished length for the hem.
❑ Handmade headings: add 25cm (10in) for a 12.5cm (5in) heading, 15cm (6in) for a 7.5cm (3in) heading.
❑ Machine-stitched headings: add 7.5cm (3in).

MAKING UP

❑ Cut the drops of face fabric. Allow for any pattern.
❑ Join the drops of fabric using French or flat-fell seams, matching the pattern if necessary.
❑ Make double 12mm (½in) side turnings. Pin and slipstitch into place, leaving 25cm (10in) top and bottom (total) for the hem and top turning.
❑ Turn up a double 5cm (2in) hem. Lace or net can be machine-stitched close to the fold. There is no need to mitre the hem of a net or other very light curtain.
❑ It is advisable to insert weights into unlined curtains, especially when they are floor length. Leadweight tape, inserted into the fold of the hem, is suitable for lightweight curtains and will help to anchor the curtain to the floor without being visible against the light. (**1**)

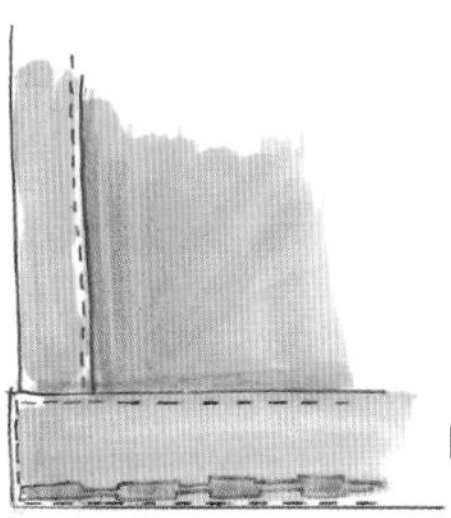

1

❑ Alternatively, for a heavier fabric, prepare standard weights by stitching them into small bags of lining fabric. (**2**)

2

❑ Mitre the lower corners, and then stitch the bags into the mitres at the base of each vertical seamline. Pin, tack and slipstitch close to the fold. (**3**)

3

❑ An unlined curtain can carry either handmade headings, stiffened with heading buckram, or have machine-stitched tapes attached to the back of the curtain. Fusible buckram is impregnated with glue that is released by a hot iron, thus attaching it to the rest of the curtain. Non-fusible buckram (more easily cleaned, see page 83) has to be hand-stitched into the heading. Handmade headings are handpleated, while machine-stitched tapes are drawn up on cords.

Handmade heading

❑ Cut heading buckram to the flat width of the curtain.
❑ Place the strip of heading buckram flush with the top edge of the fabric, under the side turnings. Tack into place. (**4**)

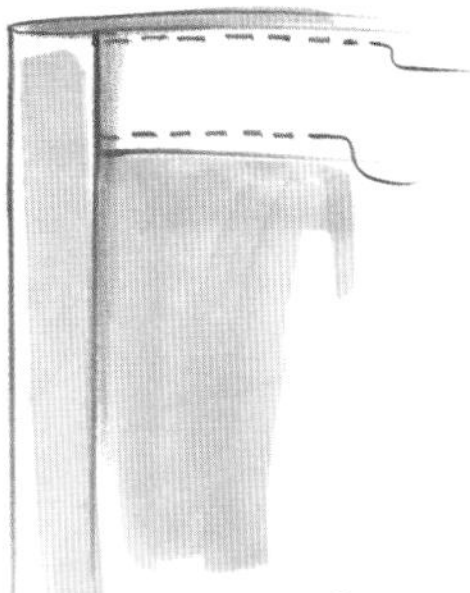

4

❑ Fold the buckram over twice so that it is encased in the fabric.
❑ Slipstitch along the base and up the sides of the stiffened heading. (**5**)

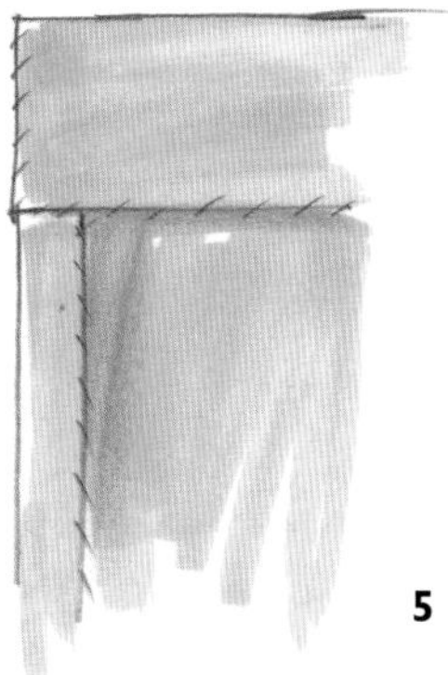

5

❑ If using fusible heading buckram, remove the tacking and press the heading with a hot iron to release the glue in the buckram, which then holds the heading in position.
❑ The tacking stitches and slipstitches will hold non-fusible buckram in place.
❑ To pleat up the handmade heading, see page 97.

Machine-stitched heading

❑ Make a 7.5cm (3in) top turning. Lay the heading tape along the back of the curtain. Pin, tack and machine-stitch the tape into position. Hold the heading taut while machine-stitching, and make sure that both rows of machine stitches start from the same side of the curtain – this will avoid puckering. Trap the heading-tape cords with machine stitches on the leading edge, and leave them free on the outer edge. In this way, as the heading is pulled up to its finished width, the cords will be pulled out to one side only, and so can be knotted and hidden behind the curtain. (**6a** & **6b**)

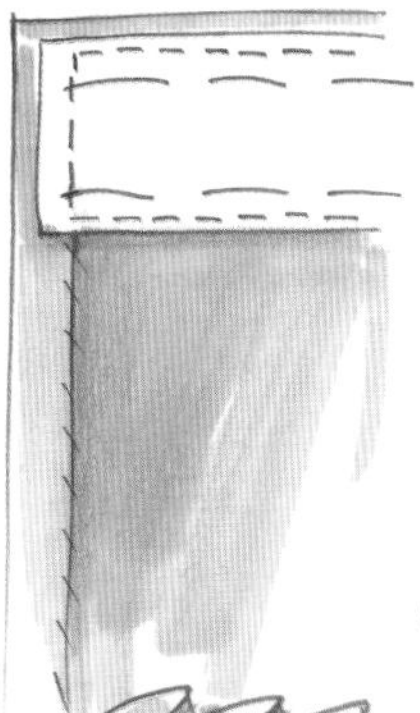

6a

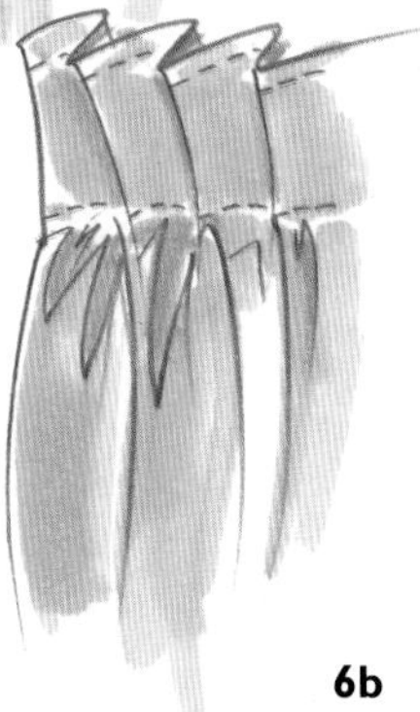

6b

❑ If a narrow (2.5cm/1in) heading tape is used and the heading is visible, not hidden behind a pelmet, the tape should be set down by at least 5cm (2in). A frill will form above the tape as it is gathered up. (**7a** & **7b** right)
❑ Wider tapes should always be set 6mm (¼in) down from the top edge. Take the position of the dropped hook into account when measuring the finished length of the curtains.

HANGING

Handmade heading

❑ Attach pin-on or sew-on hooks to the back of the heading (see page 98).

Machine-stitched heading

❑ Pull up the cords in the heading tape to the required width, making sure to form even pleats. Excess cord should never be cut, but should be looped up and hidden behind the curtain. When the curtains are washed or cleaned the cords can then simply be untied.
❑ Insert the hooks into the pockets provided.
❑ There is usually no necessity to dress unlined curtains, as they may lack the body needed to form uniform pleats. In any case, an informal look is often more appropriate to this style of curtaining.

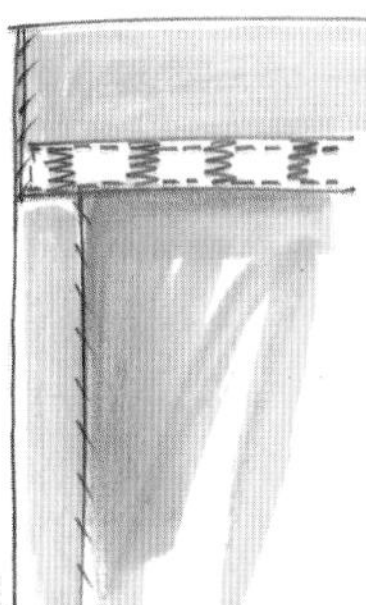

7a

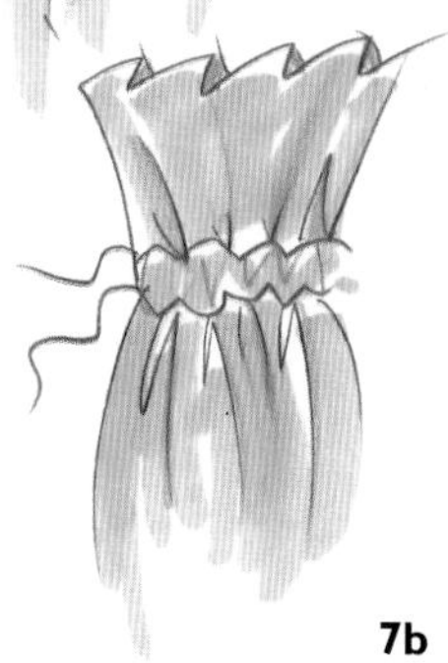

7b

Lined Curtains

Simple lined curtains are the best solution in a wide variety of situations. They are not difficult to make and, depending on the lining, can be light and billowing or, with a blackout or milium lining, defend against draughts and strong sunlight. A simple cotton lining will give curtains some substance – more than unlined curtains and less than interlined.

Use lined rather than interlined curtains for small windows and sill-length curtains: interlining can safely be reserved for larger projects, once a few successful unlined and lined curtains have provided the necessary confidence to embark on more ambitious schemes. The techniques involved in making a simple lined curtain are not difficult to master and are an excellent way to familiarize yourself with the basic curtainmaking skills.

If cleaning problems are likely to arise, use detachable linings. The curtains are made in much the same way, but with the use of a special double heading tape. The lining can then be removed from the face fabric and both elements washed separately. Washing lined curtains is not usually advisable, as the face fabric and lining may shrink to different degrees.

This lined curtain is part of a jolly arrangement of wooden pelmet and gathered valance. Linings can be plain or patterned: here, a highly original use is made of a traditional floral cotton, which is revealed when the curtains are folded back from Italian stringing. Once closed, only passers-by will enjoy the unusual choice of lining fabric. One note of caution, however – the face fabric may take on a mottled look when a lining with a busy design is lit from behind by the sunlight. (LEFT)

INSPIRATION *30, 34, 39, 42, 63*
LININGS (FABRICS) *83*
BUCKRAM (FABRICS) *83*
MEASURING *86*
MATCHING PATTERNS *89*
HEADING TAPES *107*
CUTTING OUT *178*
HERRINGBONE STITCH *179*
SLIPSTITCH *180*
LOCKSTITCH *180*
MITRING CORNERS *181*

MATERIALS

❑ Face fabric
❑ Lining
❑ Weights
❑ Heading buckram (handmade headings)
❑ Heading tape (machine-stitched headings)

MEASURING

❑ Width: the flat, unpleated width should be two and a half times the finished width. For the face fabric, add 8cm (3in) for side turnings; for the lining, add 5cm (2in).
❑ Length: for the face fabric, add 15cm (6in) for the hem plus 7.5cm (3in) for the top turning; for the lining, add 10cm (4in) plus 2.5cm (1in).

MAKING IT UP

❑ Cut out the drops in face fabric and lining.
❑ Join the drops of fabric, and lining, matching the pattern if necessary.
❑ Trim the selvedges and press open seams.
❑ Turn up a double 5cm (2in) hem in the lining and machine-stitch close to the fold.
❑ Lay fabric face down. Make 4 cm (1½in) side turnings. Herringbone-stitch into position, ending 25cm (10in) from the base and top.
❑ Stitch the weights into lining bags (see page 91).
❑ Turn up a double 7.5cm (3in) hem, mitre the corners and stitch the bags into the mitres and at the base of each vertical seamline.
❑ Slipstitch the hem.
❑ If you are handmaking the heading, this is the moment to insert the stiffening, before the lining is attached to the back of the curtain. If you are using a machine-stitched tape, this is stitched on when the rest of the curtain is complete, after the lining has been attached.

Handmade heading

❑ Cut the heading buckram to the flat width of the curtain and lay into position along the back of the face fabric, ending at the finished side and top edges of the curtain. Tack into place (fusible buckram). (**1**)

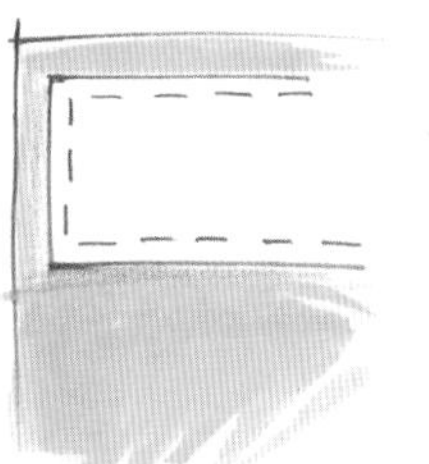

1

❑ Herringbone-stitch the buckram into position around all four sides (non-fusible buckram). (**2**)

2

❑ Turn back the top and side edges of the face fabric over the buckram.

Locking in the lining

❑ Lay the lining over the back of the curtain. The hem of the lining should lie 2.5cm (1in) above that of the finished curtain.
❑ Turn in the edge of the lining 2.5cm (1in) from the edge of the curtain. Slipstitch along the fold ending at the base of the buckram. Then fold the lining back on itself, forming a fold along the centre of the lining. Lockstitch the length of the fold. Repeat this process along every seamline and half-width, until you reach the other side of the curtain. (**3** right)
❑ When you reach the other side, turn the lining in again and slipstitch 2.5cm (1in) from the edge.
❑ If you are handmaking a heading, turn in the top of the lining and slipstitch. Remove the tacking and release the glue with a hot iron

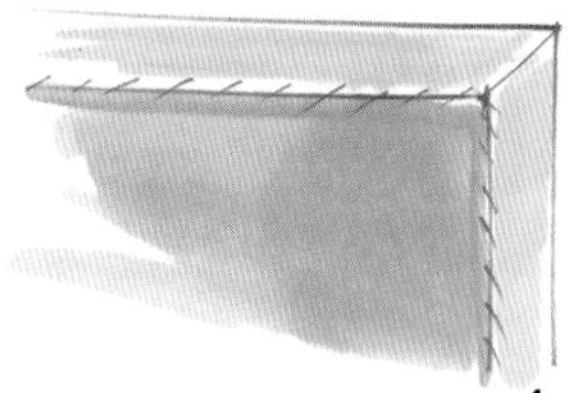

4

(fusible buckram). (**4**)
❑ If you are handmaking the heading, pleat or gather it (see pages 97, 99 for more details on how to do this).

Machine-stitched headings

❑ Make sure that the top raw edges of the face fabric and lining are aligned, trimming if necessary. Make a 7.5cm (3in) top turning. Pin, tack and machine-stitch the tape into position over the turning (see page 91). (**5** right).
❑ If the heading is visible and narrow 2.5cm (1in) tape is being used, the tape will need to be set down by at least 5cm (2in). A frill then forms along the top of the heading.

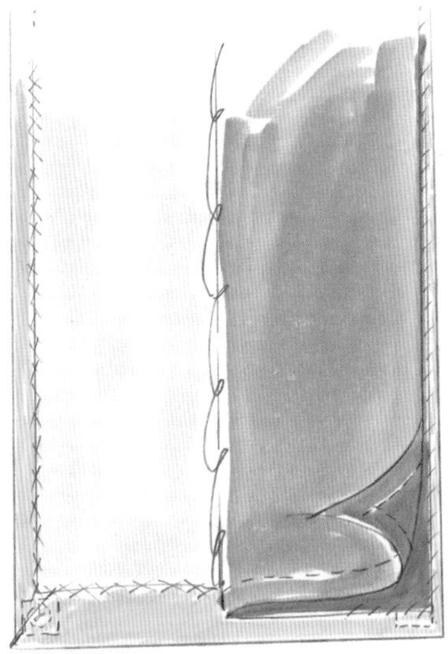

3

Other machine-stitched tapes are stitched 12mm (½in) from the top edge of the curtain.

HANGING

Handmade heading

❑ Attach pin-on or sew-on hooks to the back of the heading (see page 98).

Machine-stitched heading

❑ Pull up the cords in the heading tape from the outer edge to the required width, making sure to form even pleats. Knot the cords and insert the hooks along the back of the heading tape.

DRESSING

❑ To help the curtain retain neat, uniform folds – particularly in the case of French-pleated headings – it should be left tied with strips of lining fabric for several days after hanging (see page 177).

5

Interlined Curtains

MATERIALS
❑ Face fabric
❑ Interlining
❑ Lining
❑ Weights
❑ Heading buckram (handmade heading)
❑ Heading tape (machine-stitched heading)

Making interlined curtains requires the core skills of a good curtainmaker. They involve manoeuvring large areas of fabric and interlining, leave you covered in fluff, and demand patience and concentration. The results, however, make all the effort worthwhile. A well-made pair of interlined curtains will reward you by lasting for many years, their plump pleats giving an expensive finish to any room. In winter they keep out the cold and in summer they exclude heat. They are shown to best effect when taken to floor length.

Interlined curtains, particularly when made up in a plain colour, can take a variety of decorative features: a generous band of contrast edging, lush fringes or a padded edge. Visible headings are greatly enhanced with a looped line of cording, finished with knots and tassels – a much-neglected and highly effective way of making even inexpensive fabrics look special.

Interlining takes three forms: synthetic, bump (a thick cotton, not unlike a heavy blanket) or domette (a lighter version, similar to flannelette). The first is inexpensive, the second wonderfully thick and heavy, and the third a delicate solution for lightweight fabrics such as silk. Domette is always used for swags and tails.

Having the correct tools and a proper worktable makes interlining curtains a much easier task. Of all the projects in this book, this one makes maximum use of the table: corners can be kept square and the time-consuming interlocking of the interlining and lining is made relatively easy and less backbreaking.

Do not forget that if a pelmet or valance is to accompany the curtains, it should carry the same lining and interlining (swags and tails being an exception). A predominantly white fabric should use bleached interlining and white lining; otherwise use an unbleached interlining and cream lining. Light will penetrate even interlined curtains (unless a blackout lining is used), so be careful not to upset the colour of the fabric by using an inappropriately coloured lining.

Points to remember

❑ Make sure that the layers of fabric, interlining and lining lie flat, without wrinkles. Use clamps or covered bricks to hold everything neatly in place.
❑ Buy lining and interlining in the same width as the fabric, so that seams align.
❑ Mark notches to identify the top and bottom of each drop.
❑ Keep to the straight grain on plain fabrics, otherwise follow the pattern if possible.
❑ Unusually long pieces of thread are needed for locking stitches: avoid knotting the thread in the middle of a seam, as this causes tension.
❑ Clip seams or trim selvedges to remove any tension.
❑ Try not to lose pins inside the curtain – use glass-headed pins for easy identification.

MEASURING
❑ Width: the flat, unpleated width should be two and a half times the finished width. For face fabric and interlining add 10cm (4in) for side turnings; for the lining, add 8cm (3in).
❑ Length: for the face fabric, add 10cm (4in) for the hem plus 5cm (2in) for the top turning; for the interlining, add 10cm (4in) for the hem; for the lining, add 10cm (4in) for the hem and 2.5cm (1in) for the top turning.

MAKING UP
❑ Cut the drops of fabric, lining and interlining. Make sure to allow for any pattern repeat.
❑ Join the drops of fabric and lining. Press open seams, trimming or clipping selvedges to relieve tension.
❑ Overlap the drops of interlining by 2.5cm (1in) and join with herringbone stitch.
❑ Turn up the lining hem with a double 5cm (2in) hem and machine-stitch close to the fold.

INSPIRATION *54, 59, 76, 100*
BUCKRAM (FABRICS) *83*
MEASURING *86*
MATCHING PATTERNS *89*
HEADING TAPES *107*
TOOLS AND EQUIPMENT *166*
DRESSING CURTAINS *177*
CUTTING OUT *178*
HERRINGBONE STITCH *179*
LOCKSTITCH *180*
MITRING CORNERS *181*

Locking in the interlining

❑ Place the fabric face down. Line up the side edge and base with the edges of the table.
❑ Lay the interlining on top, smoothing out any creases. Clamp, or hold in position with a covered brick.
❑ Fold the interlining over onto itself, so that a fold is formed along the centre. Run locking stitches from the finished top edge to the finished bottom edge, moving the fabric and interlining together up the table if necessary to finish the line of stitching. (**1**)

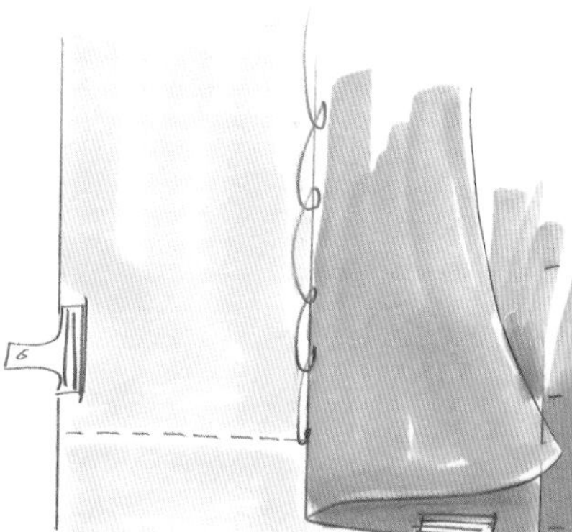

1

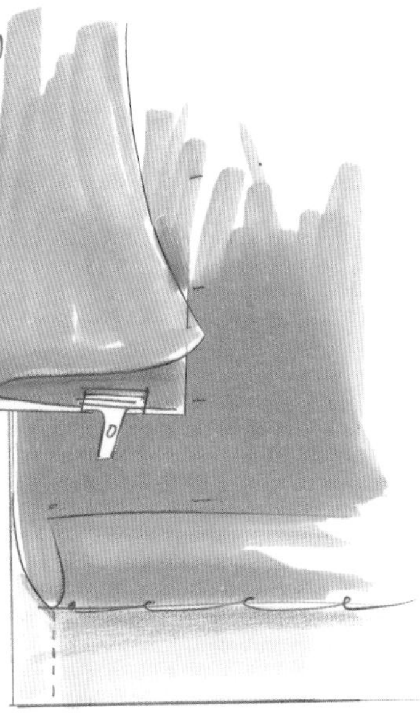

2

❑ Working out from the centre of the curtain, continue to fold the interlining back on itself every half-width, running parallel lines of locking stitches along every seamline and half-width until you reach the side of the curtain. The final row of locking stitches runs along the foldline that will become the finished side edge, holding the interlining tightly into the side turning.
❑ When the lines of locking stitches run from the leading edge to the outer edge, fold back the hem and lockstitch along the horizontal fold.
❑ Make sure to smooth the layers flat every time the curtain is moved on the table. (**2**)
❑ Flap over the side turnings and herring-bone-stitch into position, picking up only the interlining, not penetrating the front of the curtain, and finishing 25cm (10in) from the top and from the base.
❑ Turn up a 10cm (4in) hem.
❑ Stitch the weights into small bags of lining fabric (see page 91). (**6**)
❑ Mitre the lower corners, folding the interlining and fabric as one layer. Stitch the bags into the mitres and at the base of each vertical seamline.
❑ Leaving the edge raw, herringbone-stitch the hem into position.
❑ Like lined curtains, interlined ones can have handmade or machine-stitched headings.
❑ If you are handmaking the heading, now insert the stiffening, before the lining is attached to the back of the curtain. If you are using a machine-stitched tape, this is stitched on when the rest of the curtain is complete, after the lining has been attached.

Handmade heading

❑ Cut the heading buckram to the flat width of the curtain and lay into position, the top edge along the top foldline, the sides against the side foldline.
Tack into place (fusible buckram). (**3**)
❑ Herringbone-stitch the buckram into

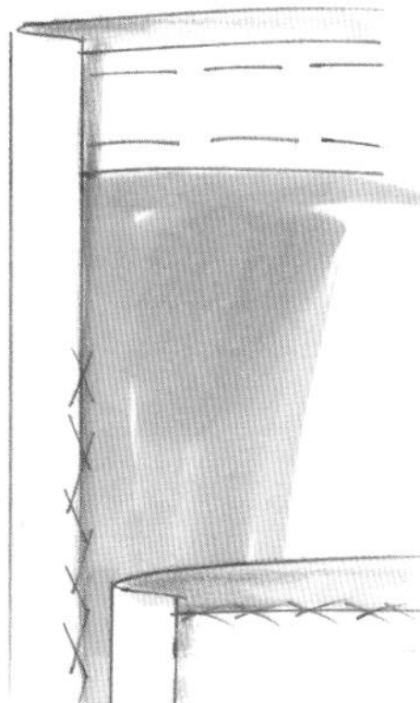

3

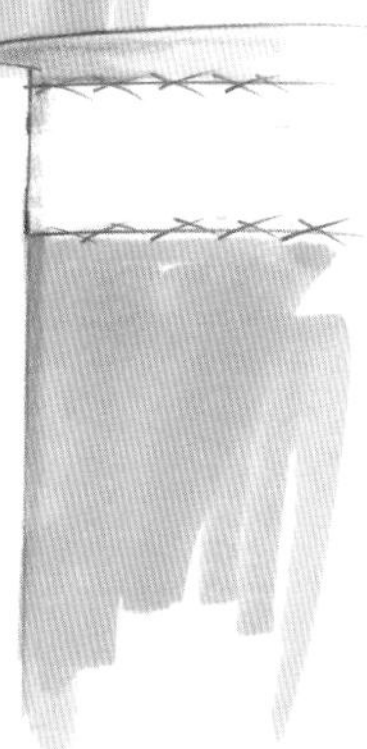

4

position around all four sides (non-fusible buckram). (**4** above)
❑ Turn back the top edge over the buckram, mitring the corners.

Locking in the lining

❑ Place the lining flat on the back of the curtain. The hem of the lining should lie 2.5cm (1in) above the base edge of the curtain.
❑ In much the same way as the interlining was attached to the face fabric, lockstitch the lining to the interlining again every half-width. (see **5** right)
❑ Turn in the sides of the lining 2.5cm (1in) from the edges. Slipstitch into place, extending the stitching 10cm (4in) around the base line. (**6**)

6

❑ If you are hand-making a heading turn in the top of the lining and slipstitch. Remove the tacking and release the glue with a hot iron (fusible buckram).
Pleat or gather (see pages 97, 99).

Machine-stitched heading

❑ Make sure that the top raw edges of the face fabric and lining are aligned, trimming if necessary. Make a 2.5cm (1in) top turning. Pin, tack and machine-stitch the tape into position over the turning (see page 91).

HANGING

Handmade heading

Attach, pin-on or sew-on hooks to back of heading (see page 98).

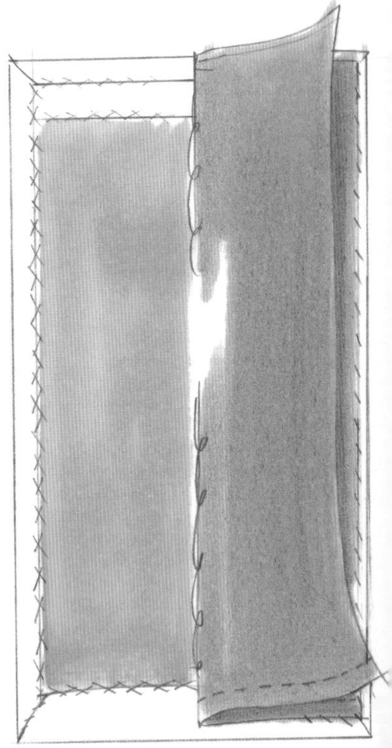

5

Machine-stitched heading

❑ Pull up the cords in the heading tape from the outer edge to the required width, making sure to form even pleats.
❑ Knot the cords and insert the hooks along the back of the heading tape. Wider tapes often have two or three choices of hook height. Brass hooks are stronger than plastic, are better for heavy, interlined curtains and will last longer.
❑ Bearing the weight of the curtain on your shoulder, mount the ladder and insert the hooks into the track or pole rings. Start from the centre of the curtain and work outwards – in this way, the weight of the curtain is distributed.

DRESSING

❑ It is essential to dress interlined curtains, particularly if they are French pleated. Leave the curtains tied up with strips of lining fabric for at least a week after hanging (see page 177).

Headings
Handmade Headings

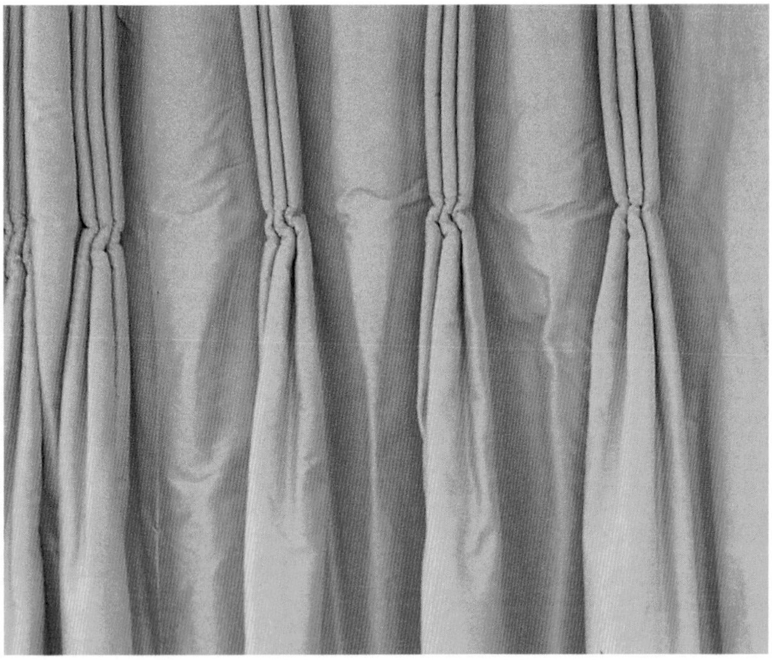

Classic French pleats are shown to effect in an apricot silk curtain, its heading free of any extraneous detail. (TOP) *A deep heading of handmade pencil pleats is decorated with striped cord and tassels.* (ABOVE)

Handmade headings have, until fairly recently, been considered the province of the professional curtainmaker. Little information was available that could help the amateur, and a request for heading buckram would have foxed the average haberdashery assistant. Now, however, things have changed: a much wider range of materials can be obtained, and the techniques needed for handmade headings are readily accessible.

Many people are unable to tell the difference between a machined or hand-stitched heading, hardly noticing the tell-tale double line of machine-stitching that attaches the sew-on tape to the rest of the curtain. As the subtleties of curtainmaking become apparent, however, so will the attractions of a hand-finished heading. It requires little more effort than the machined equivalent, but gives greater flexibility of hook position and dispenses with untidy cords. To the connoisseur, a handmade heading is an essential part of professional-looking curtains, and there is a certain pride associated with producing an entirely hand-stitched article.

The base of a handmade heading is a band of stiffening inserted behind the lining. This is known as 'heading buckram' and is made from a heavily stiffened cotton. 'Fusible' buckrams are impregnated with a glue that is released when the heading is pressed with a hot iron, thereby fixing them in position. 'Non-fusible' buckram has to be herringbone-stitched into place, but is more easily dry cleaned.

Once in place, the heading is pleated up by hand and stitched into position. If a heading is to be hidden behind a pelmet or valance, a sew-on heading is perfectly acceptable.

INSPIRATION *18, 30, 39, 41, 50, 54*
BUCKRAM (FABRICS) *83*
HERRINGBONE STITCH *179*
SLIPSTITCH *180*
TACKING *180*
PRICKSTITCH *180*

French Pleats

French pleats are the most commonly used heading shape. The curtain falls into folds that can be easily dressed and tied back, while the triple pleats are an excellent vehicle for cording shapes and can vary in depth from 7.5 to 20cm (3 to 8in).

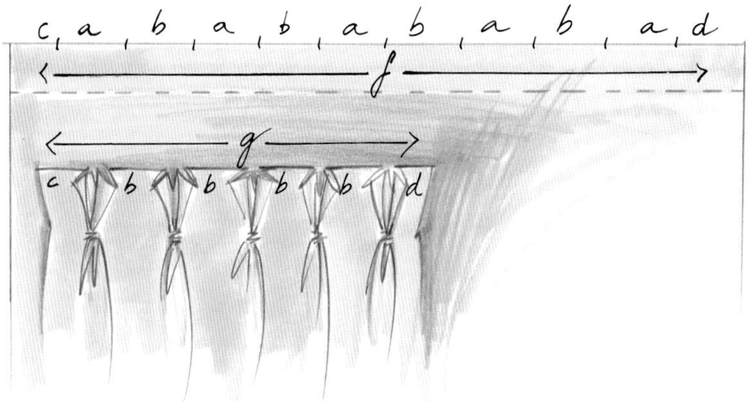

1

2

MEASURING

❑ Width: the flat, unpleated width should be two and a half times the finished width. (**1** & **2** above)

❑ Decide on the length of the return (*c*) and the overlap (*d*), usually 7.5cm (3in). The flat areas between the pleats (*b*) plus the return (*c*) and the overlap (*d*) will add up to the finished width of the curtain (*g*). Each flat area (*b*) should measure about 15cm (6in).

❑ First subtract (*c*) and (*d*) from your finished width (*g*). Then work out how many times (*b*) will fit into what is left.

❑ You now know how many spaces there will be between the pleats (*b*); add one to arrive at the total number of pleats (*a*). Now subtract the finished width (*g*) from the unfinished width (*f*) to calculate the excess that will be used up by the pleating. Divide your answer by the total number of pleats to arrive at your (*a*) measurement.

❑ For example, if the finished width of the curtain is 1.1m (45in), the return (*c*) is 12cm (5in) and the overlap (*d*) is 8cm (3in), there will be 90cm (36in) left for the flat areas between the pleats (*b*). There will therefore be room for six flat areas (*b*) and seven pleats (*a*). Bearing in mind that the unfinished heading (*f*) should be two and a half times wider than the finished, pleated-up heading (*g*), (*f*) will be 1.1m (45in) x 2.5 = 2.75m (112½ in). From this, subtract (6 x *b*) + *c* + *d* = *g* = 1.1m (45in) and you are left with 1.65m (67½ in). Divide this by the seven pleats and you are left with an (*a*) measurement of just over 23.5cm (9½in).

MAKING UP

❑ Using pins, mark out the heading.

❑ Pleat up and machine down the back of the pleats. The baseline of each pleat should be about 12mm (½in) above the baseline of the heading buckram. (**3**)

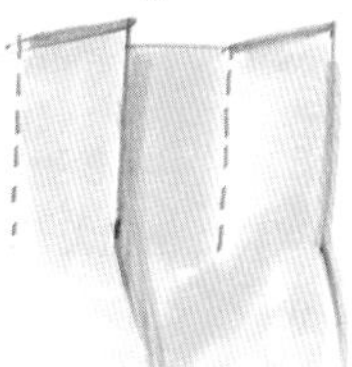

3

❑ Form the pleats into three sections, pressing the buckram into sharp edges. (**4**)

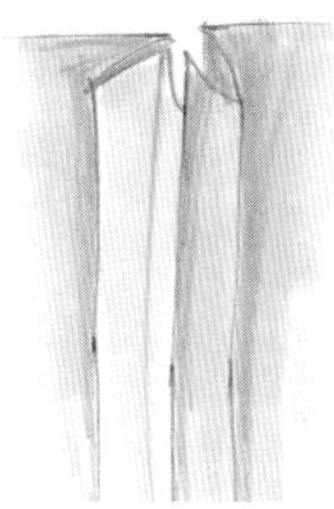

4

❑ Hand-stitch or machine across the base of the pleats. (**5** & **6**)

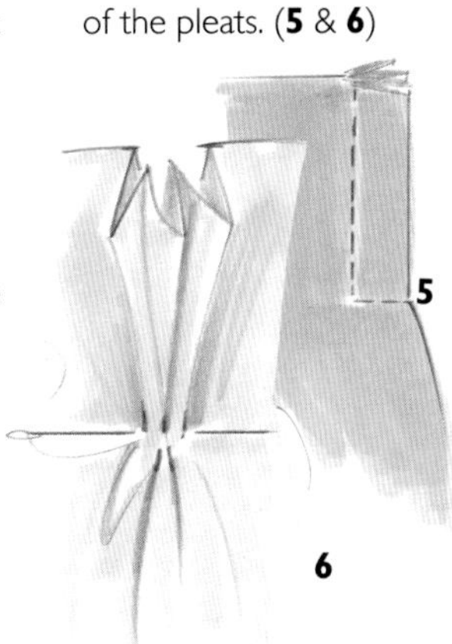

5

6

Goblet Pleats

Goblet pleats are closely related to French pleats and have much the same uses. The curve formed by the 'goblet' gives a more rhythmical, less regimented finish to the heading and seems to work outstandingly well in combination with a curved pelmet board and fixed heading. Like the French pleat, this heading lends itself to the use of cording in figures-of-eight, loops, knots and tassels. A covered button sewn to the base of each goblet can make an attractive finishing touch.

MAKING UP

❑ Form the triple pleat at the base, stitch into place and push out the upper section into a cup shape.

❑ Stuff the cup with a piece of wadding or interlining. (**7**)

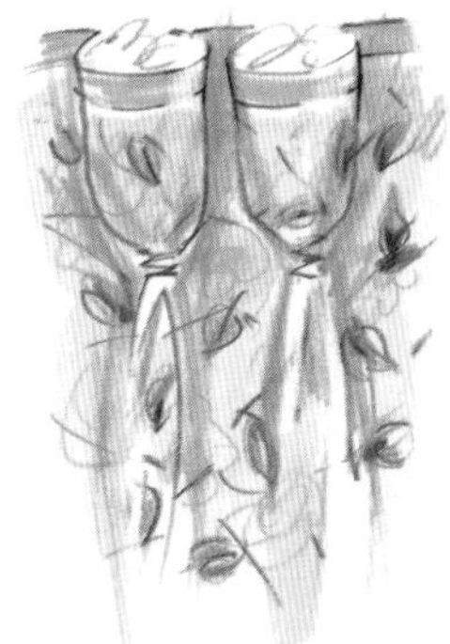

7

Pencil Pleats

Handmade pencil pleats are something of a luxury, as heading tape will do the job quite adequately. Like all handmade headings, however, they give a luxurious and professional finish to a pair of curtains, which will not have the double line of machine-stitching showing on the front of the heading. Another advantage in making your own is the freedom to choose the precise depth of heading you want. Sew-on hooks, the alternative to pin-on hooks, are also usually the province of professional workrooms, but there is no reason why they should not be used by the amateur. All that is needed is accurate measuring – unlike pin-on hooks, it is difficult to vary the hook positions.

MEASURING

❑ Width: the flat, unpleated width should be two and a half times the finished width.

MAKING UP

❑ Hand-sew a double line of matched stitches along the stiffened heading using strong thread. Leave one end loose. If handling a curtain with multiple drops, use a fresh piece of thread for every width of fabric. (**8**)

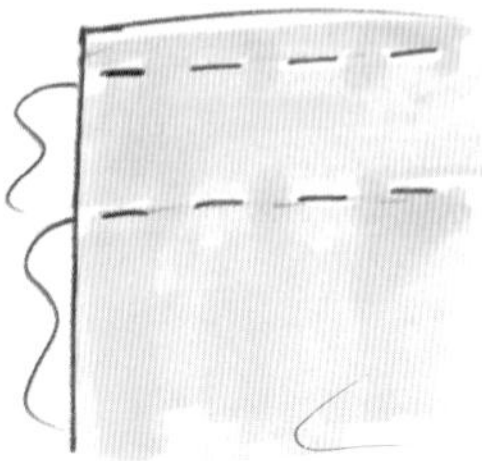

8

❑ Pull the threads up to the finished width.

❑ Cut a length of webbing to run along the back of the gathered heading. Cut a piece of lining to the same length, but double the width of the webbing. Stitch the strip of lining to the back of the webbing. (**9**)

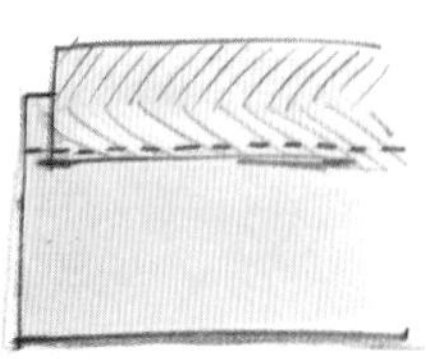

9

❑ Stitch the webbing to the back of the heading. It should run 6-12mm (¼-½in) below the top of the curtain. Use a double row of backstitch, picking up the heading buckram each time.

❑ Stitch the sew-on hooks to the webbing. Send the needle through all the layers, forming small, strong stitches that will be hidden in the back of the folds. (**10a** & **10b**).

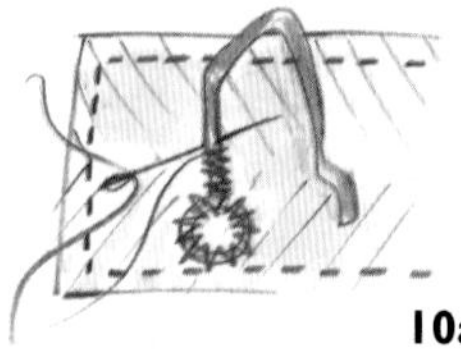

10a

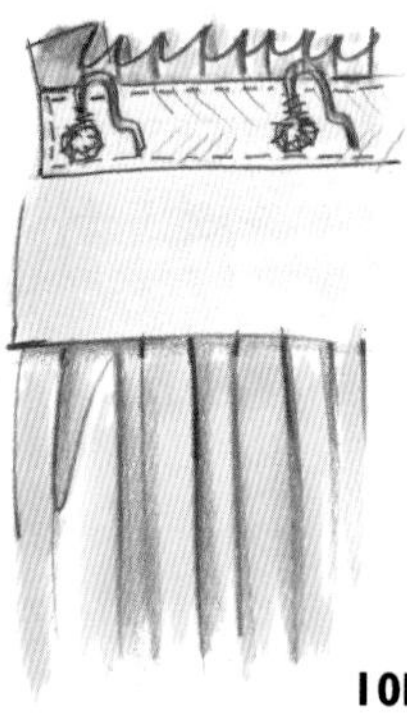

10b

❑ Turn the strip of lining over so that it covers the webbing, leaving the front of the hooks showing. (**11**)

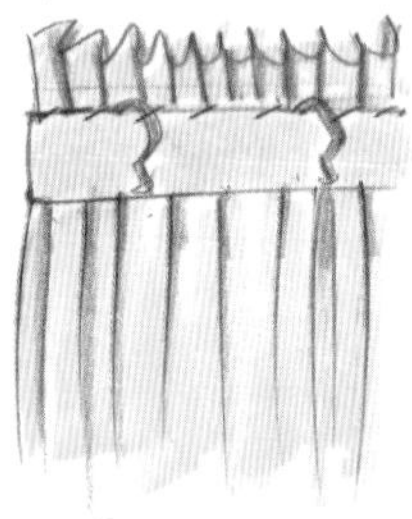

11

❑ Slipstitch along the top and sides of the lining strip.

Smocked Heading

A smocked heading to a pair of curtains looks most impressive. To sew such a heading is time-consuming but requires no special skill. Based on a pencil-pleated heading the pleats are alternately linked, using small hand-stitches, to form the lattice-work surface. Machine-sewn tapes are available that provide an outline for the smocking, but even these need to be finished by hand. Smocked headings are suitable for use with fixed-headed curtains which never need to be drawn back as the smocking prevents the curtains from stacking back in a uniform manner. The overlap of fixed-headed curtains makes an ideal position for a decorative bow, rosette or Maltese cross.

MAKING UP

❑ A smocked heading can vary in width and scale according to the dimensions of the curtain.

❑ Proceed as for pencil pleats (see left). When the pleats are made, mark alternating stitching points and catch the pleats together. (**12**)

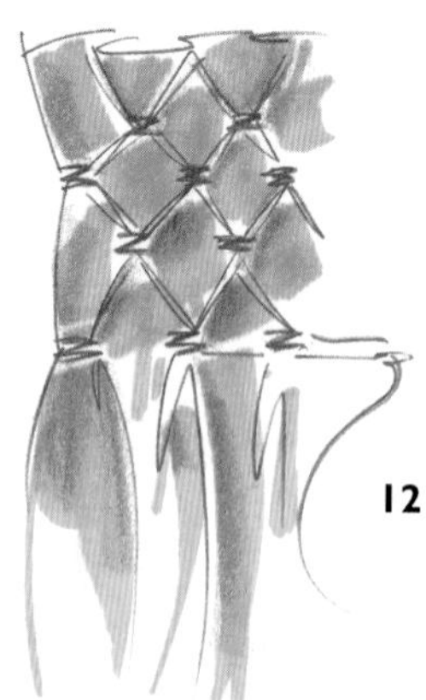

12

Gathered Heading

A narrow gathered heading gives a charming finish to small, dainty curtains. Heading buckrams are often too stiff for this type of heading and should be avoided. If a little extra padding is needed, fold a strip of domette interlining into the heading before it is gathered.

MEASURING

❑ Width: the flat, ungathered width should be two and a half times the finished width.

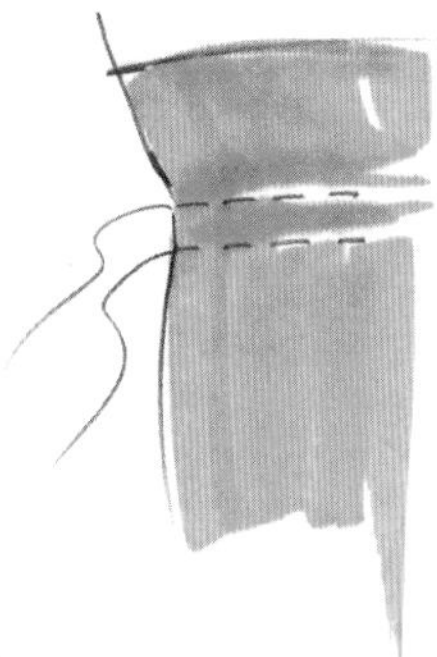

13a

MAKING UP

❑ Run a double line of matching stitches along the heading and gather up in a similar way to pencil pleats. (**13a** & **13b**)

❑ Secure the pleats with a strip of webbing stitched to the back of the heading. Pin-on or sew-on hooks can then be attached. To save time, consider using a narrow machine-stitched tape – the finished result will be much the same.

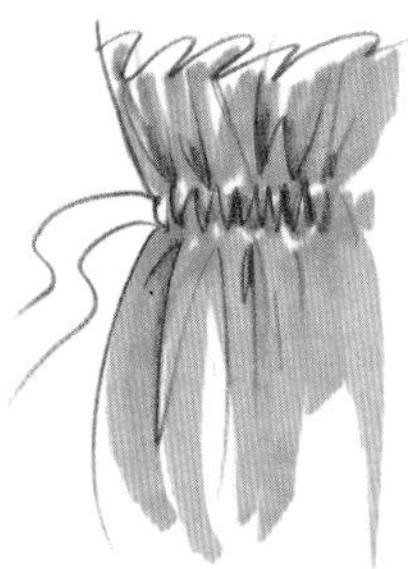

13b

Puffed Heading

When the gathering above a slotted or gathered heading is flattened out it becomes a 'puffed' heading. Instead of standing up from the pole in a stiff frill, a fat ruffle is formed along the heading. Little expertise is needed for this heading – the ruffle is merely pulled and teased until a satisfactory result is achieved. A layer of domette interlining, folded into the heading, makes for a more solid effect.

MAKING UP

❑ Make up as for a slotted heading, or gathered heading, leaving a generous frill along the top. The frill is then puffed out to form the fat ruffle that gives this heading its name. (**15**)

15

Cased Heading

A simple cased heading is used with light curtains or voiles. A more sophisticated version, known as a slotted heading, is described in detail in the project on page 104.

MEASURING

❑ Width: the flat, ungathered width should be two and a half times the finished width.

MAKING UP

❑ Turn in the top edge twice and run a line of machine-stitching close to the fold to form a slot.

❑ Gather the curtain on to a piece of dowel and fix to the window using rod sockets. (**14**)

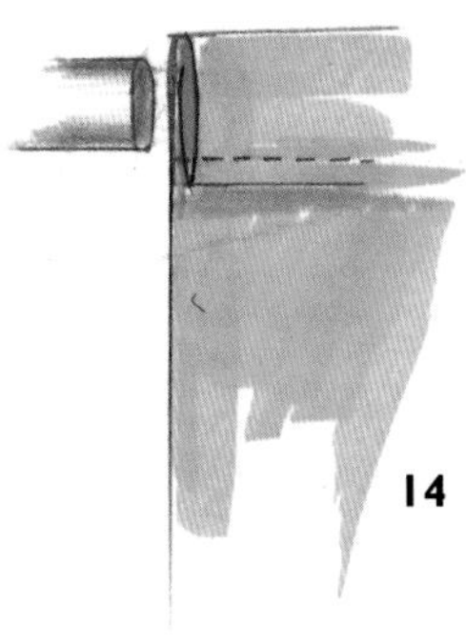

14

Unpleated Heading

Unpleated headings should only be used when the top of the curtain is visible and hanging from a decorative pole and rings, in which case the gently waved surface and lack of fussy heading shapes are quite a tonic. This type of heading usually carries ties that attach the curtain to the rings. The no-sew curtain on page 136 has an unpleated heading. In this particular instance, however, the stiffness of the fabric eliminates the need for heading buckram.

MEASURING

❑ Width: a curtain with an unpleated heading is only one and a half, not the usual two and a half, times wider than the window space that it is to occupy.

MAKING UP

❑ Insert the heading buckram behind the lining in the usual way, but do not pleat or gather the heading.

❑ Stitch ties to the back of the heading (see page 101) and tie in bows or knots to the curtain rings or directly onto the pole. (**16**)

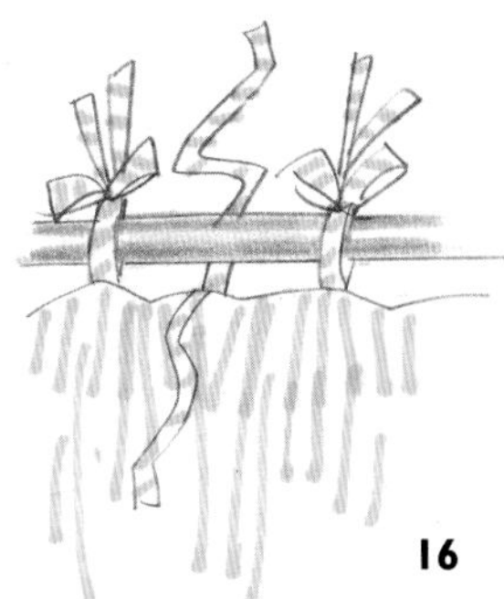

16

Corded Heading

A decorative line of cording gives an elegant finish to grand curtains. The cord is stitched at the base of the pleats and the loops are left to find their own lines. There are many different ways of looping and tying cord and tassels – care should be taken not to overburden a heading; simplicity is often the key to success.

MAKING UP

❑ Pin the cord to the front of the heading. Using a long, fine needle attach it with firm stitches in strong thread. The needle picks up a few threads from the front of the curtain and the back of the cord with each stitch. (**17**)

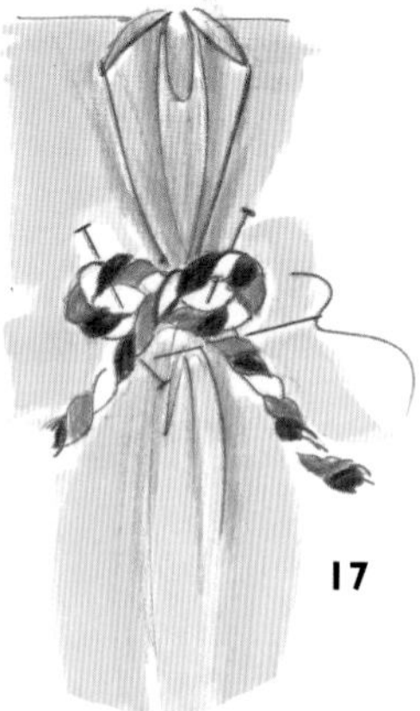

17

❑ Never try to attach a cord once the curtains are hung – working on a ladder for long periods with the arms held high is exhausting.

PROJECT

Curtain with Tied Heading

Tied or tab headings are among the simplest ways of hanging curtains. The headings may either be knotted to wooden or brass curtain rings, or looped over the pole itself. Tied to rings, the curtains will slide back smoothly. Fabric ties, however, will tend to stick when drawn over a pole, and may therefore be more suitable if the curtains are not intended to be opened and closed regularly. Headings cannot easily be tied to corded or uncorded metal or plastic tracks, which need curtain hooks to operate effectively.

Tied headings can give an informal look and work well for light kitchen or bathroom curtains, although they sometimes also suit the stiffened headings of heavy interlined curtains. By varying the shape and size of the ties, from narrow ribbons to fat bows, the effect can range from the floating to the voluptuous.

To avoid fussiness – pleats, ties, bows, pole, rings and finials all vying for attention – ties are often best used with plainer curtains. Remember that well-stiffened headings are less likely to droop between the ties. Otherwise, avoid sagging by placing the ties at frequent intervals.

For this cheerful kitchen curtain, a piece of checked fabric has been lined with striped material and tied to a simple wooden dowel. By day the curtain is caught with a bow to reveal the rooftop view. It is easy to remove for cleaning, and the absence of stiffening in the heading reduces the risk of shrinkage.

MATERIALS

❑ Face fabric
❑ Lining

FITTINGS

❑ Dowel
❑ Rod sockets

TOOLS

❑ Drill or bradawl

FITTING

❑ Attach a length of dowel to the top of the window using top- or face-fixing rod sockets. (**1a** & **1b**)

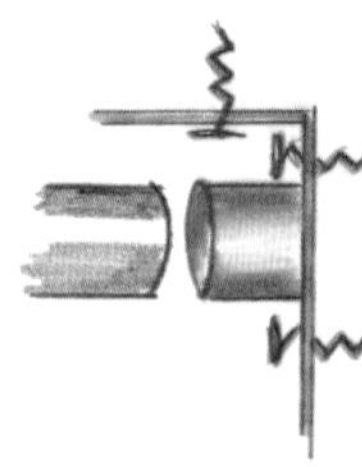

1a

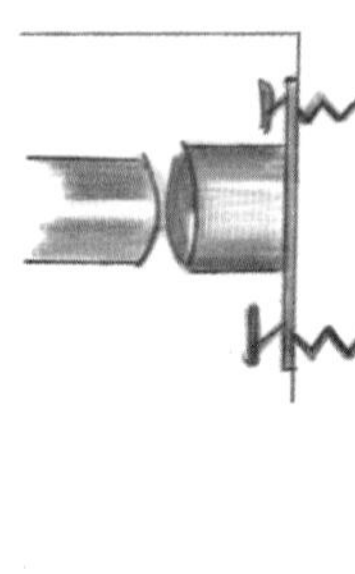

1b

MAKING UP

❑ Cut one square of face fabric to the length of the window, adding 30cm (12in) to the width to allow the curtain to drape slightly between ties.
❑ Cut one square of lining, allowing an extra 15cm (6in) all round.
❑ Cut the required number of ties in strips measuring 90 x 15cm (36 x 6in).
❑ Pin the square of face fabric to the lining, right sides together, down the side edges, leaving 15cm (6in) of lining showing top and bottom. Stitch, turn and press. Equal bands of lining will show to either side. (**2** right)
❑ Turn the lower and upper edges of the lining over to the front of the curtain, tuck in, pin and slipstitch into place.
❑ Fold the strips of fabric in half lengthwise, right sides together, and machine-stitch around two sides. Trim the corners, turn and press. Tuck in the open ends and hand- or machine-stitch across.
❑ Fold all but one of the ties in half. Pin the folded ties to the back of the curtain at regular intervals, 10cm (4in) from the top edge. Machine-stitch into place. (**3** & **4**)

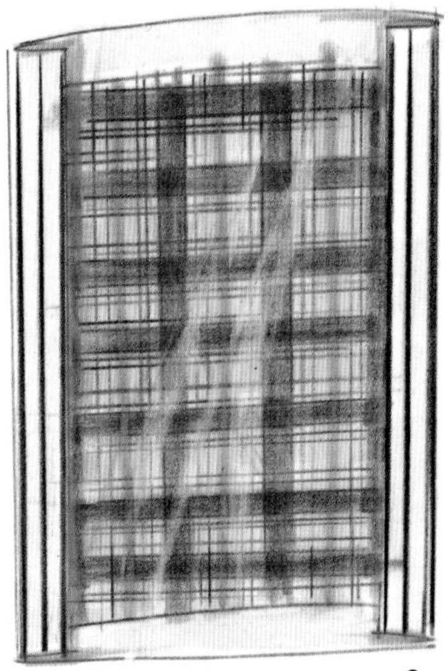

2

3

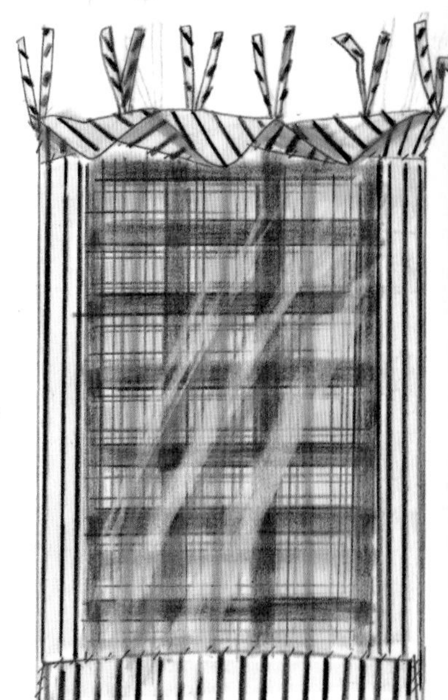

4

HANGING

❑ Tie the finished curtain to the pole or dowel.
❑ Tie one strip around the centre of the curtain.

PROJECT

Tab Heading

One of the most straightforward ways of slotting a curtain onto a pole is by means of a tab heading. No knots, bows, hooks or rings are necessary. Instead, simple strips of fabric fold over the pole, attached to the back of a pleated or unpleated, stiffened or unstiffened, heading. Made in a white or cream cotton or linen, the effect is one of classical purity.

This tab heading runs along an unlined curtain whose top edge has merely been given a double 19mm (¾in) turning. The loops are secured with a double line of machine-stitches. Because of the lightness of the curtain, the closely spaced tabs and the lack of any extra fullness, the heading does not drape between the loops.

MAKING UP

❑ Measure the circumference of the curtain pole and allow for the ties to fit around, allowing extra length for them to be sewn to the back of the heading. The width of the ties should be twice the finished width plus two seam allowances. Cut the required number of ties.

❑ Fold the strips in half lengthwise, right sides together.

❑ Pin and machine-stitch along the side and one end.

❑ Turn, trim the corners and press.

❑ Fold in half to form a loop.

❑ Pin the tabs at regular intervals along the back of the heading. Machine into place with two lines of stitching. (**1**)

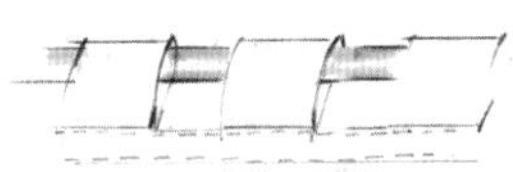

1

HANGING

❑ Slot the pole through the tabs.

PROJECT

Cable Top

These stencilled curtains use webbing to stiffen their headings. A line of metal eyelets is then threaded with cord to link the heading and the pole. This strong, plain treatment is suitable for unlined curtains that are scarcely wider than the window.

MAKING UP

❑ Pin a length of 5cm (2in) cotton webbing to the top of the curtain and attach with two lines of machine-stitching.

❑ Using a special eyelet tool, insert a line of eyelets at regular intervals along the length of the webbing.

❑ Measure out cord to slot through the eyelets and round the pole. Cut to length. Knot each length of cord around the pole. (**1**)

HANGING

❑ Run the pole through the loops of cord and fix into place.

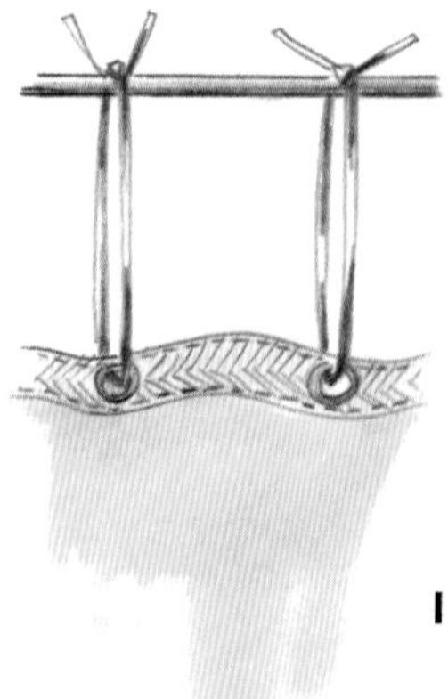

1

VARIATION
Swedish Bow

Bows set against a floating muslin curtain make for a simple but graceful scheme. The curtains have been given wide, pencil-pleated headings (see page 98) behind which lengths of narrow ribbon have been stitched. The lightness of the curtains means that even the most delicate ribbon will be strong enough to hold them in place. (**1**)

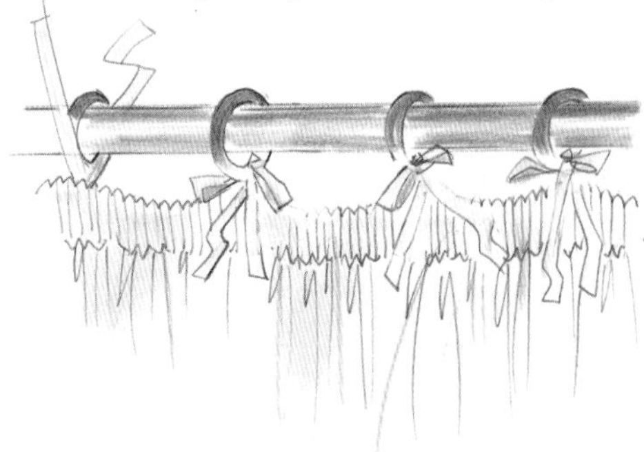

1

A plain stiffened heading is pierced with eyelets and slotted along a metal rod. (ABOVE)

VARIATION
Zig-zag Top

Shaped tops such as these zig-zags are easy to make and lend an amusing air to a small cotton curtain.

MAKING UP

- ❑ Cut the face fabric and lining to the shape of the window, adding 10cm (4in) to the length of the face fabric and 7.5cm (3in) to the lining. Add 2.5cm (1in) to the width.
- ❑ Using a template, cut out a zig-zag pattern along the top of the face fabric and lining.
- ❑ Place the fabric and lining right sides together. Pin, tack and machine-stitch around the zig-zags and three-quarters of the side seams. (**1**)

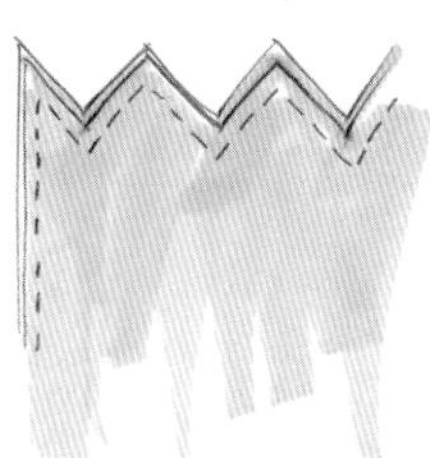

1

- ❑ Turn and press.
- ❑ Make double 5cm (2in) hems in the fabric and lining. Herringbone-stitch the hem of the face fabric, machine the lining hem. Finish the side seams with slipstitches.
- ❑ Insert eyelets with an eyelet tool.

HANGING

- ❑ Use split brass rings to hang the curtain from the brass pole. (**2**)

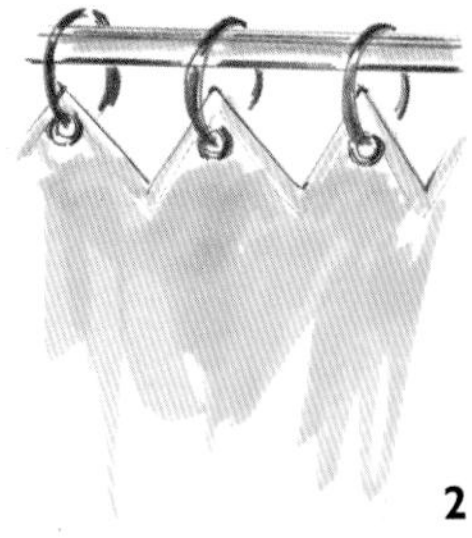

2

PROJECT
Plaid Bordered Curtain with Slotted Heading

A slotted heading is one of the simplest headings – nothing more than a glorified version of the cased heading. Two lines of stitching the length of the unstiffened heading create a slot into which a pole is inserted. As the curtain is pushed onto the pole a frill is created which, depending on the depth of the area above the slot, can be anything from squat and stiff to wide and swaying. A slotted heading cannot easily be drawn but remains fixed, tied back or – as here – draped across an ombra. An elegant pair of finials will complete the effect.

This single curtain is bordered in a wide contrast band – unusually a combination of bias and straight grain – and makes a dramatic sweeping gesture across the opening between two rooms. An undercurtain, its purpose again strictly decorative, loops back into an antique embrasure. It is made using a simple cased heading and is slotted onto a second pole. Being visible from behind, it should be made using the same fabric for lining. If the project is adapted for use as a window treatment the undercurtain can be made as an ordinary unlined or lined curtain.

As seen in the accompanying illustration, the main curtain has a deep undulating frill: 20cm (8in) vertical borders, a 15cm (6in) top frill and 5cm (2in) socket are allowed for – these can be reduced in size but care should be taken to narrow all borders – they are designed to be of equal width. If the frill above a slotted heading is opened up and flattened it becomes a 'puffed' heading (see page 99).

MATERIALS
- ❑ Face fabric
- ❑ Interlining
- ❑ Lining
- ❑ Contrast fabric
- ❑ Braid

FITTINGS
- ❑ Pole
- ❑ Cornice brackets
- ❑ Ombra

MEASURING
❑ Width: the flat, ungathered width should be twice the finished width.
❑ Length: allow an extra 20cm (8in) plus one seam allowance for the top frill, 10cm (4in) for the hem: 30cm (12in) in total.
❑ Contrast fabric: allow for a 28cm (11in) bias strip twice the finished length of the curtain plus hem allowances. Allow for a 23cm (9in) deep border cut on the straight grain for the top border.

FITTING
❑ Fix a pole above the aperture using cornice brackets (see page 171). Overlap the aperture by 30cm (12in) on each side, not including the length of the finials. The brackets should be flush with the edges of the finials.

MAKING UP
❑ Cut the required number of drops in face fabric, lining and interlining.
❑ Cut a 28cm (11in) bias strip of contrast fabric to run along the outer and leading edges.
❑ Cut a 23cm (9in) strip of contrast fabric on the straight grain for the top curtain border.
❑ Join the drops of face fabric and attach the

bias-cut borders to either side (see page 182). Press open seams.
❑ If seams are needed along the top border, use flat-fell seams to avoid problems when inserting the pole.
❑ Make up as for an ordinary interlined curtain (see page 94), but leave the top edge raw and unstiffened. At this stage the curtain is the finished length plus one seam allowance.
❑ Make double 12mm (½in) turnings in the side edges of the remaining contrast border (straight grain).
❑ Machine-stitch into place close to the fold.
❑ Place the right side of the contrast border against the wrong side of the curtain top. Pin, tack and machine-stitch the two sections together. (**1**)

1

❑ Turn the border over the top of the curtain. Turn under the lower edge of the border and slipstitch into place.
❑ Mark parallel lines above and below the slot for the pole. A 5cm (2in) space between the lines of stitching is usually enough. The lower line should be positioned just above the lower edge of the contrast border. Tack and machine-stitch the two lines, leaving the ends open. The slot should allow the pole to fit in snugly, and should be neither too loose nor too tight. (**2**)

2

❑ Run two short lines of slipstitching to close up the open ends of the frill.
❑ Pin and hand-stitch the braid to the curtain.
❑ Gather the curtain onto the pole.
❑ Drape the curtain over the ombra.

VARIATION

Green Silk Curtains

This pair of slotted-headed curtains is perhaps more typical of the genre than the single curtain described previously. The heading is made using the face fabric, giving the impression of being simply folded over the front of the curtains. The frill formed above the slot is restrained in its dimensions and complemented by a disciplined self-frill along the leading edges.

A gilded surface is always best seen against a rich colour and fabric. Here the dull gold of the ombras is set off most effectively against the folds of deep green silk.

MAKING UP

❑ Make up as for the single curtain in the main project, taking note of these points:
1. The pole has no finials. Accommodate the cornice brackets between the front of the slot and the pole (see page 173) via the holes in the back of the slot. Close the open ends of the slot with a line of slipstitches, and tack to the end surface of the pole using small-headed nails. (**1**)

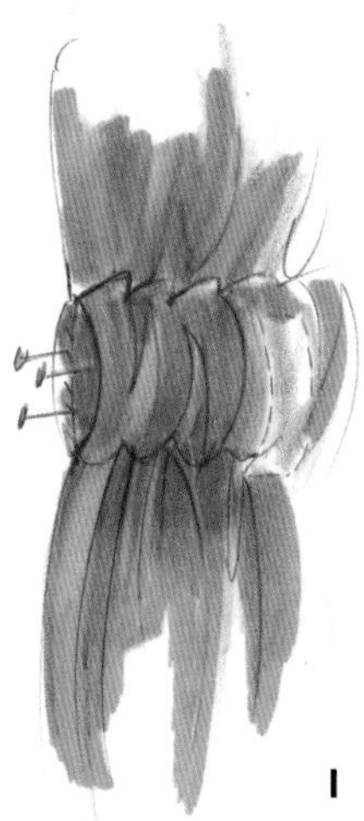

1

2. As the curtains cover the whole length of the pole instead of two-thirds, make the flat width of each curtain two and a half times the finished width.
3. Instead of a contrast top border, allow for a band of the same fabric. Reduce the dimensions to allow for a narrower frill. The band should measure the depth of the frill plus an allowance for the slot plus two seam allowances.
4. Position the ombras well inside the outer edge of the curtains.
5. A frill (see page 183) decorates the leading edges.

PROJECT

Muslin Curtain with Fan-pleated Heading

Made in white muslin and contrast banded, this heading shape – an accordion-pleated scallop – is unusual and charming. It is well adapted to the light cotton fabric: a heavier cloth would not pleat up so effectively.

MATERIALS
- ❑ Face fabric
- ❑ Lining
- ❑ Contrast fabric
- ❑ 15cm (6in) heading buckram
- ❑ Pin-on hooks

MEASURING
- ❑ Width: the flat unpleated width should be two and a half times the finished width.

MAKING UP
- ❑ Calculate the dimensions of the heading (see page 97). Make a newspaper template of the looped and curved heading shape. The curves (*a*) will be pleated, the loops (*b*) will form the linking sections.
- ❑ Cut out in the face fabric, leaving 12mm (½in) for the top turning.
- ❑ Cut out the same in a strip of white lining fabric, 15cm (6in) deep. Make a small turning along the base of the lining and machine-stitch close to the fold.
- ❑ Lay the heading buckram on the back of the heading.
- ❑ Pin and herringbone-stitch the base of the buckram to the fabric (non-fusible buckram). (**1**) Otherwise tack into place.
- ❑ Turn the top of the fabric over the buckram, clipping where necessary. Tack close to the edge.
- ❑ Lay the lining strip over the back of the heading. Pin and turn in the top edge, clipping where necessary. Tack.
- ❑ Turn in the sides and hem of the curtain and stitch in the usual way (see page 181).
- ❑ Cut a bias strip in the contrast fabric and attach (see page 182).
- ❑ Pleat up the scalloped sections into five small pleats, stitching the base of each to hold it in position. (**2a** & **2b**)

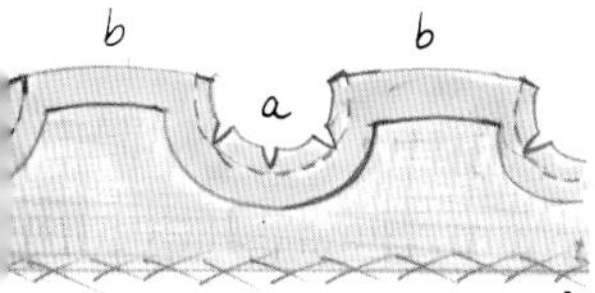

1

2a

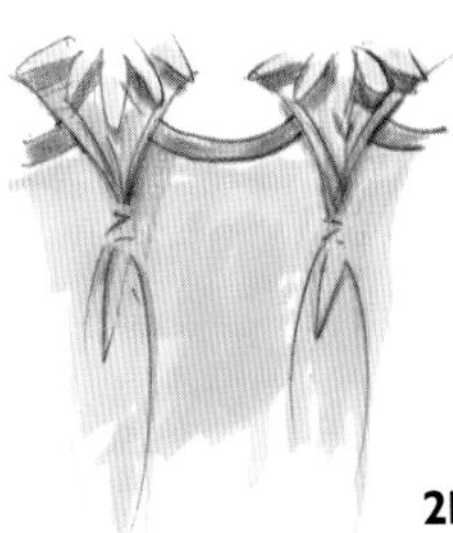
2b

HANGING
- ❑ Pierce the back of the pleats with pin-on hooks and hang the curtains in the usual way.

Heading Tapes

Sewn-in heading tapes stiffen curtain headings, contain pockets into which hooks are slotted and are machine-stitched to the backs of curtain headings. Parallel lines of cord run through the tapes, which are pulled up once the curtain is made to form the requisite heading shapes. Available in a selection of widths – 2.5cm, 7.5cm and 12.5cm (1in, 3in and 5in) are the most common – heading tapes vary widely in quality and detail.

GATHERED

A narrow 2.5cm (1in) tape will give a gathered heading to a light curtain or valance. With a hidden heading, the tape runs along the top edge; with an exposed heading, when a frill is appropriate, the tape is set down by at least 5cm (2in). (**1**)

PENCIL PLEATS

A 5cm (2in) or 7.5mm (3in) tape is the choice for formal pencil pleats. Suitable for lined or interlined curtains and valances. (**2**)

FRENCH PLEATS

A 7.5cm (3in) or 12.5cm (5in) tape will draw the heading up into pleats, which are then secured by hand-stitching. Suitable for lined or interlined curtains and valances. (**3**)

SMOCKED

This tape – usually 9cm (3½in) deep – gives the heading a smocked outline which is then hand-stitched. These headings will not draw back satisfactorily as the smocking will not form regular folds, and the curtains are draped back and held in place with tiebacks. Suitable for interlined curtains with exposed, fixed headings.

NET

This open-mesh tape is less opaque than other tapes and will complement translucent net or lace fabrics.

DETACHABLE LINING

A special tape is used when a detachable lining is required.

TOUCH-AND-CLOSE

A newly invented tape which does not need hooks, but is drawn up to form a rear surface suitable for attaching to touch-and-close fastening. This tape eliminates the need to stitch lines of touch-and-close tape to the backs of pull-up blinds or valances.

HOOKS

Plastic hooks are best for holding nets, unlined and simple lined curtains, but use brass for heavier, interlined curtains. A woven slot, available on the more expensive tapes, will hold the hook firmly in place and avoid the sagging that cheaper, corded pockets sometimes cause. A 2.5cm (1in) tape has only one hook pocket while wider tapes have two or three, allowing the length of the curtains to be varied. An uncorded tape uses pronged hooks. These slot into vertical pockets to form French or cartridge pleats. (**4**)

1

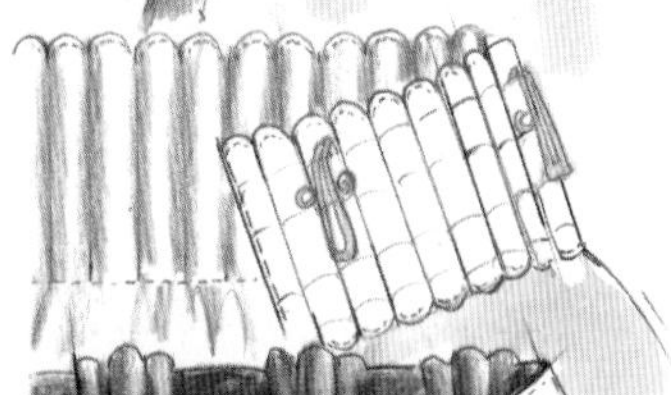
2

3

4

Valances

MATERIALS
❑ Face fabric
❑ Lining
❑ Heading buckram
❑ Touch-and-close fastening
❑ Cord
❑ Fringe
❑ Stiff brown paper or newspaper (template)

FITTINGS
❑ Pelmet board
❑ Brackets
❑ Curtain rail
❑ Tieback hooks

TOOLS
❑ Drill
❑ Bradawl
❑ Staple gun or hammer and tacks

FITTING
❑ Prepare the pelmet board in the usual way.
❑ Staple or tack a line of touch-and-close fastening to the front edges and returns.
❑ Attach the curtain rail to the board, and the board to the wall, in the usual way.
❑ Fix the tieback hooks in position.

A valance is like a miniature curtain, hung over the top of the window from the pelmet board. Valances can take many forms, from a simple band of lace, unsupported by curtains of any sort, to an elaborate arrangement of gathering and pleating, made to accompany a pair of heavy curtains below. A pelmet or lambrequin has a flat surface, pulled over a stiff backing; a valance is soft, either draped, gathered or folded, and can be lined and interlined. Its purpose is partly decorative, partly practical. Visually, a valance balances the curtains below, making a room seem cosier, the ceiling lower. Decoratively, they can make a considerable contribution – the permutations of cording, swagging, pleating and trimming are almost endless and, on a practical note, they serve to hide the curtain track.

The lower edge of a valance can be treated in numerous ways – cut into a serpentine shape, edged in contrast banding, fringe or fan-edging. The upper edge, too, can be put to use – a looped cord or line of rosettes to name just two of the many possibilities.

The valance should be in proportion to the window, never shallow and mean-looking, but may then blot out too much light and make a room dark. If this is the case, consider either raising the pelmet board slightly so that the valance covers some of the wall above the window, or use an attached valance that pulls back with the curtains.

Like so many other treatments, one basic shape, made up in different fabrics and with a variety of trimmings, can be used in any number of settings.

PROJECT
Bell-pleated Damask Valance

In this project the valance, made up in sections and edged in silky fringe, was taken from an 1840 upholsterer's manual. The delicate cream damask and gently tapering bells lend tranquil symmetry to a London drawing room.

The valance and curtains are backed in plain lining fabric and decorated with fringe and cording to match the tassel tiebacks. The curtains themselves have been lightly gathered, the flat width being only one and a half times the finished width, while the pelmet boards have been given a slight bow to the front edges, lending a subtle rhythm to the line of windows that permit the morning light to flood the room.

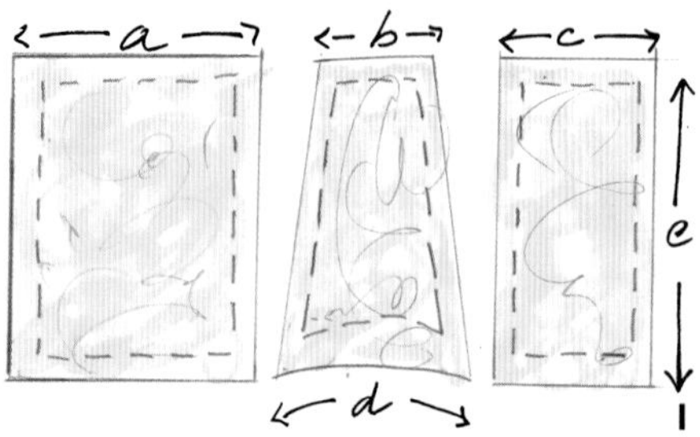

MAKING UP
❑ The valance is made from alternating pieces of fabric: tapered to form the bells, rectangular to form the linking panels. Longer side panels take the valance around the returns of the pelmet board.
❑ By working out how many flat sections (between bells) will fit along the front of the pelmet board, assess how many bells there will be (see French pleats, page 97).
❑ Experiment with paper cut-outs to find the correct proportions for the window in question. Make templates (see page 115) that include a seam allowance.
❑ Cut out the two side panels, the bells and the rectangular panels in face fabric and lining. Each bell and each panel should show the same part of any pattern. (**1** left)

INSPIRATION *34, 39, 43, 76*
TRIMMINGS *76*
BUCKRAM (FABRICS) *83*
MEASURING *86*
MATCHING PATTERNS *89*
HEADING TAPES *107*
FITTING PELMET BOARDS *168*
CUTTING OUT *178*
HERRINGBONE STITCH *179*
SLIPSTITCH *180*
CUTTING BIAS STRIP *182*
ATTACHING FRINGE *182*
PIPING *182*
BOX PLEATS *183*

❑ Join the alternating pieces, first in the face fabric, then in the lining. Press open seams. (**2**)
❑ Cut out pieces of buckram, 7.5cm (3in) deep, to stiffen the valance heading. Each piece (fusible buckram) will fit under the seam turnings, 3.8cm (1½in) below the top edge. (**2**)
❑ Tack into position. Herringbone-stitch around each section (non-fusible buckram).
❑ Place the lining and face fabric right sides together. Pin and stitch along the base, leaving 3.8cm (1½in) free at each end for turnings. Turn and press the lower edge.
❑ Turn the lining in around the other three sides. Slipstitch into place.
❑ Taking one panel at a time, remove the tacking and press to release the glue (fusible buckram).

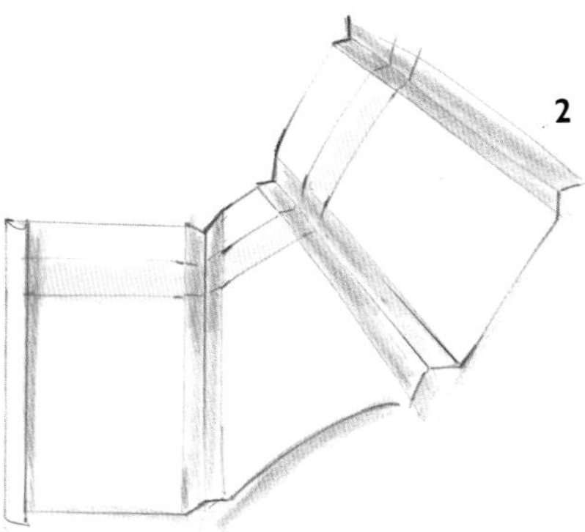

2

❑ Pleat up the valance by bringing the vertical seams together behind each pleat, and tack the pleats into position. (**3**)

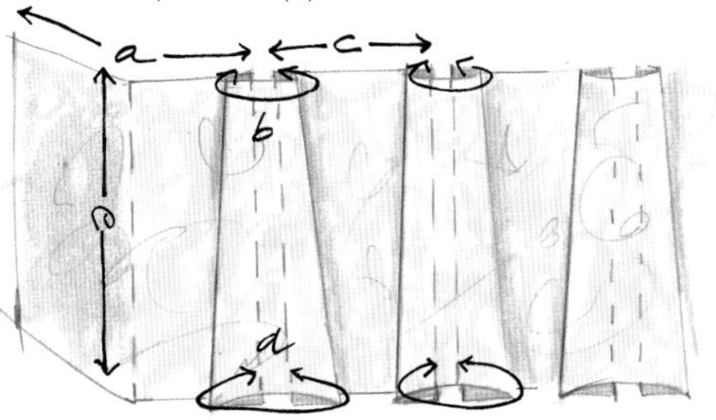

3

❑ Pin and hand-stitch the touch-and-close fastening to the back of the heading 3.8cm (1½in) below the top edge. (**5**)

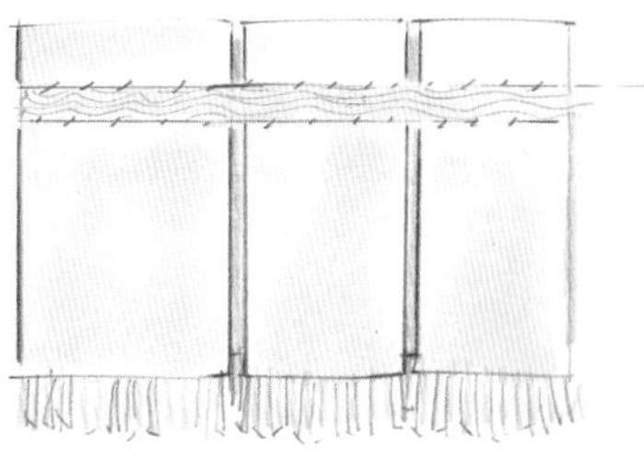

5

❑ Attach the fringe to the lower edge.
❑ Pin the cord along the front and hand-stitch into position. (**4**)

4

HANGING
❑ Join the lines of touch-and-close fastening.

VARIATION

Ruched Bell-pleated Valance

This feminine concoction of bell pleats and miniature swags has its main part cut out in one continuous strip, which is then ruched and pleated onto a band of covered buckram. The valance dips down a little at either end, framing the window in an attractive repeated loop. If you wish to make the valance appear more substantial use domette as a light interlining – anything heavier will cause too much bulk – and treat as a single layer with the face fabric.

Pale Roman blinds pull down behind the curtains, offering an alternative means of covering the window and making for a most effective blackout system.

MATERIALS

- ❑ Face fabric
- ❑ Interlining (to cover buckram band)
- ❑ Lining
- ❑ Pelmet buckram
- ❑ Contrast fabric
- ❑ Piping cord
- ❑ Touch-and-close fastening

FITTINGS

- ❑ Pelmet board
- ❑ Curtain track
- ❑ Roman blind batten and fittings

FITTING

❑ Prepare a wooden pelmet board to the required width. Make sure that it is sufficiently deep to house a curtain track and Roman blind fittings.

❑ Screw in a 5 x 5cm (2 x 2in) wooden batten to the back edge of the board. Fix a curtain track in front of the blind fittings. Run screw eyes along the base of the blind batten. Staple touch-and-close fastening to the front edge of the board.

❑ Fix the pelmet board to the wall using particularly strong brackets. With the blinds and the curtains the board will take much strain. If the board is hung well above the reveal there may be room to have an independent Roman blind fitting directly above the window's architrave.

MAKING UP

❑ Cut a strip of pelmet buckram to the finished depth of the band and the width of the pelmet board, allowing extra for returns. Make vertical scorelines on the back of the buckram at the corner points to facilitate a sharp edge when the returns are bent back.

❑ Using the buckram as a template, cut out the face fabric, interlining and lining allowing 2.5cm (1in) extra all around for the fabric, 19mm (¾in) for the interlining and 12mm (½in) for the lining.

❑ Lay the buckram over the interlining. Stretch the overlap of the interlining over the edge of the buckram. Trim the corners to remove bulk. Herringbone-stitch around all four sides (non-fusible buckram). Press the turning with a hot iron to release the glue in the buckram (fusible buckram).

❑ Lay the buckram strip on the face fabric, turn in the edges on all four sides. (**1**)

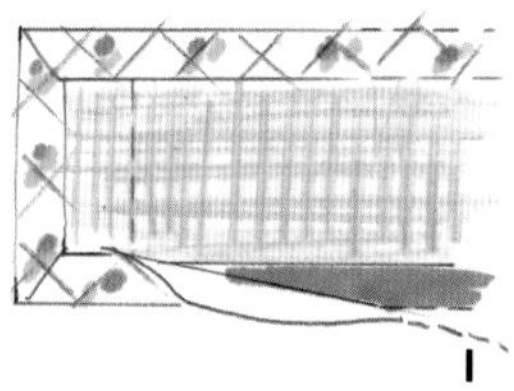

1

❑ Herringbone-stitch the fabric to the interlining beneath (non-fusible buckram). Press the edges with a hot iron to fuse the fabric and buckram (fusible buckram).

❑ Cut a bias strip of contrast fabric and prepare the piping (see page 182) to the length of the buckram strip plus 2.5cm (1in) for end turnings. Pin and slipstitch the piping to the base of the buckram strip. (**2a** & **2b**)

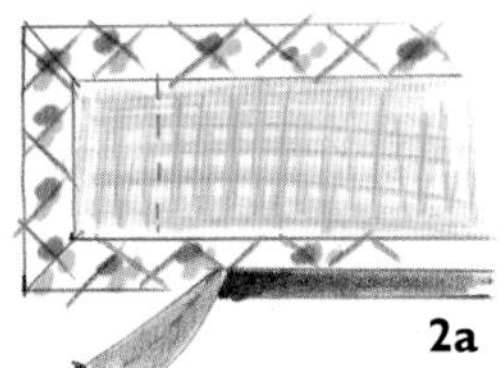

2a

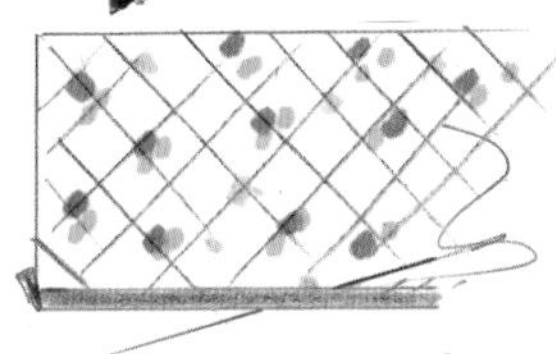

2b

❑ Prepare a second bias strip for the contrast edging along the top of the band. Fold the strip in half lengthwise and press. Make a single 12mm (½in) turning and press. Place the fold of the bias strip along the top edge of the buckram band with the turned edge to the front and the raw edge running along the back. Pin and slipstitch along the front of the band. Tack the back of the edging to the fabric and interlining.

❑ Prepare a template for the frill section of the valance. (**3** right)

❑ The distances (*c-e*) and (*d-f*) are equal to the depth of the buckram strip and will be the side edges of the triple pleats – the (*c-d*) measurement will fold into the triple pleats themselves. The pleats appear to be part of the buckram bands but are actually sewn on separately. The (*a-b*) measurement represents the distance between the bell pleats. The depth of the valance should be about one fifth of the overall length of the curtains, dipping to slightly more at the sides. The curving lower edge gives the valance its lower edge of alternating loops.

❑ The ruched effect between the bell sections is achieved by gathering (*b-k*) onto (*e-k*) and (*a-l*) onto (*f-l*); (*b-k*) and (*f-l*) should be one and a half times the length of (*e-k*) or (*f-l*).

❑ Cut out the template in face fabric and in lining. Pleat or gather (*b-k*) and (*a-l*) either by hand or using gathering stitches, and pin onto (*e-k*) and (*f-l*) respectively. Tack and machine-stitch ending 19mm (¾in) from the end (where *b* meets e and *a* meets *f*). (**4** right) Repeat the same process in the lining fabric.

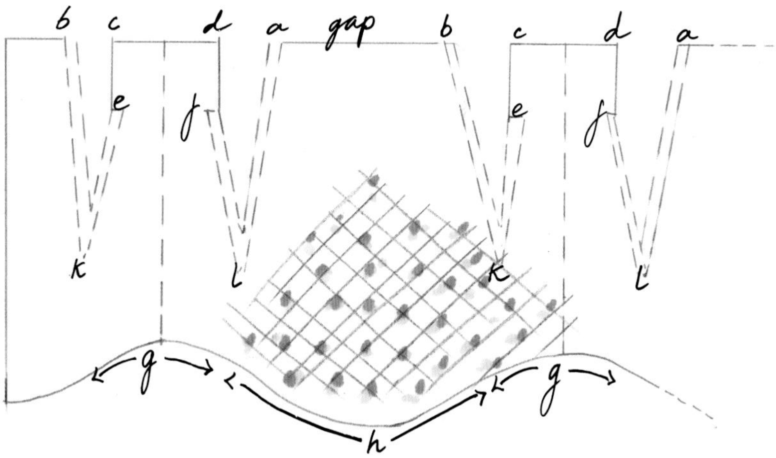

3

❑ Lay the face fabric and lining with right sides together. Pin, tack and machine-stitch along the lower edge and sides. Press the seams, trim the corners and turn. Tack around the top, 12mm (½in) from the edge.

❑ Cut the contrast bias strip for the lower edge. Lay against the edge, pin, tack and machine-stitch. Fold the contrast fabric over to the back and slipstitch into place (see page 180).

❑ Turn in the lining and face fabric around the triple-pleat section (*e-c-d-f*) and slipstitch around the three sides.

4

❑ Prepare another bias strip in contrast fabric and attach to the top of the pleat section (*c-d*) in the same way as for the lower edge of the valance.

❑ Form the pleated sections into triple pleats, pin and secure with hand-stitches at the base.

❑ Join the buckram band to the frill. The pleat sections lie along the surface of the band, the top seam allowances of the swag sections are slotted behind the lower edge of the band. Pin, tack and slipstitch the frill into place. (**5a** & **5b**)

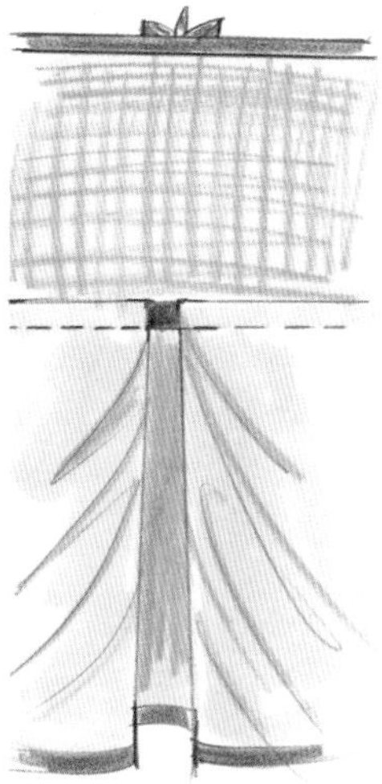

5a

❑ Pin, tack and machine-stitch a line of touch-and-close fastening along the front of the buckram band lining 12mm (½in) from the top edge. Lay the lining over the back of the buckram strip, turn in on all four sides and slipstitch into place. (**6** right)

❑ Prickstitch below the line of fastening (non-fusible buckram). Press with hot iron to release glue (fusible buckram).

❑ Remove all pins and visible tacking stitches.

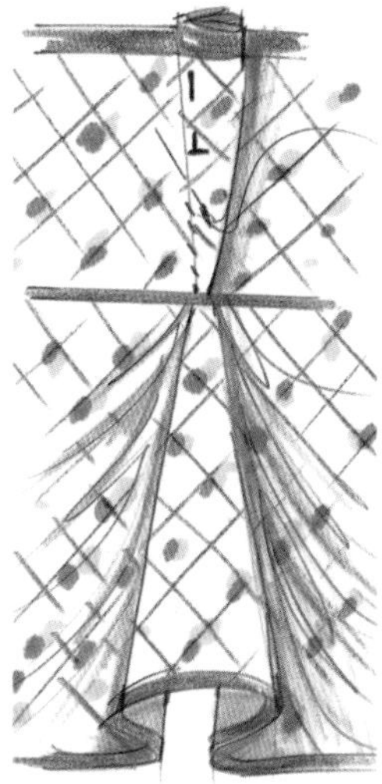

5b

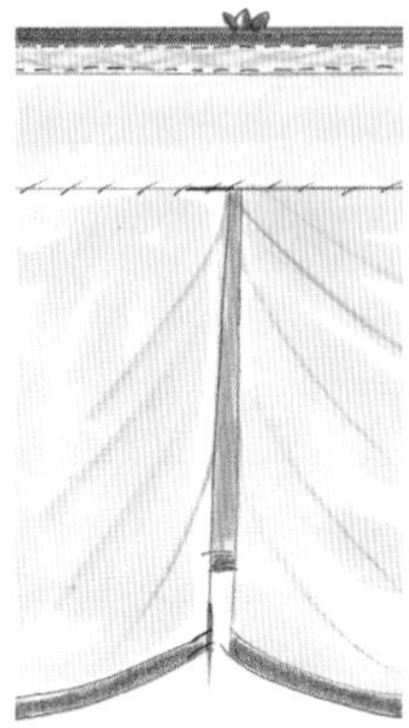

6

HANGING

Join the lines of touch-and-close fastening.

PROJECT

Box-pleated Valance

A box-pleated frill brings a touch of formality to a soft valance. Made in a sprigged cotton, it is well adapted to this bedroom window; made in a more sophisticated fabric it can take on a much grander look, particularly if bordered in a matching or coordinated fringe.

MATERIALS

❑ Face fabric
❑ Interlining (domette)
❑ Lining
❑ Pelmet buckram
❑ Piping cord
❑ Contrast fabric
❑ Touch-and-close fastening

FITTINGS

❑ Pelmet board
❑ Brackets
❑ Curtain track

MEASURING

❑ Depth: the depth of the valance should be one-fifth of the curtain length. The box-pleated frill is twice the depth of the flat panel.

Panel

❑ Width: equal to the front and returns of the pelmet board plus 2.5cm (1in) for corners (buckram); the same plus 5cm (2in) for turnings (fabric and lining); the same plus 2.5cm (1in) for turnings (interlining).

❑ Depth: equal to the finished depth (buckram); the same plus 5cm (2in) for turnings (fabric and lining); the same plus 2.5cm (1in) for turnings (interlining).

Box-pleated frill

❑ Width: the flat, unpleated width should be two and a half times the finished width plus 5cm (2in) for turnings (fabric, lining and interlining). For box pleats that abut one another, without a gap, allow three times the width.

❑ Depth: add 5cm (2in) to the finished depth for hem and seam allowance (fabric, lining and interlining).

Piping cord and bias strip

❑ Length: both are equal to the width of the pelmet board plus returns plus two seam allowances.

FITTING

❑ Fix the curtain track to the base of the pelmet board.

❑ Staple touch-and-close fastening to the front edge of the board.

❑ Fix the pelmet board above the window using strong brackets.

MAKING UP

❑ Cut out the buckram strip using a heavy duty craft knife. Score the buckram to make bending the returns easier.

❑ Cut and join the drops of fabric, interlining and lining for the panel and then for the box-pleated frill. Match and position any pattern carefully, using central and side panels if more than one drop is being used.

❑ Prepare the piping.

❑ Lay the buckram over the fabric and interlining. Starting at the centre and working outwards, stretch first the interlining and then the fabric over the back of the buckram, and secure with herringbone stitch (non-fusible buckram) or by releasing the glue with the tip of a hot iron thereby fusing the layers together (fusible buckram). Trim any bulk at the corners. (**1**)

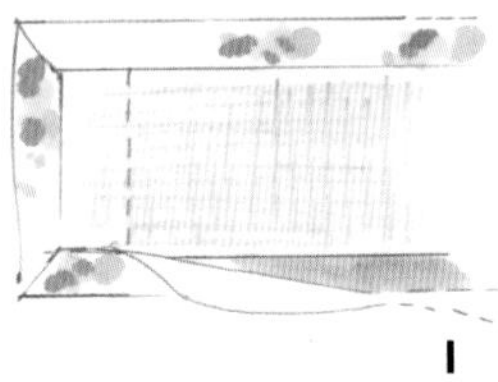

1

❑ Pin and slipstitch the piping to the lower edge of the panel. (**2a** & **2b**)

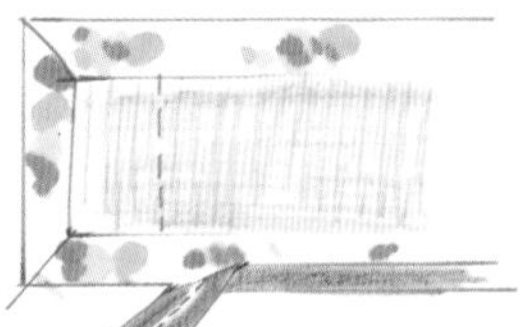

2a

2b

❑ Prepare a bias strip in the contrast fabric (see page 182). Fold in half lengthways and press. Turn in one edge and press. Lay over the top edge of the buckram band. Pin and slipstitch the turned edge to the front of the band. Tack the back to the fabric/interlining turning.

❑ Machine-stitch the lining and fabric for the box-pleated frill along the lower edge, right sides together. Trim and press so that the fabric extends 12mm (½in) up the back of the lining.

❑ Open out and lay the interlining so that its raw bottom edge fits into the base fold. Herringbone-stitch the interlining into position around all four sides. (**3**)

3

❑ Fold the lining back over, turn in the sides and slipstitch. Tack along the seamline. (**4**)

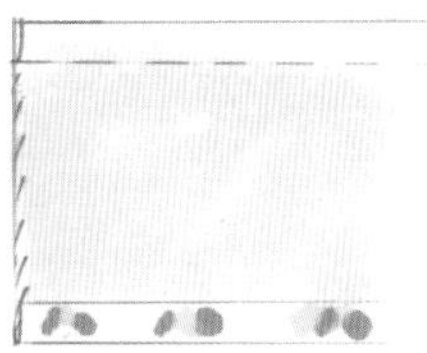

4

❑ Using pins, mark the centre point of the frill.

❑ Decide how many pleats will be accommodated and where they will fall. If using a patterned fabric, try to repeat the same part of the design on the front of each box pleat. Mark out with pins dividing each pleat and flat area into eight equal parts: (*a-h*). Match the foldlines and pleat up into half the flat width (*j*) to form (*k*). (**5a** & **5b**) Tack the pleats into position.

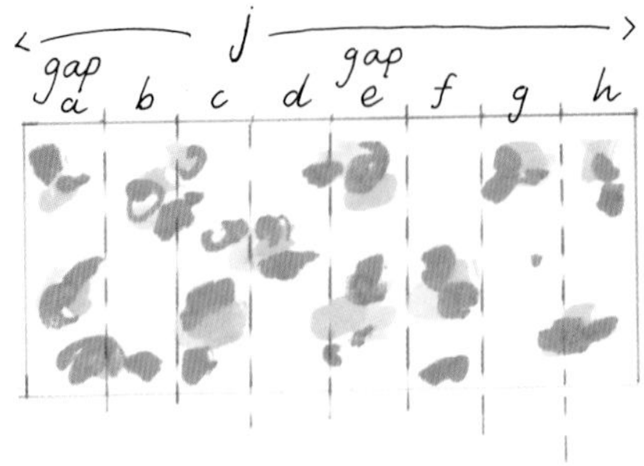

5a

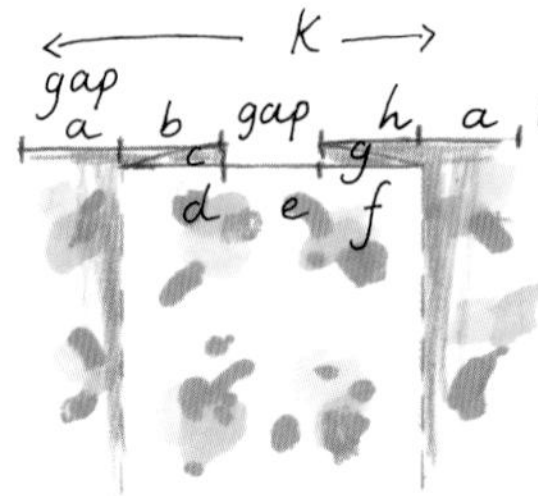

5b

❑ Starting from the centre and marrying the centre points of the panel and frill, pin the frill to the panel, picking up the turnings on the back of the buckram panel. Slipstitch into place below the piping. (**6a** & **6b**)

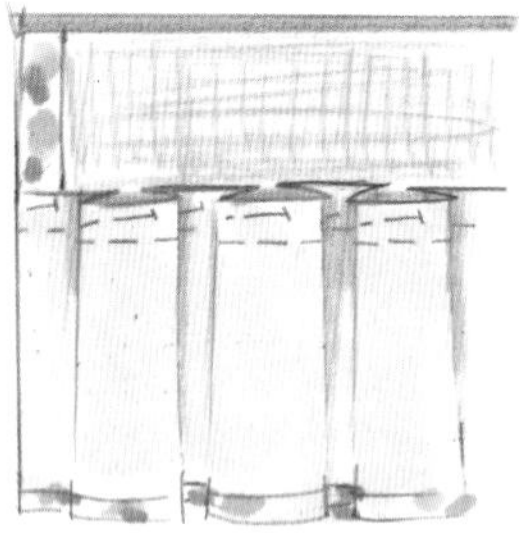

6a

6b

❑ Pin, tack and machine-stitch a line of touch-and-close fastening 2.5cm (1in) below the top, raw edge of the lining.

❑ Lay the lining over the back of the buckram panel, turn in and slipstitch around all four sides. (**7**)

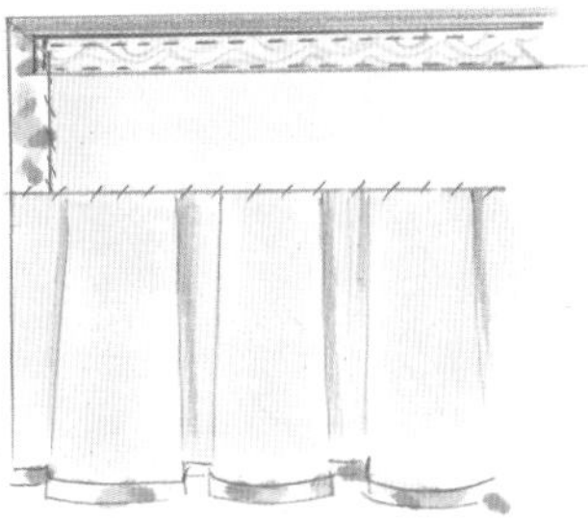

7

❑ Press with a hot iron to release the glue and secure the lining (fusible buckram). Using long stitches to minimize visibility, prickstitch just below the line of the fastening to hold firmly in position (non-fusible buckram).

HANGING

❑ Bend the valance at the corners and pinch to give a sharp edge. Mark the centre of the board and the valance. Starting at the centre point and working outwards, join the lines of touch-and-close fastening.

PROJECT

Serpentine Valance

A single basic technique may be used in scores of ways to create as many different effects as you like. A slight change of outline, trimming or detail can create an entirely new look – the only limit is your imagination.

Here, a curved edge and gathered heading give the valance its particular features. The standard serpentine valance has a plain gathered heading and is often decorated with a line of fringe or contrast binding along the lower and upper edges. In this example, white lining overlaps the edge to emphasize the curve and bring a welcome horizontal line to the busy vertical stripes. In addition to its interesting shape and contrast trimming, this valance could carry a fringe, cording, rosettes or even bows.

Making a gathered valance requires much the same technique as making a lined or interlined curtain: the layers of fabric, interlining and lining are assembled, and the heading is made up and pleated. There is one difference: unless the valance is unusually deep, you do not need to interlock the layers. If the curtains are interlined, the valance should be too. Floor-length curtains and a valance of this sort could take either domette or bump interlining.

MATERIALS
❑ Face fabric
❑ Lining
❑ Interlining (optional)
❑ Pencil-pleated heading tape or heading buckram
❑ Touch-and-close fastening
❑ Stiff brown paper or newspaper (template)

FITTINGS
❑ Pelmet board
❑ Curtain track
❑ Brackets
❑ Roman blind fittings
❑ Tieback hooks

MEASURING
❑ Width: the flat, ungathered width should be two and a half times the finished width.
❑ Depth: the side depth is one-fifth of the length of the curtain, narrowing in this case to only one-eighth of the overall length at the centre.
❑ Work out how many drops of fabric will be needed and multiply by the side depth, plus two seam allowances, to arrive at the total fabric quantity.

FITTING
❑ Prepare and fix the pelmet board, curtain and blind fittings, and tieback hooks in the usual way.

❑ Staple touch-and-close fastening to the front and side edges of the board.

MAKING UP

❑ Cut out the drops of face fabric, lining and interlining to the same length, i.e. the longest part of the valance plus two seam allowances.
❑ Avoid a central seamline by using a central panel of face fabric, lining and interlining, adding the rest to either side.
❑ Join the drops of face fabric, lining and interlining. Either overlap the interlining and herringbone-stitch, or turn on its side to avoid the need for joins altogether. Join the drops of face fabric and lining in the usual way, and press.
❑ Make a template of the flat valance in newspaper. Fold the paper in half lengthways and make a mark on the fold to show the narrowest part of the valance. With a fluid motion, describe the curve from the centre to the outer edge of the pelmet, using a felt pen or dotted pencil line. (**1**)

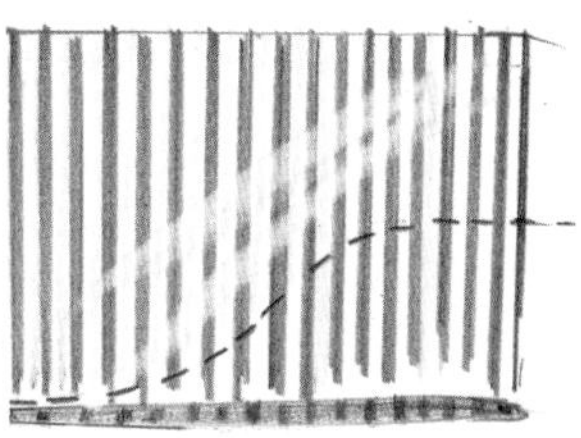

1

❑ Cut along the line and open out.
❑ Using the template, cut out the shape in interlining.
❑ Herringbone-stitch the interlining pieces together (if necessary) and remove the pins.
❑ Cut the same shape in the face fabric, allowing an extra 2.5cm (1in) along the top for the turning. Make sure that any pattern falls correctly in the centre.
❑ Cut out the same in lining, allowing 2.5cm (1in) extra along the top and the base for turnings.
❑ Lay down the fabric and lining, right sides together, lower edges flush with one another. Pin, tack and machine-stitch along the lower edge. (**2**)

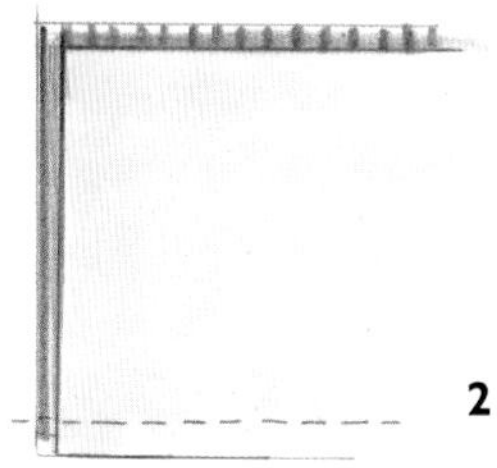

2

❑ Turn and press the seam, with both parts over the fabric side of the seamline.
❑ Clip to relieve any tension on the curve.
❑ Place the wrong sides of the lining and fabric together and press so that the base of the lining overlaps the front of the pelmet by 12mm (½in).
❑ If you do not wish a band of lining to show, make the seamline along the back of the valance, 12mm (½in) above the fold.
❑ Lay the valance fabric side down. Open out and use the ironed fold as a guide for the interlining.
❑ Lay the interlining against the back of the fabric so that the base of the interlining runs along the foldline. Pin into place and run a line of herringbone stitches along the bottom edge.
❑ Pick up only a few threads of fabric with each stitch. (**3**) Remove the pins.

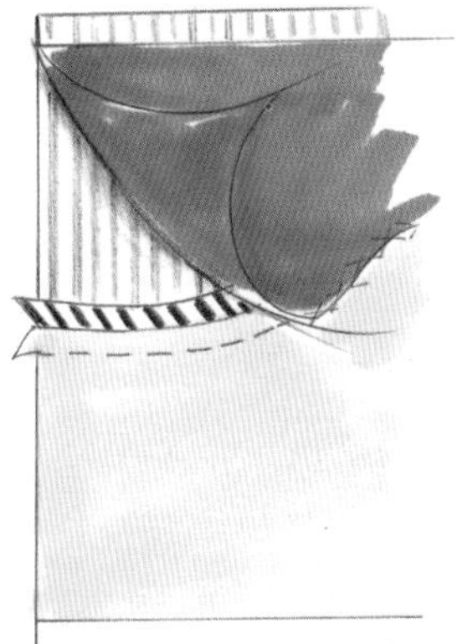

3

❑ If a heading buckram is being used insert it now. It should lie 9cm (3½in) below the top edge.
❑ Herringbone-stitch into place (non-fusible buckram) or tack (fusible buckram).
❑ Fold the lining back over the interlining. Pin the layers together at intervals.
❑ Make side and top turnings in the fabric and interlining. Turn under the side edges and top of the lining and slipstitch around all three sides.
❑ Press with a hot iron to release glue (fusible buckram).
❑ Run two lines of matched stitches 12mm (½in) from the upper and lower edges of the buckram, penetrating all layers.
❑ If using heading tape place it over the back, set down by 7.5cm (3in).
❑ Pin, tack and machine-stitch, starting both lines of stitching from the same end to avoid puckering. Leave the cords in the tape free at either end. (**4**)

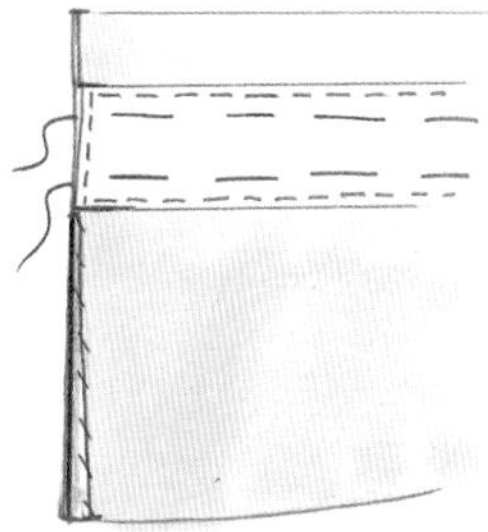

4

❑ Pull up the cords or thread to the finished width of the valance, forming tighter gathers at 10cm (4in) intervals, thus forming the scalloped shape that runs along the top of the valance. Slipstitch the touch-and-close-fastening to the back of the heading. (**5** & **6**)

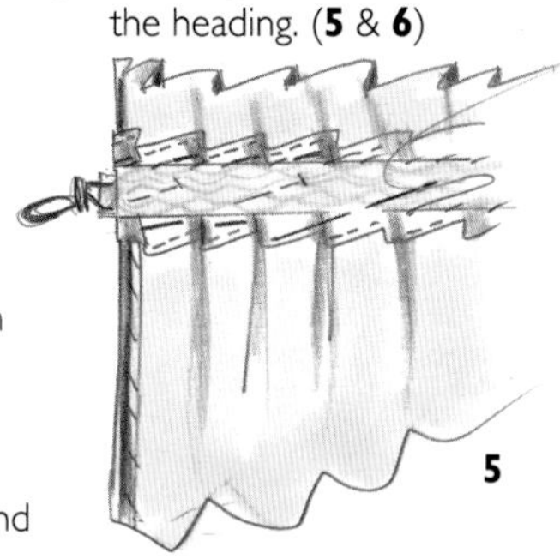

5

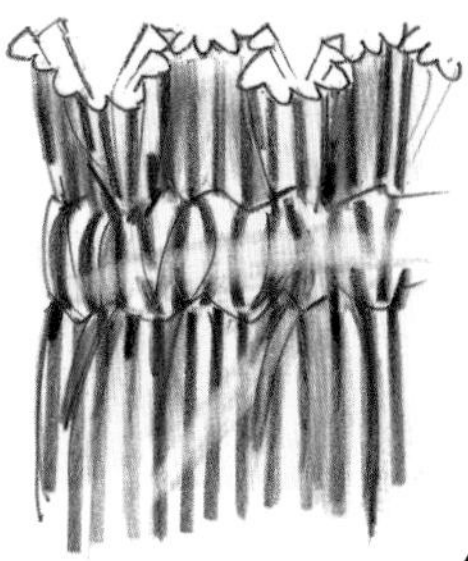

6

HANGING

❑ Hang the valance after the blind and curtains. Make sure that there is plenty of room for the curtains and blind to operate efficiently without interfering with the back of the valance.
❑ Join the lines of touch-and-close fastening on the valance and pelmet board.

PROJECT
Ogee Valance

MATERIALS
- ❑ Fabric
- ❑ Pendants
- ❑ Stiff brown paper or newspaper (template)

FITTINGS
- ❑ Curtain pole
- ❑ Brackets
- ❑ Roller blind

This ogee valance lends an air of stately sophistication to a high window, but the actual sewing techniques themselves are not difficult. This valance needs no stiffening, hooks or obscure equipment and hangs from a simple pole. However, like all projects that involve drapery, a little extra concentration is required in order to ensure that preliminary calculations are correct.

The valance softens the daylight that comes through the top of the window, its majestic appearance well suited to the surroundings. Heavy pendants pull the tips into shape but, if these are difficult to find, they could be replaced by improvised objects, perhaps tassels or decorative beads.

A roller blind in the same fabric pulls down at night to blank out the window.

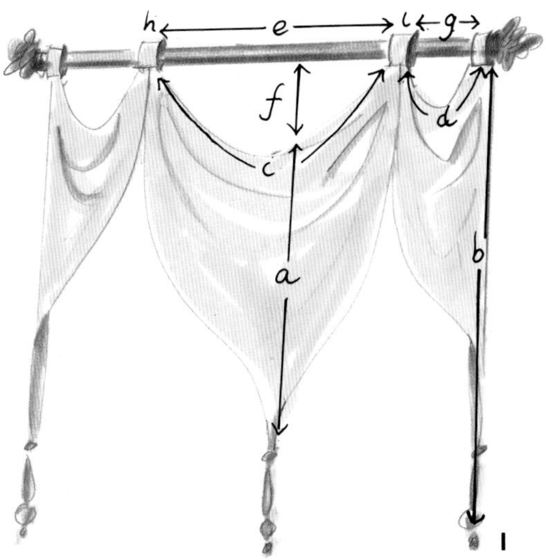

1

MEASURING

(**1** above)

❑ The valance is self-lined and so requires double the basic quantity of fabric. Patterned or heavier fabrics can be backed with normal lining.

❑ The flat width of the valance should be one and a half times the length of the pole.

❑ Each section is cut out separately and is complete, without seamlines running through it. As a first step, therefore, it is safest to cut out your shapes in templates and work out your layout. Design repeats and the width of the chosen fabric will make considerable differences to the fabric requirements and how the valance is cut out.

❑ One complete central section and two partial side sections are ideal for this window. Add more central sections for a wider window, but always retain a complete section in the middle with additional ones to either side.

❑ The central section occupies twice the pole length of the side sections, as they are suspended from their centre points; (*e*) is therefore double (*g*). To allow the central and side pendants to hang at the same level, the depth of the side section (*b*) is greater than that of the central section (*a*). Work out the finished distance from pole to pendant. This will give you the (*b*) measurement.

❑ Now calculate (*f*). To do this, drape a light chain or piece of string from your pole in imitation of the top edge of the central section, from point (*h*) to point (*i*). Measure the distance from the pole to the deepest point in the swag; this gives you the (*f*) measurement. Subtract (*f*) from (*b*) and you have (*a*).

❑ For a simple reckoning for plain fabrics, calculate the top width of each section (based on the top edge being one and a half times the length of the pole that it covers), and then assess how many sections can be cut in each width of fabric. Then multiply the number of drops needed by the deepest part of the pelmet (*b*), and add an extra 50cm (½yd) for seam allowances and the ties.

❑ Allow the same basic quantity of lining fabric.

FITTING

❑ Fix the curtain pole and roller blind fittings in the usual way, ensuring if possible that the roller will be hidden once the valance is in place.

MAKING UP

❑ Make a newspaper template of the central section and cut out twice in fabric to allow for the self-lining. (**2**)

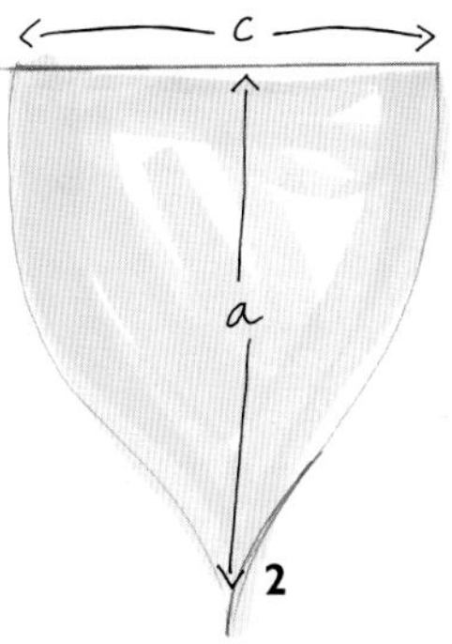

2

❑ Make a template of the side section. Only half of the shape will be visible, but allow extra width beyond the centre point for the soft wrap-around on either side. (**3**)

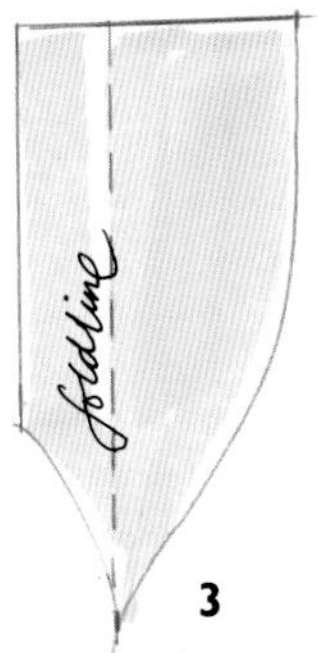

3

❑ Cut out two side sections in fabric and two lining pieces.

❑ Cut out four ties in fabric to wrap around the curtain pole. Each should be 15cm (6in) wide, and equal to the circumference of the pole plus 15cm (6in) in length.

❑ Place the pairs of ogees together, right sides together. Pin, tack and machine-stitch around the curved sides 12mm (½in) from the edge. Clip to relieve tension, turn and press. (**4**)

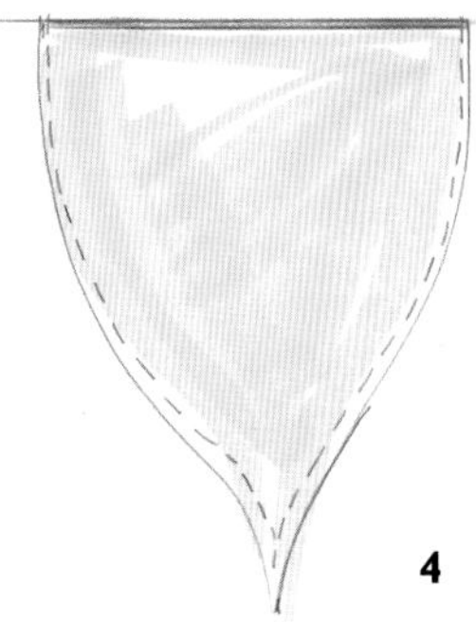
4

❑ Turn in the top edge and either machine or slipstitch it closed.

❑ Line up the sections side by side and slipstitch the top 5cm (2in) together.

❑ Fold the ties lengthwise, right sides together, and machine-stitch along the side and one end. Trim across the corner and turn. Press.

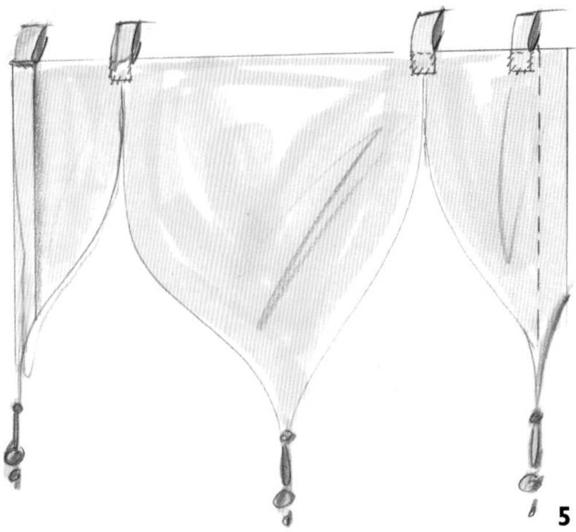
5

❑ Fold the ties in half and pin them along the back of the valance 5cm (2in) below the top edge. The ties are positioned at the join of the central and outer sections, and directly above the tips of the outer sections. Slipstitch the ties to the back of the pelmet.

❑ Fold the outer edges back and slipstitch to the back of the outer edges of the valance. Stitch the pendants to the tips. (**5** above)

HANGING

❑ Hang the roller blind.

❑ Slot the valance onto the pole.

PROJECT
Attached Valance

To get the best of both worlds – plenty of light and a generously deep valance – an attached or integral valance is the solution. When the curtains are closed the valance looks like any other. As the curtains draw back, so too does the valance, leaving the window clear. A fringe along the base of the valance will highlight it to great effect. Otherwise, run a contrast edge around the valance, leading edges and the base of the curtains. Here, a combination of wool fringe and edging provides a most effective contrast to the cream crewelwork of the curtains.

Attached valances are at their best hung from a handsome pole. It is also possible to hang them from a covered board and fascia.

The curtains shown in the illustration are interlined but this is not essential. Follow the general instructions for interlined or lined curtains for guidance in making the main section of these curtains (see pages 92-5). Sew-on heading tapes are not suitable for use with attached valances. If the heading needs stiffening (there are sometimes sufficient layers to hold the heading up without extra stiffening) use heading buckram.

MATERIALS
- ❑ Face fabric
- ❑ Lining
- ❑ Interlining (optional)
- ❑ Heading buckram
- ❑ Fringe
- ❑ Contrast fabric for edging

MEASURING
❑ Allow for the flat width of the curtains and the valance sections to be two and a half times their pleated or gathered width.

Valance
❑ The depth of the valance section should be one fifth of the curtains' overall length plus two seam allowances (face fabric and lining).

Curtains
❑ To finished length add 10cm (4in) for hem and one seam allowance (face fabric and lining). To finished length add 10cm (4in) for hem (interlining).

MAKING UP
❑ Cut out the required number of drops for the main curtain in face fabric, lining and interlining. Cut the drops for the valance section in face fabric and lining.

❑ Join the drops for the curtain, then the valance section. Overlap the drops of interlining; join with a herringbone stitch.

❑ Lock the curtain fabric, interlining and lining, following the instructions for interlined curtains

(see page 94). Herringbone-stitch the top edge of the interlining to the face fabric 12mm (½in) below the top. Leave the top edges of the face fabric and the lining raw.

❑ If the fabric is relatively lightweight insert a strip of heading buckram 19mm (¾in) below the top, raw edge, between the lining and the interlining. Attach either with herringbone stitches around all four sides (non-fusible buckram) or fuse layers together using a hot iron (fusible buckram).

❑ Run a line of tacking stitches through the face fabric and the lining 12mm (½in) below the top edge.

❑ Place the valance face fabric and lining with right sides together. Pin, tack and machine-stitch along the base and up the sides, finishing 10cm (4in) from the top. (**1a** & **1b**) Trim the corners, turn and press.

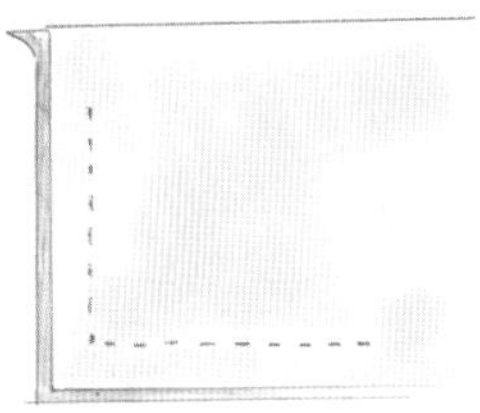

1a

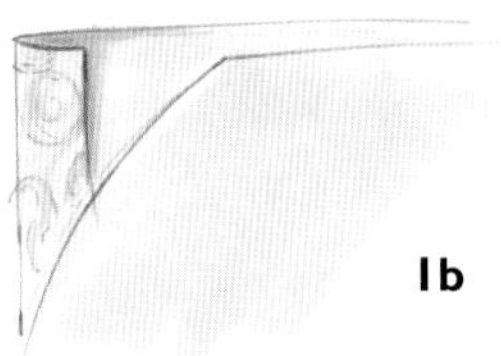

1b

❑ With the right side of the valance against the wrong side of the curtain, pin the valance face fabric to the curtain 12mm (½in) from the top edge. Machine-stitch, trim bulk and press seam open. Remove tacking. (**2a** & **2b**)

2a

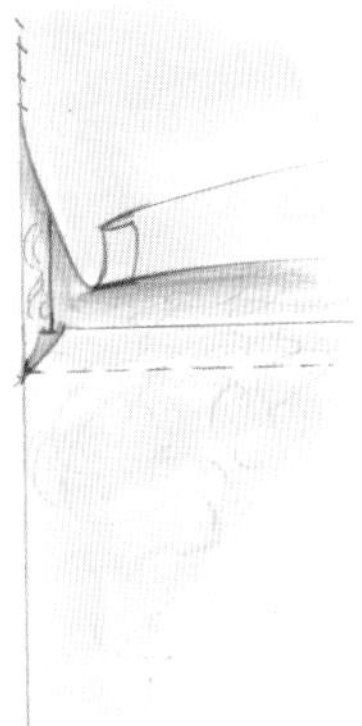

2b

❑ Fold in the remaining edges of the valance lining and slipstitch into place. (**3**)

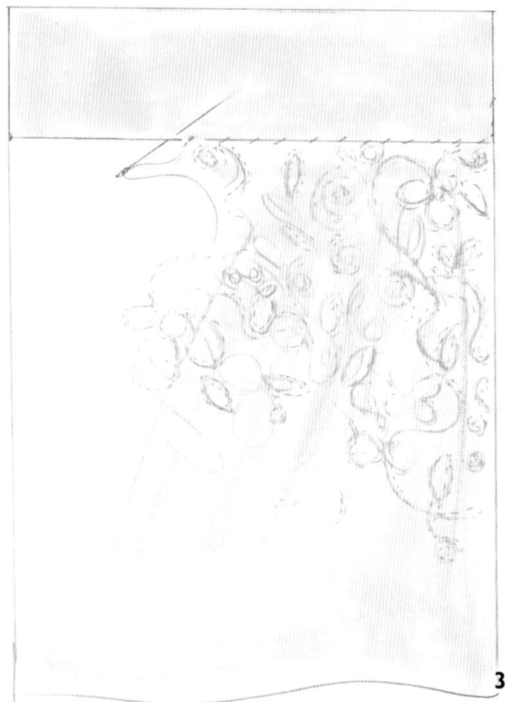

3

❑ Place the contrast band over the seamline that joins the curtain to the valance and turn in at either end. Pin and slipstitch. (**4**)

4

❑ Turn valance over the front of the curtain and tack into place. (**5**)

5

❑ Pleat or gather heading in the usual way (see page 97) and remove tacking stitches.

HANGING

Insert pin-on hooks or use sew-on hooks attached to a covered band of webbing (see page 98).

Pelmets

While sharing the practical advantages of all pelmets and valances, hard pelmets are generally simpler to make, economical with fabric and give a professional finish. Their clean lines can be particularly effective where a fabric design might be lost in the folds of a fussier, gathered treatment, and shapes can range from the discreet to the flamboyant.

Proportion is crucial with pelmets of any description: they should balance the rest of the treatment and must never look mean in relation to the size of the window.

MATERIALS

- ❑ Face fabric
- ❑ Lining
- ❑ Interlining (bump or domette)
- ❑ Contrast binding
- ❑ Small tassels
- ❑ Pelmet buckram or 6mm (¼in) plywood
- ❑ Touch-and close fastening
- ❑ Fabric glue and stapler (plywood)
- ❑ Stiff brown paper or newspaper (template)

FITTINGS

- ❑ Pelmet board
- ❑ Brackets
- ❑ Curtain rail

TOOLS

- ❑ Drill
- ❑ Staple gun or hammer and tacks
- ❑ Heavy-duty craft knife (buckram backing)
- ❑ Jigsaw (plywood backing)

FITTING

- ❑ Prepare the pelmet board in the usual way.
- ❑ Staple or tack a line of touch-and-close fastening to the front edge and returns.
- ❑ Attach the curtain rail to the board, and the board to the wall, in the usual way.

PROJECT

Gothic Pelmet

Often, finding the right shape for a pelmet can take longer than its actual construction. In this case, the designer has found inspiration in the shape of the window itself. The pelmet serves to emphasize, not disguise, its shape, drawing attention to the window's magnificent pointed arches.

MAKING UP

- ❑ For most windows buckram is a suitable backing material. Plywood, cut with a jigsaw, is better for large-scale schemes or when damp in the air (in a kitchen or bathroom, for example) will warp the buckram.
- ❑ Cut a template in stiff brown paper or newspaper. To achieve symmetry, fold the paper in half before drawing the shape. Do not forget to allow for returns, if necessary.
- ❑ Draw the design on to the buckram or plywood and cut it out using a heavy-duty craft knife (buckram) or jigsaw (plywood).
- ❑ When cutting out a curve, try to avoid hesitation and attempt a confident, sweeping motion. Always have enough materials to allow you to try again if necessary.
- ❑ To allow the returns to be bent back easily, score the buckram. Plywood returns should be cut separately and given a hinge by glueing a strip of fabric over the join.
- ❑ Join the widths of face fabric and lining. Match the pattern with care – any misalignment will be very obvious. Press open seams. Interlining should not be seamed or overlapped, as this would cause an uneven surface. It can either be used lengthwise or sections can be laid side by side.
- ❑ Make sure that the pelmet has a central panel of fabric with any extra added to either side. Check that the right section of the design shows in the centre, and that the pattern is not chopped inelegantly.
- ❑ Place the template in turn on the fabric, lining and interlining. Cut to shape, allowing an extra 6cm (2½in) all round for the face fabric, 4cm (1½in) for the interlining and 19mm (¾in) for the lining.
- ❑ Cut out strips of contrast binding on the cross grain. Fold in

INSPIRATION *59, 62*
BUCKRAM (FABRICS) *83*
MEASURING *86*
MATCHING PATTERNS *89*
CUTTING A TEMPLATE *115*
FITTING A PELMET BOARD *168*
CUTTING OUT *178*
CUTTING A BIAS STRIP *182*

half lengthwise, press. Fold in one 12mm (½in) turning and press again. (**1**)

1

❑ Machine-stitch the touch-and-close fastening to the front of the lining, 2.5cm (1in) below its top edge.
❑ Lay the face fabric, interlining and buckram face down. Make sure that the fabric is absolutely flat.
❑ Starting at the centre top, fold the interlining over the buckram and attach by pressing the turning with a hot iron to release the glue. Do not touch the buckram itself with the iron. If you are using plywood or non-fusible buckram, stick the interlining into place with fabric glue. Trim away any bulk on the corners and clip where necessary.
❑ Repeat with the face fabric, overlapping the interlining. (**2**)

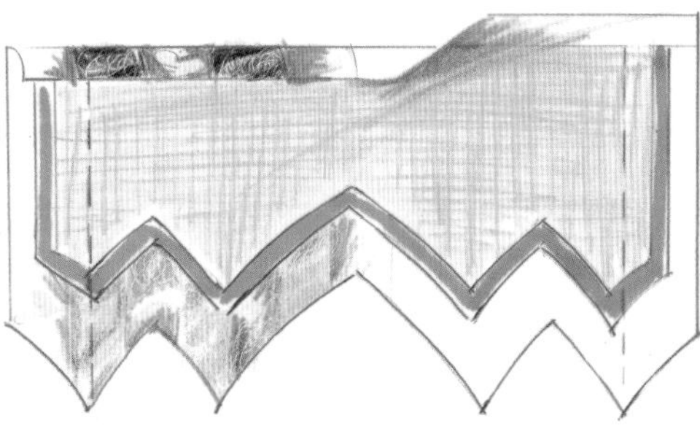

2

❑ Pin the folded edge of the contrast binding along the pelmet, marrying the fold of the binding with the edge of the pelmet. Fold the binding at the corners to eliminate tension. Using a semi-circular needle, slipstitch into place along the front. Tack the back edge to the fabric turning. (**3**)

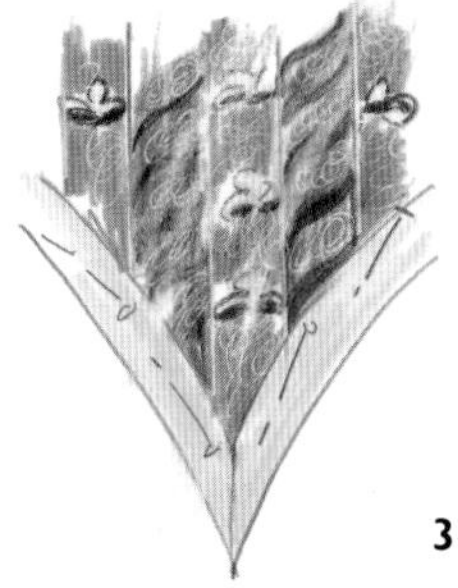

3

❑ Turn the pelmet over. Hand-stitch the tassels to the base of the pelmet using tiny stitches, or attach with fabric glue. Pin the lining to the back, turning in and clipping the overlap. The touch-and-close fastening should run just below the top edge. The lining should be slip-stitched into place. (**4**)

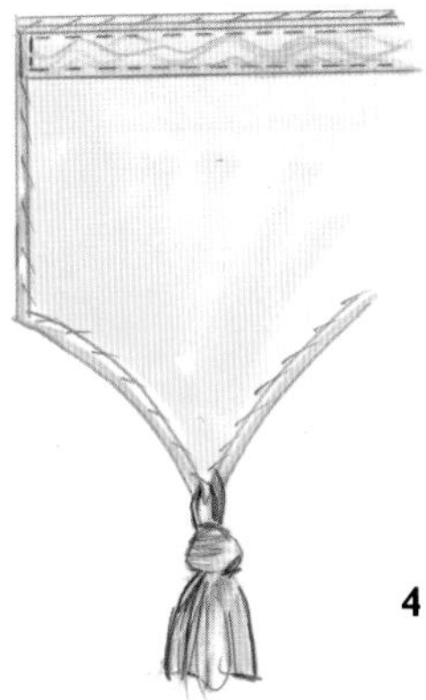

4

❑ Press the back of the pelmet through the lining to release the glue (fusible buckram).
❑ Run a line of prickstitches along the base of the touch-and-close fastening to hold it firmly in position.

Plywood

❑ Machine-stitch the touch-and-close fastening to the front of the lining, 2.5cm (1in) below the top edge.
❑ Lay the interlining and plywood face down. Make sure that the interlining is absolutely flat.

❑ Starting from the centre top and working outwards, turn the top edge of the interlining over to the back of the plywood and staple into position. Repeat for the lower edge, again starting in the centre.

❑ Turn the side edges to the back and staple. Make sure the fabric is not too tight for returns to swing back.

❑ Lay the pelmet on the fabric and repeat the stapling process.

❑ Place the bias strip along the base edge. It can either be glued or slipstitched along the front to secure it, but should be only lightly glued to the back surface of the plywood.

❑ Turn the pelmet over. Glue or staple the tassels into place.

❑ Lay the lining over the back.

❑ Again starting from the centre top, turn under the edges and staple neatly around all four sides, close to the fold, the staples parallel to the outer edge. Run a line of staples below the touch-and-close fastening.

HANGING

❑ Mark a centre point on the back of the pelmet and the front of the board. With a second person to help if the window is high or wide, marry the centre points and join the lines of touch-and-close fastening. If the pelmet is particularly heavy, a small-headed nail at each end will hold it firmly in place. (Work the head of the nail behind the fabric). (**5** below)

❑ If curtains or blinds are to accompany the pelmet, make sure that these are hung first.

❑ Try to avoid rolling or bending the pelmet. If it needs to be rolled, keep the lining facing outwards. This prevents any stretching of the face fabric.

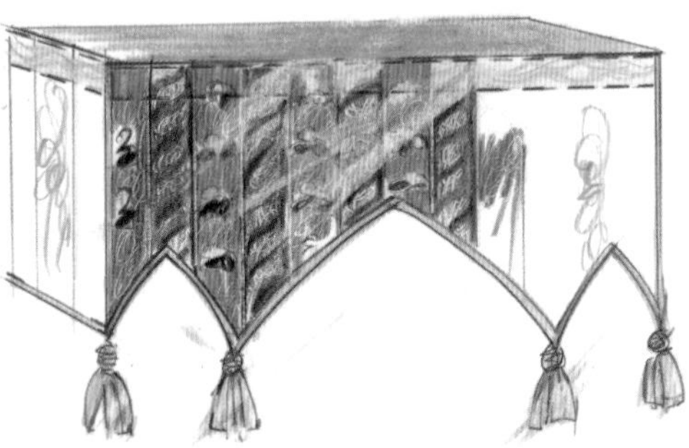

5

VARIATION

Tartan Pelmet

A double row of piping provides a quietly extravagant finish to this pelmet which encapsulates the three most important themes of this book: scale, simplicity and appropriateness. The depth of the pelmet is in proportion to the length of the curtains – it is generous without being exaggerated. Its line is classic: neither unnecessarily fussy nor dull. Finally, the deeply coloured, sober tartan from which the curtains and pelmets are made adds just the right note of restraint, providing a gently luxurious backdrop to the room.

VARIATION
Striped Pelmet

Pelmets need not always match the curtains. Here, a bold contrast has been struck between a striped pelmet – edged in cord and finished with tassels – and floral curtains. (ABOVE)

VARIATION
Grecian Urn Pelmet

Wide banding, juxtaposed with the massive shapes of antique urns, creates a bold effect. Make up in the same way as the Gothic pelmet in the main project on page 120. (LEFT)

VARIATION

Pagoda Pelmet

The top edge of the pelmet is a neglected area of design. Almost invariably pelmets are given flat tops, while any artistic effort goes into looping lower edges. However, there is ample scope for more interesting outlines if there is room above the window and the pelmet does not project far from the wall (the pagoda pelmet does not wrap round the pelmet board and would leave the sides exposed).

The shape of this pelmet evokes Regency chinoiserie or willow-pattern china. Despite its sober black-and-white checks outlined in black banding, its shape adds a frivolous note to a decorative scheme. The banding emphasizes the pagoda outline, which is set off by a pair of plain white curtains.

The pelmet is made in just the same way as any other hard pelmet. The curved banding is made using a bias strip, ironed first to give the central fold and turnings. The banding can then be placed over the edge of the pelmet, giving an equal depth to either side. If a basic colour is required, use dressmaker's bias binding – as here – fixed using fabric glue or slipstitching.

A projecting pelmet board need not rule out such an imaginative pelmet, but it calls for action to hide the side of the board and the workings of the curtain track. Cover two pieces of buckram or plywood in the pelmet fabric and attach them to the side edges of the board.

Pelmet Shapes

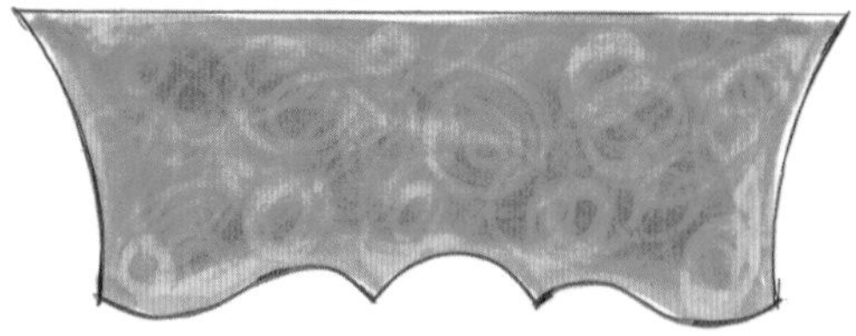

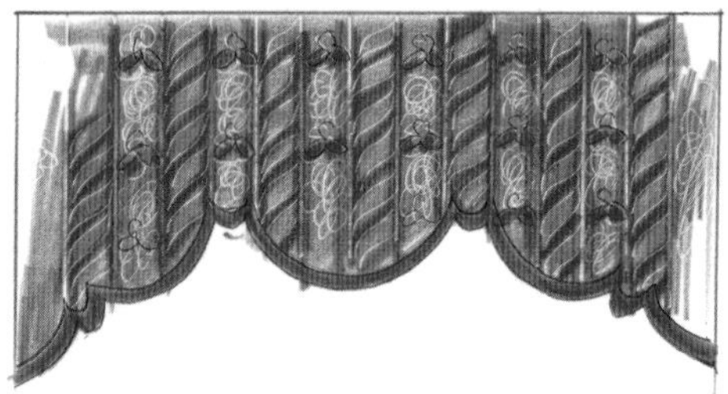

Lambrequins

Lambrequins became highly fashionable in the last century, only to disappear almost completely, and the mention of a lambrequin today will attract many a blank look. Quite simply, a lambrequin is a glorified pelmet. It is made in the same way – backed in pelmet buckram or plywood – and frames the window, generally extending to sill level. When used alone it is purely ornamental; otherwise, it can hide a roller or Roman blind to be drawn down at night. To soften the inner edge, a piece of soft muslin or organdie can be hung inside.

Lambrequins are a delight. They offer great scope for theatricality and can turn the dullest window into a striking feature. Converted attics, for example, will often have tiny windows that are difficult to curtain and a shaped lambrequin will give such a window unaccustomed prominence, the hidden blind taking care of the practical business of screening the light. A flamboyant fixed lambrequin might also be appropriate for a single window on a staircase, often inaccessible and therefore impractical for raising blinds or opening curtains, but frequently the first to be seen by a visitor.

Painted Pelmet with Tassels

If your room needs a touch of fantasy, how about a cut-out pelmet? Something painted in midnight blue, edged in gold and decorated with alternating blue and gold tassels or any other colour combinations might just be the answer!

As this pelmet is made of plywood, you should cut out the returns separately and glue a strip of fabric behind the join to make a hinge.

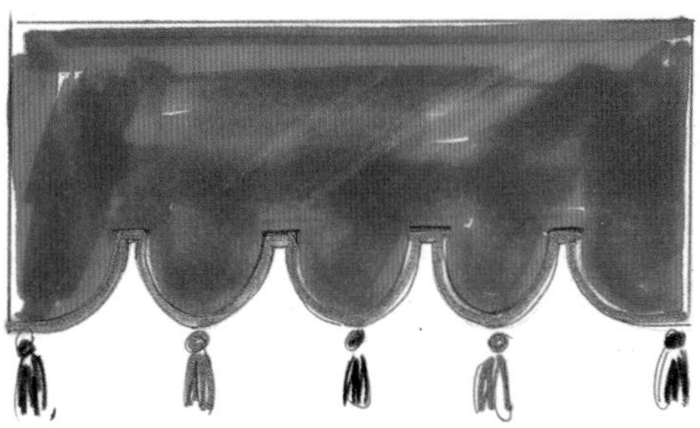

Swags and Tails

❑ Formal swags and tails are best used with full-length curtains on large-scale windows.
❑ Choose the fabric carefully – try to find one that has a natural tendency to drape well.
❑ Don't be afraid to sacrifice the odd piece of lining fabric for experimental purposes.
❑ Best results come with swags cut on the crossgrain of the fabric, so try to avoid patterned fabrics, or obvious naps, that must be cut on the straight grain.
❑ Use the best trimmings that you can afford – swags and tails are lifted by well-matched, good quality fringes and cords.
❑ Keep the proportions generous – the depth of swag and length of tails should balance the length of the curtains and the width of the window.
❑ Measure with care.
❑ Domette interlining will help the fabric to drape.
❑ Nails or long pins and a pinboard ease the task of arranging pleats.

Swags and tails, with all their permutations, have long occupied the centre stage of curtainmaking. Traditionally associated with heavily draped, large-scale windows, they have recently translated themselves into a multitude of less formal variations.

Formal swags and tails are made from separate pieces of cloth, each interlined, lined and pleated, then hung, each in its turn, from a pelmet board to create the illusion of continuous drapery. On windows too wide for a single swag multiple swags are used (see page 13), the joins either overlapped or hidden beneath 'pipes' or 'flutes'. The proportions of swags should be generous and tails need length to be seen at their best, usually about half the overall length of the curtains.

Although it is possible to generalize on the subject of swags, tails take many different forms. For example, they can be pleated in concertina fashion, each pleat either hiding the one below or spread out into a line, or they can be made in a spiral, with the fabric rolled up and flattened. Tails can lie over or under the edges of the swag.

Take care in choosing lining fabrics for the tail, pipe or flute sections. These will play an important part in the colour scheme as they are clearly visible in the zig-zag lower edges. The lining should complement the face fabric – usually in a paler colour – and can be taken up in the choice of trimming colours.

The draped pole, made popular by the recent revival of interest in all things Empire, has fooled many a home curtainmaker, whose attempts to reproduce Grecian folds in a single length of cloth have often ended in failure. In fact, these too are made up from separate sections, the joins carefully hidden along the top of the pole. Of all the variations, the loose drape (the name for this type of swag) is perhaps the most difficult – often involving complicated asymmetrical sections – and only to be attempted by the most confident of curtainmakers.

Informal swags and tails – more gathered than pleated and accessible to one and all – are made from a single piece of cloth, its ends cut into opposing diagonals. Used simply to soften and enhance the top of the window, usually without curtains or blinds, results can be quick and encouraging. Such arrangements can be interlined, lined or unlined – many voiles, silks and laces can be shown off to great effect, the daylight making the most of a delicate design.

The scope for decoration makes swags and tails the subject of some of the most elaborate trimming arrangements. The sweep of the swag can be followed with a line of cording or fringe; the cord can be tied into any number of decorative knots to either side, sometimes weighted down with a pair of handsome tassels, hanging in line with the tails. In fact, fringing is an essential element in every formal swag and tail.

Make use of choux, rosettes, bows and Maltese crosses – they will give an expensive-looking finish and serve to disguise the points at which the elements join. Lighter, informal swags are generally unsuitable for any trimming heavier than a white bobble fringe or a garland of silk flowers, set against the curved gathers of floating muslin or lace.

A generously proportioned swag and tail, decorated with a subtle fringe and a pair of choux, complements an elegant arched window. (RIGHT)

INSPIRATION 12, 70
LININGS & INTERLININGS 83
MEASURING SWAGS & TAILS 88
INTERLINED CURTAINS 94
CHOUX 160
PADDED EDGES 161
FIXING PELMET BOARDS 168
HERRINGBONE STITCH 179
LOCKING STITCH 180

MATERIALS

Swag and tails

- ❑ Face fabric
- ❑ Interlining (domette: bump is too heavy)
- ❑ Milium or blackout lining (swags)
- ❑ Contrast lining (tails)
- ❑ Paper and lining (template)
- ❑ Fringe

Curtains

- ❑ Fabric
- ❑ Interlining (bump)
- ❑ Lining
- ❑ Contrast fabric (for leading edge)
- ❑ Cord
- ❑ Heading buckram (handmade heading) or heading tape (machine-stitched heading)

FITTINGS

- ❑ Pelmet board
- ❑ Curtain track
- ❑ Brackets

TOOLS

- ❑ Leadweight tape or light chain
- ❑ Large pinboard and heavy-duty pins or fine nails (optional)

FITTING

- ❑ Attach the curtain track to the pelmet board, and the board to the wall, in the usual way.

PROJECT

Silk Swag and Tails

A classic single swag is balanced by tails finished in choux (see page 127). Tussah silk is ideal for this type of treatment as it drapes well and falls into soft, irregular folds. A wide linen fringe links the cream coloured silk with the moss-green damask lining. To avoid an imbalance of translucency between the heavily interlined curtain and lightly interlined swag, block the light that comes through the swag with milium or blackout lining.

The curtains are notable in three ways. First, they hang straight down from the track, unencumbered by tiebacks. This allows the swags and tails the prominence that is their due, and provides a welcome vertical line. Second, they drape discreetly on the floor. Third, they carry padded leading edges with a band of dove-grey cotton, edged in a line of cord, to give a discreet air of luxury.

MEASURING AND CUTTING THE TEMPLATE

(see Measuring, page 88)

Swag

❑ Hang the leadweight tape or light chain from the pelmet board in imitation of the swag's lower edge. The deepest part of the swag should occupy about one-fifth of the overall length from pelmet board to floor. Use this measurement as the base edge of the unpleated swag. The top edge of the unpleated swag is the length of the pelmet board.

❑ Allow for the unpleated depth of the swag to be twice the pleated depth. The base of the flat swag should be given a slight curve to assist it in forming an effective curve.

❑ Using the measurements, mark out a template. Allow for a seam allowance around the sides and base of the template. Allow a double seam allowance along the top edge.

❑ Cut out in lining fabric and pin the pleats (using a pinboard if possible), teasing them into curving, matching drapes. Allow for the curve of the swag to run out at either edge of the board. Trim the sides so that when the lining template is flattened the sides form a zig-zag, each representing one pleat. (**1** right)

❑ For plain fabrics, the swag will be cut on the crossgrain of the face fabric. Obvious patterns, which cannot successfully be tilted at a 45° angle, must be cut on the straight grain.

❑ If the fabric is not wide enough to take the whole template, cut a central section of fabric and add the extra in equal additions to either side. Make sure to run the seams vertically, even if the sections are cut on the crossgrain. (**2** right)

❑ Allow for an extra strip of fabric the length of the board plus two seam allowances by a depth of 9cm (3½in). This will bind the top edge of the swag and provide the fixing.

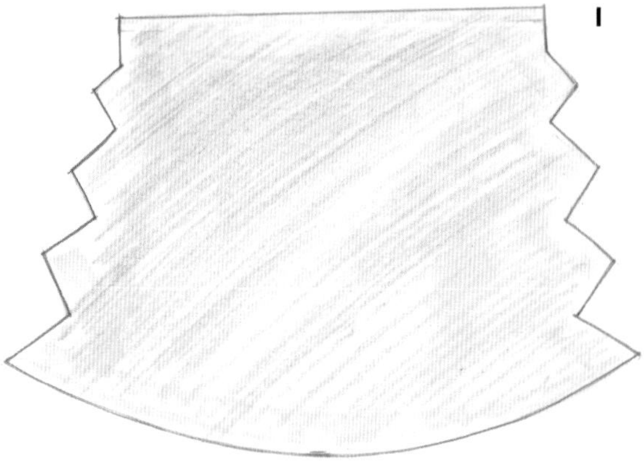

1

2

3a

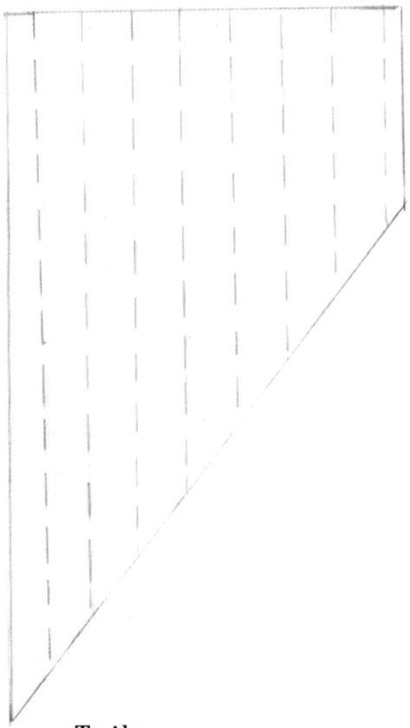

3b

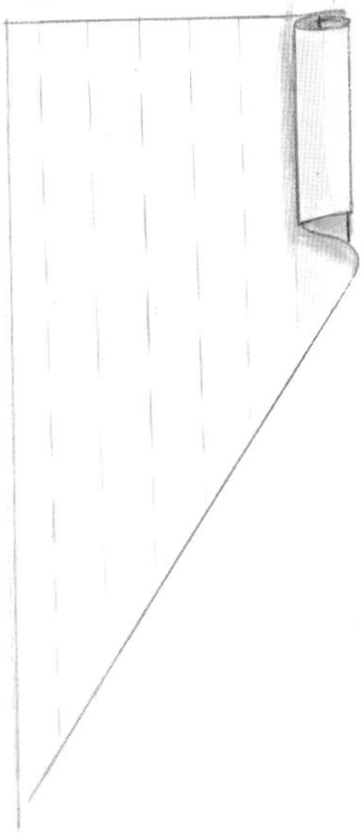

Tails

❑ The outer edge of the tail should extend halfway down the curtains. The inner edge of the tail is equal to the depth of the swag. The flat width of the tail is seven times its pleated width, plus the length of the returns, plus an extra 5cm (2in) to turn around the inner edge of the tail. Calculate for a seam allowance all around. Give the edges a slight flare – in this way the tails will widen towards the base. (**3a** & **3b** above)

Choux

See page 160.

Curtains

❑ The flat width should be two and a half times the finished gathered width. One drop of contrast fabric will be needed for the leading edge, plus the same in cord.

❑ Add 5-7.5cm (2-3in) to the finished length for the draped hem.

MAKING UP

Swag

❑ Lay the lining template on a piece of stiff brown paper or newspaper, trace around the edge and cut out two versions, one with and one without seam allowances. The fabric and lining should be cut with seam allowances, the interlining without seam allowances.

❑ Using the first template, cut out the fabric, on the crossgrain if possible, but on the straight grain for obvious designs or stripes. Join the sections if necessary, and press open seams.

❑ Cut out the interlining and lining on the straight grain. If necessary, turn the interlining or lining on its side to avoid joins.

❑ Lay the fabric face down. Lay the domette over the back of the fabric. Fold back the domette every 10cm (4in) and run vertical lines of locking stitches, attaching it to the face fabric. (**4**)

4

❑ Fold the base turning of the fabric over the edge of the domette and herringbone-stitch into place. (**5**)

5

❑ Lay the lining face down on the back of the swag and lock to the interlining in the same way. The lines of locking stitches should end a few centimetres from the base edge to allow the lining to be turned in.

❑ Tack along the raw top and side edges of the swag.

❑ Turn in the base edge of the lining and slipstitch into position. (**6**)

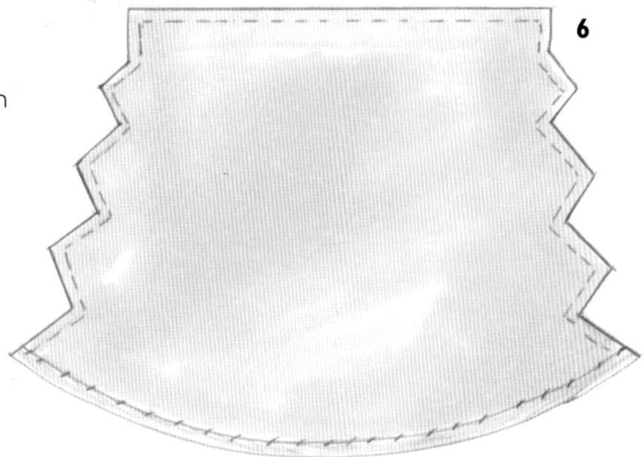

6

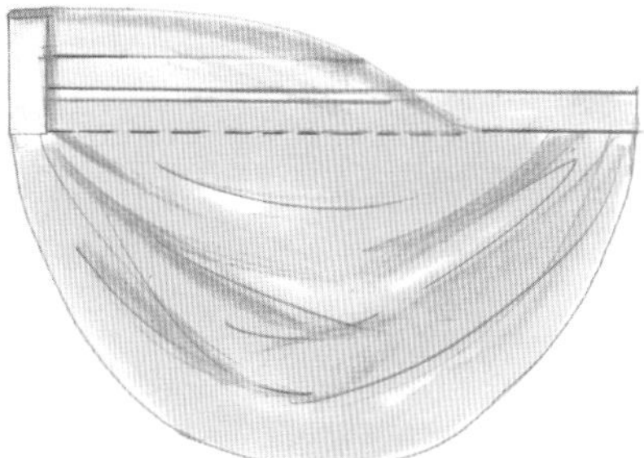

7

❑ Pleat up the swag and bind the top edge, using the prepared strip. Fold the strip in half lengthwise and turn in a seam allowance along the edges and the ends. Press to keep the turnings in place. Pin, tack and slipstitch the band over the top edge of the swag. (**7** above)

❑ Attach the fringe to the lower edge.

Tails

❑ Cut out the tails in fabric and lining, allowing a seam allowance all around. Use the straight grain, making sure to place and match any obvious pattern.

❑ Cut the interlining without any seam allowance.

❑ Lock the interlining to the fabric and the lining to the interlining in the same way as the swag. Turn in the lining around all four sides.

❑ Attach the fringe to the base of each tail.

❑ Pleat up each tail, leaving the return free and turning in 5cm (2in) to create a fold along the inner edge. (**8**)

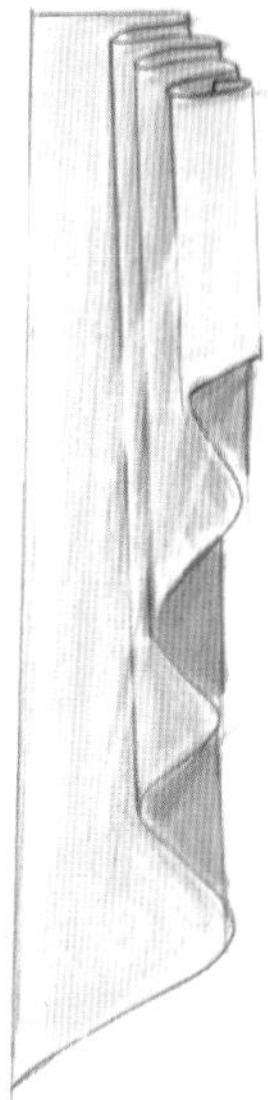

8

❑ Secure the pleats with a line of tacking stitches.

Choux

See page 160.

Curtains

Make up as for interlined curtains. Give each edge a 4cm (1½in) border in contrast fabric (see page 161), insert the padded edge (see page 161) and attach a line of cording to the join of the border and main section.

HANGING

❑ Hang and dress the curtains in the usual way.

❑ Position the swag and tack the bound top edge to the top of the board.

❑ Tack the tails to the front of the pelmet board.

❑ Attach choux.

VARIATION

Swagged Valance

One of the simplest and most attractive ways to decorate the top section of a window is by using a single length of cloth, draped over a pair of hooks.

MATERIALS

❏ Fabric
❏ Lining

FITTINGS

❏ 5cm (2in) square wooden batten
❏ Pair of hooks

FITTING

❏ Fix the batten above the architrave. Attach the hooks to the window frame below the batten. Make sure that the hooks project sufficiently to carry the swag.

MEASURING

❏ Hang leadweight tape, light chain or cord between the hooks in imitation of the projected swag (see pages 88, 128). Decide on the length of the outer edge of the valance (*a*).
❏ Measure the inner-edge of the swag (*b*).
❏ Calculate the depth of the swag (*c*) and multiply by two. (**1**)

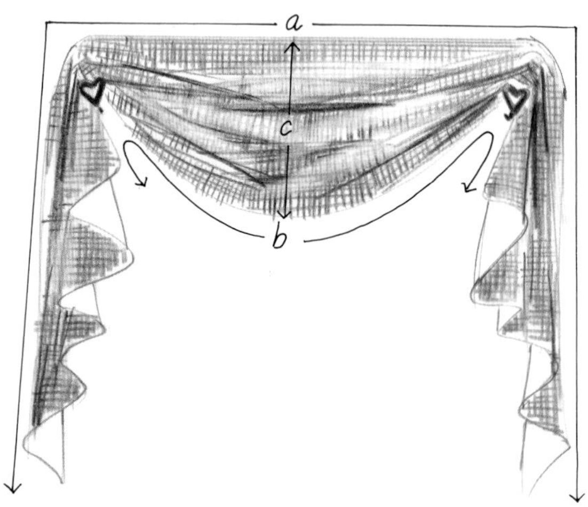

1

MAKING UP

❏ Cut a template, allowing a seam allowance on all four sides. (**2**)
❏ Cut out in the fabric and the lining. Place the two pieces of fabric with right sides together. Pin, tack and machine-stitch around three sides. Turn and press. Turn in the fourth edge and slipstitch.

HANGING

❏ Tack the top of the valance to the top surface of the batten.
❏ Lay the swag over the hooks and tease the folds into place.

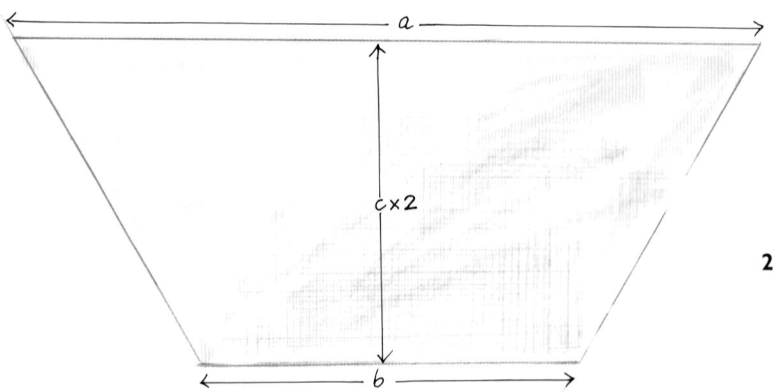

2

VARIATION

Art Deco Swag and Tails

A modern interpretation of the traditional swag and tails is used here in a most original fashion as an accompaniment to a translucent, striped roller blind. The swag and tails are made in the same way as the main project – the difference lies in the small crested tabs that adorn the top section of the tails. These are not integral, but are made separately and fixed on to the front of the tails. In keeping with the zany modernity of the room, the usual rules on swag-and-tail proportions do not apply.

VARIATIONS

Flute, Spiral and Pipe Tails

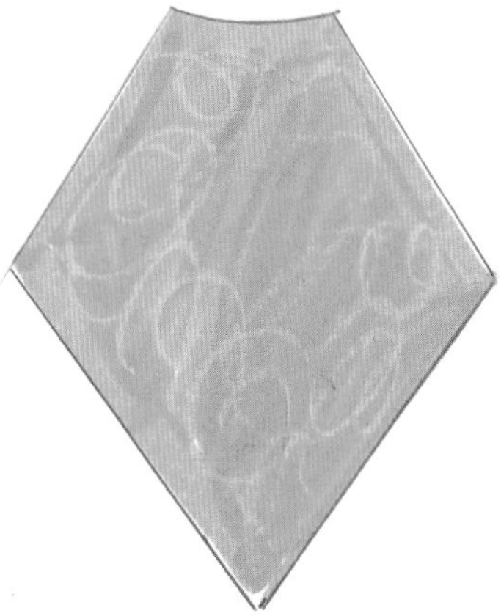

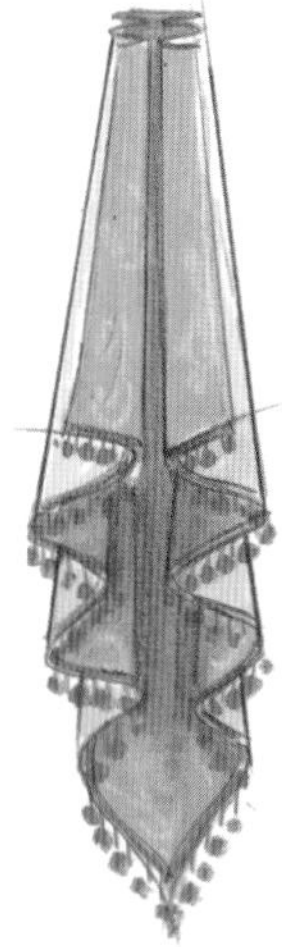

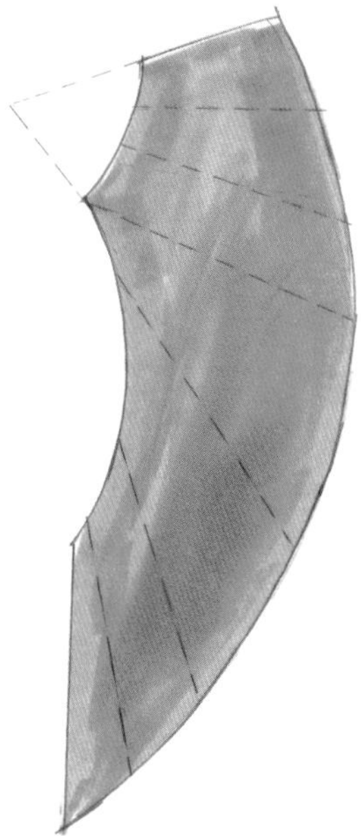

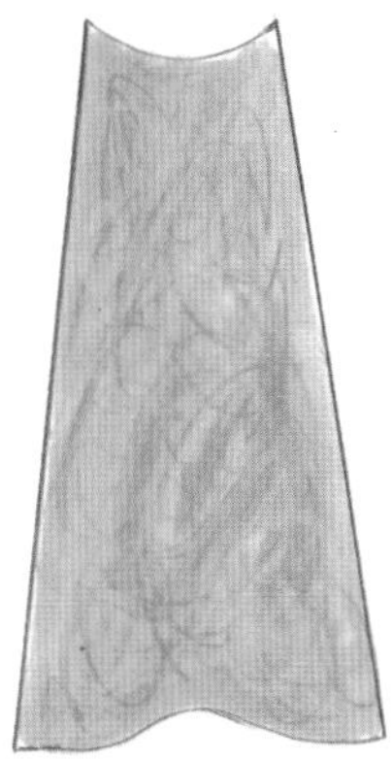

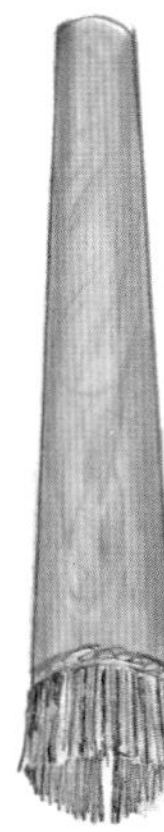

VARIATION

Muslin Swag with Choux

This fan swag is a variation on the more conventional version. It forms the graceful curve typical of the style without masking any of the daylight entering a room. Deeply looped curtains follow the curve of the swag, filtering and diffusing the light. These curtains clear the floor, but could equally well be made to floor-length. Fat choux punctuate the top edge of the fan, hiding the side edges of the pelmet board.

MATERIALS

- ❑ Muslin
- ❑ Touch-and-close fastening
- ❑ Small-headed nails
- ❑ Lining (template)

FITTINGS

- ❑ Pelmet board (as shallow as possible: there are no tails or returns to hide the side of the board)
- ❑ Brackets
- ❑ Curtain track
- ❑ Tieback arms

FITTING

- ❑ Prepare the pelmet board in the usual way.
- ❑ Attach the curtain track to the board, and the board to the wall.
- ❑ Fix the tieback arms into position.

MEASURING

- ❑ Measure the length of the swag (*a*) using a chain or leadweight tape (see pages 88, 128). (**1** below)
- ❑ Measure the depth of the swag (*b*) and measure the length of the pelmet board (*c*).
- ❑ Make a template in lining fabric, experimenting with relative dimensions. (**2** below right) When (*c*) gathers to form the curve (*a*), (*d*) comes up either side to form part of the top edge; (*e*) is gathered up to form the end points of the swag.

MAKING UP

Swag

- ❑ Allow an extra 2.5cm (1in) all around the template. Cut out in the fabric.
- ❑ Make a double 12mm (½in) turning along the base edge and slipstitch into place.
- ❑ Run a line of gathering stitches along (c) and both (e) sections. Pull up gathering stitches and secure.
- ❑ Measure out and cut a strip of fabric the length of the pelmet board by 7.5cm (3in) to bind the top edge of the swag and provide the fixing. If you are using muslin, use plain lining fabric or white cotton webbing for this job – muslin is too flimsy.
- ❑ Fold the strip in half lengthwise, turn in a seam allowance along each long edge and turn in the ends. Press to secure the folds.
- ❑ Place over the top edge of the swag and back- or machine-stitch into place.
- ❑ The swag can be held to the pelmet board using either touch-and-close fastening or tacks. If the first technique is chosen, attach the touch-and-close fastening to the back of the bound top edge.

Choux

See page 160.

Curtains

- ❑ Make up as for unlined curtains (see page 90).

HANGING

- ❑ Hang the curtains in the usual way and loop them up into the tieback arms.
- ❑ Staple or tack the swag to the top surface and just behind the front edge of the pelmet board. If touch-and-close fastening is used, attach it along the same position on the pelmet board and join it to the back of the swag.
- ❑ Tack choux to either end around the front corners of the board, using small-headed nails.

1

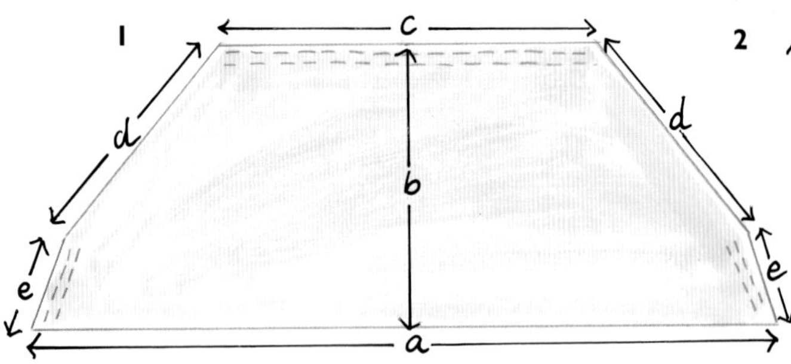

2

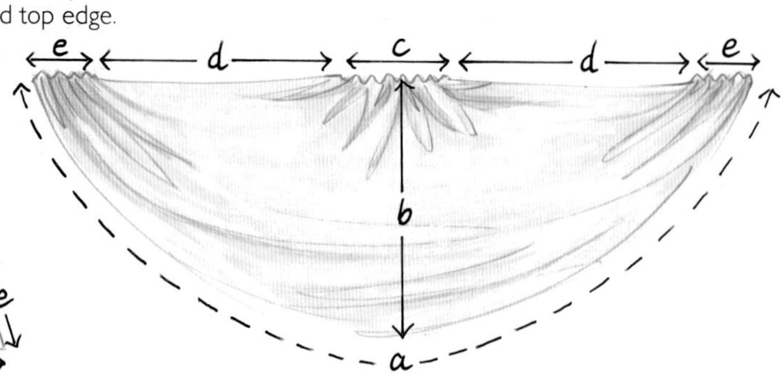

Italian Stringing
Checked Curtains

MATERIALS
- ❑ Fabric
- ❑ Lining
- ❑ Interlining
- ❑ Weights
- ❑ Brass or plastic rings

FITTINGS
- ❑ Pole
- ❑ Cornice brackets
- ❑ 5 x 2.5cm (2 x 1in) board
- ❑ Screw eyes
- ❑ Cord
- ❑ S-ring
- ❑ Acorn or tassel
- ❑ Cleat or pair of small brass or wooden knobs

TOOLS
- ❑ Drill
- ❑ Bradawl

Italian-strung curtains, drawn by a system of cords running through rings sewn in a diagonal line to the back of the curtain, are not difficult to make, and have considerable practical and decorative charms: a single pulley ensures that both curtains will open evenly without any handling; the height of the stringing allows more light to penetrate; and the vertical sweep of the curtain is uninterrupted by a tieback. The treatment works well for interlined curtains, whose weight helps to create a lush, draped effect.

Italian stringing is only appropriate with fixed headings and is not suitable for curtains that draw back on a rail. With a fixed heading, a decorative motif can be attached to the overlap. Similarly, cording, looped along the heading, remains undisturbed as the curtains are opened and closed.

Slotted headings (by nature static or fixed) offer an opportunity to show decorative finials. Ordinary fixed headings allow the use of a curve-fronted pelmet board, giving an elegant bow front to the scheme.

Italian-strung curtains may crush slightly more than those held back by conventional tiebacks, particularly if silk or other delicate fabrics are used. Heavier weights in the hem will ease the problem; alternatively, the curtains can be kept open at all times, with a blind placed behind to pull down at night.

A brass acorn or heavy tassel attached to the cording may pull on the leading edges and cause a continuous dent even when the curtains are closed. To overcome this, relieve the pressure by tying up the cord.

FITTING

❑ Insert three screw eyes into the front of the board, as shown. Fix the board flat to the wall immediately above the window. Fix the pole immediately above the board.

❑ At points (*a*) and (*b*) fix screw eyes to the wall or window frame. These will carry the cord from the edge of the curtains up to the board and should be in line with the outer screw eyes. (**1**)

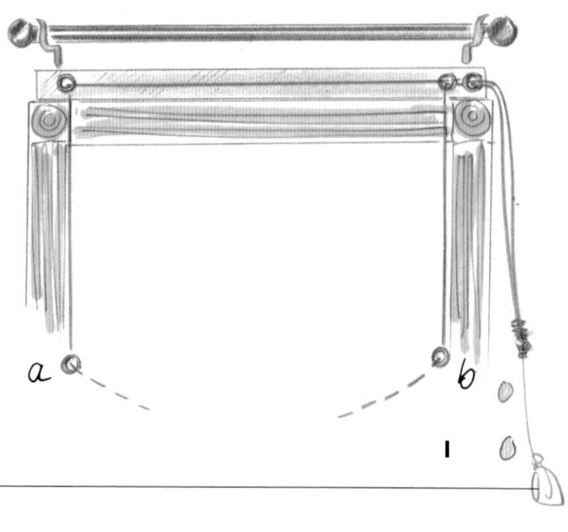

1

INSPIRATION *30*
INTERLINED CURTAINS *94*
SLOTTED HEADING *104*
POLES *173*
FITTING *176*

❑ At about chest height, fix either a cleat or pair of small knobs about 12cm (5in) apart (in scale with the overall size of the window) in line with the pull cord. This will anchor the cording.

MAKING UP

❑ Measure and make up the curtains in the usual way. This pair has a slotted heading and uses a curtain pole. The cornice brackets holding the pole are hidden between the front of the slot and the pole itself (see page 173).

❑ Dress the curtains.

❑ Use chalk to mark a diagonal line on the back of the curtain folds. This runs from the point on the leading edge where the first ring will be positioned (*c*), up to the point on the outer edge of the curtain (*a*) or (*b*), where a screw eye will lead the cord up to the pelmet board. The distance from (c) to the top of the curtain should be approximately one-third of the overall length. The distance from (*a*) and (*b*) to the top should be about one-quarter to one-fifth of the overall length. (**2** left)

❑ Stitch rings to the back of each fold using the chalk marks. Penetrate all layers, using small stitches and strong thread.

❑ Having decided which side the pull cord should hang, cut two lengths of cord. The shorter cord runs from the leading edge to the outer edge of the curtain, through the screw eye (*a*) up to the outer screw eye and down to the pull cord (or vice versa if the pull cord hangs on the other side of the window). The longer cord travels much the same path, but runs through the screw eyes on the pelmet board to join its companion on the pull cord side.

❑ Knot the cords to the first rings (see page 148) and run them through their allotted paths. (**3** left)

❑ With the curtains closed and the cords evenly tensioned, stitch the raw ends to the S-ring (see page 51).

❑ Attach a short piece of cord finished with a tassel or acorn to the other half of the S-ring. (see page 151). The acorn or tassel should hang just below waist height.

2

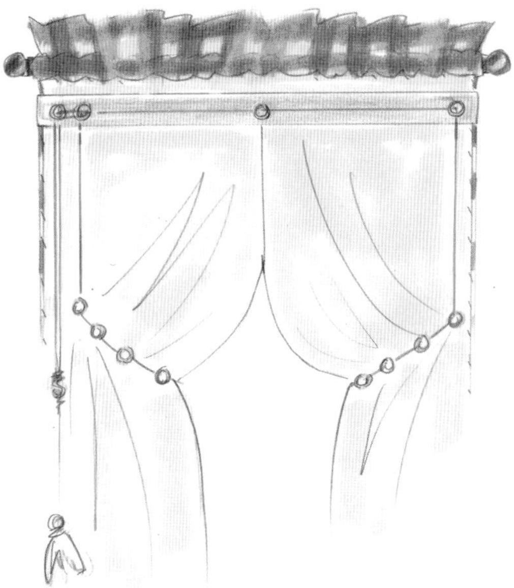

3

VARIATION

White Curtains

Here, a dramatic effect has been achieved by extending the curtaining between the two windows. A batten has been fixed along the length of the wall, touch-and-close fastening along the front surface holds the drapery in place, and screw eyes in the base of the batten operate the Italian stringing. (**1** below)

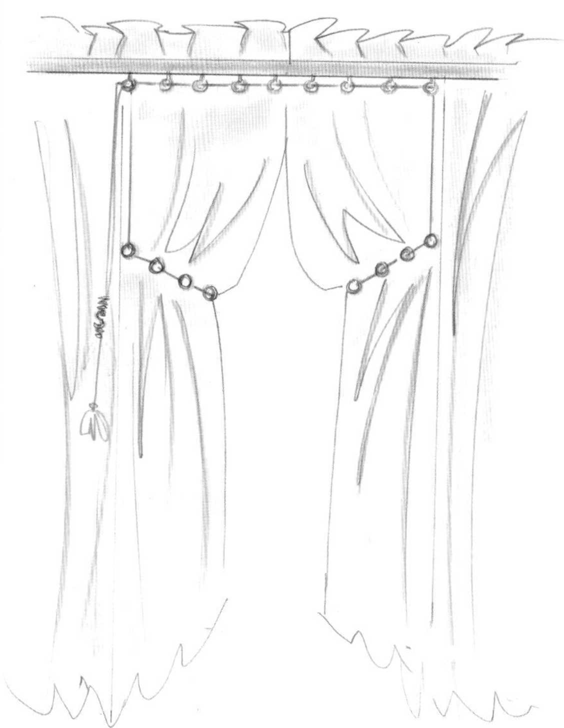

1

No-sew Curtains

MATERIALS
❑ Fabric (heavy calico or cotton duck)
❑ Pin-on hooks
❑ Fabric glue
❑ Stiff brown paper or newspaper (templates)

TOOLS
❑ Pinking scissors

FITTINGS
❑ Pole
❑ Cornice brackets
❑ Rings
❑ Finials

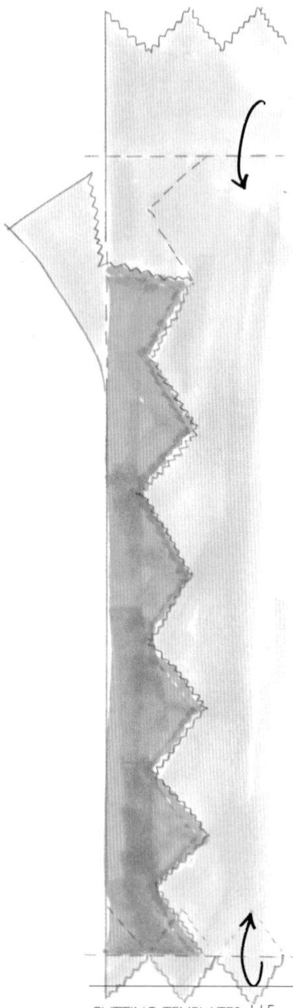

1

There are numerous short cuts to curtaining a window, and no-sew curtains can be among the most successful. Held together with fabric glue they take little time or skill to assemble once the basic shapes are cut.

These curtains are unlined and, to work efficiently, should be made of heavy calico or cotton duck. A shaped border is cut out in the same fabric, using pinking scissors, and glued to the edges of the curtain. The light penetrating the curtain highlights the appliquéd shape, shading from a lovely gentle honey colour in the centre to a deeper caramel at the sides. The top edge can either carry an extension to the side border or, as here, be cut into a zig-zag and flapped over to form an informal valance. A Matisse-style collage could provide one variation on the no-sew curtain, using cut-out fish and shell shapes. Equally flowers, leaves, the sun or the moon could provide inspiration.

The simplicity of the design calls for the use of a pole and rings, whether finished off with gilded finials and brass rings or amore austere wrought iron arrangement. Because heavy cotton duck is too stiff to form soft drapes, tiebacks will not work here, so the curtains are not dressed in a formal manner, but are left to billow.

If possible, no-sew curtains should be made from a single width of fabric. Cotton duck and calico is available in much bigger widths than ordinary fabrics, wide enough to cover all but the very largest windows. This treatment lacks the pleating or gathering of conventional curtains – much of their appeal lies in the gently wavy surface – so the flat curtain width is about one and a half times the length of pole that it occupies.

No-sew curtains are most suited to the bedroom and it is a particular delight to wake up to sunlight filtered through the appliquéd shapes.

MEASURING
❑ Width: the flat width should be one and a half times the length of pole that the curtain occupies. There are no side turnings, so nothing need be added. Joining drops is not really advisable with such heavy fabric and the see-through pattern would be spoiled by a visible seam, so try to find fabric of the right width to start with. If there is no other solution, overlap the drops by 2.5cm (1in) and either glue together or run a double line of machine stitches.
❑ Length: add 15cm (6in) for the hem and one-fifth of the finished length of the curtain for the pelmet flap.
❑ Side borders: one extra drop of fabric.

FITTING
❑ Fix the pole and finials in the usual way.

MAKING UP
❑ Prepare a paper template of:
1. Border shape
2. Hem zig-zag
3. Pelmet zig-zag
(see page 148).
❑ Cut the drop.
❑ Cut the side borders to the finished length plus 5cm (2in) to turn under the hem. Allow 2.5cm (1in) extra on the width to wrap around the side edge of the main panel.
❑ Lay the main panel face down. Cut the zig-zag in the hem.
❑ Turn up the hem and glue sparingly (an excess of glue will show through, discolour and cause a range of other problems).
❑ Turn the curtain over and position the side panels to overlap the edges by 2.5cm (1in) and the hem by 5cm (2in). (**1** left)
❑ Glue into place. Do not allow any glue to seep from under the border.
❑ Turn over the pelmet flap and secure with intermittent dabs of glue. (**2** right)

HANGING
❑ Position pin-on hooks along the back and hang. (**3** right)

CUTTING TEMPLATES *115*
POLES *173*
CUTTING BIAS STRIP *182*

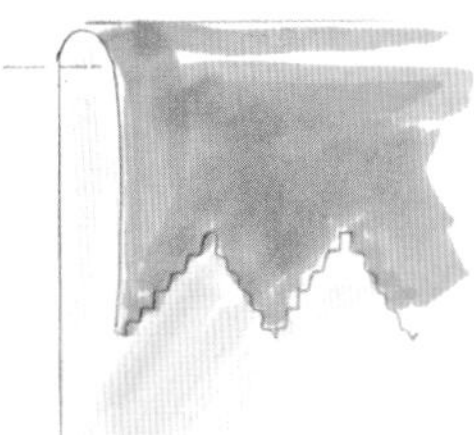

2

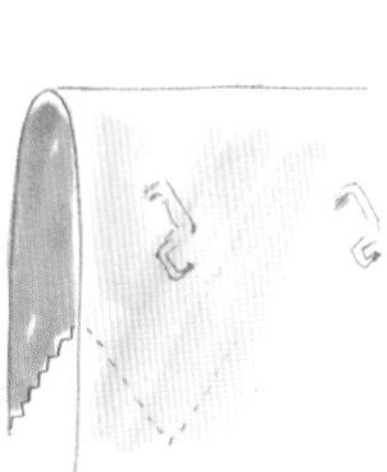

3

Border Shapes

Tiebacks

I never used to understand why tiebacks were considered necessary. They seemed to assist little in the job of clearing the curtain away from the window, and would often hang limp and redundant once their novelty had worn off.

Seeing them used correctly has converted me. Except in exceptional circumstances, curtains are seen at their best gently draped into tiebacks, forming a graceful frame to the window. It takes some effort to wrap the tiebacks around the curtains each morning, teasing the folds into place, but the effort is well rewarded. Keen to retain the elegant folds of a newly hung curtain, some leave the curtains permanently tied back, drawing down a hidden roller blind for seclusion at night.

Tiebacks take many forms. Brass arms or pairs of tassels can embrace the leading edge, or curtains may be draped over lion-faced ombras. I favour the use of simple, stiffened tiebacks, made in the same fabric as the curtain. These can be positioned two-thirds of the way to the floor or high up, opening up the window rather in the manner of an Italian-strung curtain (see page 134). You may prefer to line the tiebacks in the face fabric so that even when hanging down at night with the curtains closed, the tieback never shows a plain lining.

Make sure that the hooks or other fixings are secure. There is nothing more irritating than collapsing tiebacks.

A contrast-banded crescent tieback unobtrusively retains the graceful folds of a matching curtain. (LEFT)

INSPIRATION *13, 18, 21, 41, 59, 62, 77*
BUCKRAM (FABRICS) *83*
CUTTING OUT *178*
HERRINGBONE STITCH *179*
CUTTING BIAS STRIP *182*
FRILL *183*

Crescent Tieback

The crescent-shaped tieback is the most conventional means of tying back a pair of curtains. Its curved shape and broad centre provide a firm hold and cause minimum creasing. Make sure that the tieback is neither too tight nor too loose – it should hug the curtain, neither squeezing it into a series of wrinkles nor flapping disconsolately against a limp leading edge. The key to a pair of well-dressed curtains – the uniform folds hanging in regimented lines – is a pair of generous tiebacks.

Tiebacks and curtains are usually made in the same fabric. An unobtrusive tieback is self-piped; for greater prominence a contrast piping, edging, or even a frill, can be used, perhaps echoing a colour taken from the fabric itself or from the rest of the room. For further decoration rosettes, choux and bows can be sewn to the front of tiebacks and the lower edge can be cut into a decorative shape – a double curve or scallops, for example. A shaped lower edge often precludes the need for piping, which fits with difficulty around the tight curves.

Most tiebacks attach to the tieback hooks by means of brass rings or D-rings. This project shows a tieback anchored with ribbons made up in the contrast fabric. (FAR LEFT)

MATERIALS FOR TIEBACKS

- ❑ Face fabric
- ❑ Interlining
- ❑ Lining
- ❑ Tieback buckram
- ❑ Contrast fabric
- ❑ Newspaper or stiff brown paper (template)
- ❑ 2 brass or plastic rings per tieback

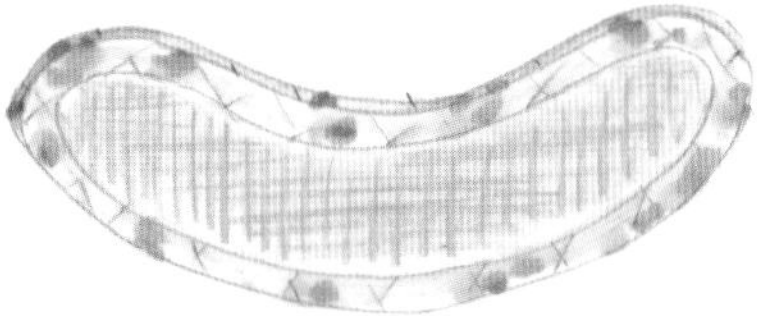

1

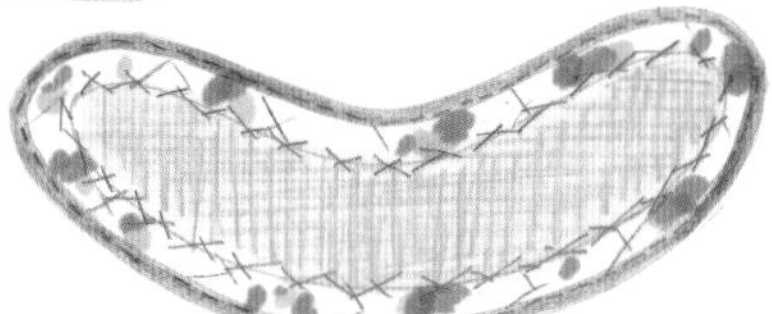

2

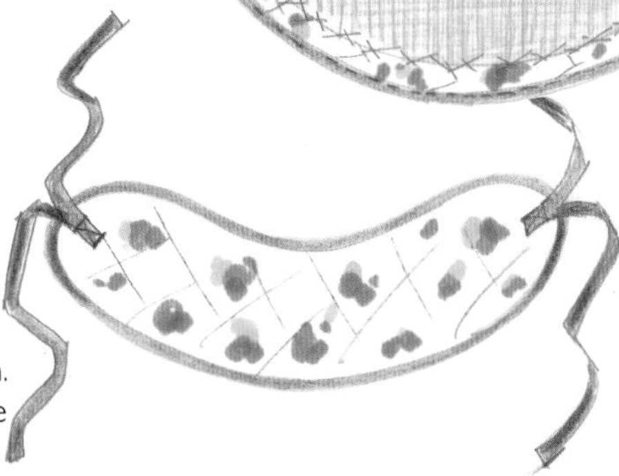

3

MAKING UP

❑ Measure around the finished curtain to assess the length of the tieback.

❑ Using a template, cut out the shape in buckram. Then cut out again in face fabric, lining and interlining, overlapping the template by 2.5 cm (1in).

❑ Overlap the interlining by 12mm (½in) (fusible buckram).

❑ Stretch the interlining, then the face fabric, around the buckram, clipping and trimming to avoid bulk. Press turnings with a hot iron (fusible buckram). (**1**) Herringbone-stitch into place (non-fusible buckram).

❑ Cut a bias strip. Fold in half lengthways and press. Turn in one edge and press. Lay the central fold along the edge of the tieback. Pin along the turned edge and slipstitch into place. Tack the back edge to the fabric turning. (**2**)

❑ Place the lining over the back of the tieback and fold in around the edges. Slipstitch into position. Press with a hot iron to release the glue (fusible buckram).

❑ For the ties, cut four strips of fabric twice the finished length and twice the finished width, plus two seam allowances. Fold each in half lengthwise, right sides together, and machine around the long side and one end. Trim , turn and press. Turn in and stitch the open end. Fold each in half and attach to tieback. (**3**)

Ruched Tieback

Best accompanied by a pair of medium- or lightweight curtains, a ruched tieback is a simple alternative to the stiffened, contrast-banded tieback described previously. It gives an informal finish to a pair of curtains, its fat ruffles complementing a pretty floral print.

MAKING UP

❑ Cut a strip of tieback buckram to length.

❑ Cut a strip of face fabric and one of interlining (domette or bump) to twice the finished length and four times the finished width, plus two seam allowances.

❑ Lay the interlining over the back of the fabric and treat as one layer.

❑ Fold the strip of fabric and interlining in half, right sides together. Stitch around the long side and one end. (**4** below)

❑ Clip the corner and turn.

❑ Insert the buckram into the tube and gather up evenly. Turn in the open end and slipstitch. Prickstitch across each end and sew on a brass or plastic ring.

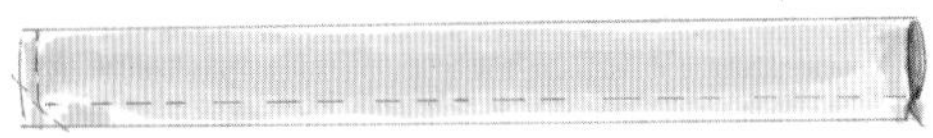

4

Frilled Tieback

A plain, crescent-shaped tieback is enhanced with a knife-pleated frill, the vivid green moiré inspired by a colour in the main fabric.

MAKING UP

❑ Make up as for the crescent tieback, but omit the contrast edging Before attaching lining, slipstitch a prepared frill to the back. (**5**)

❑ Lay the lining over the back, slipstitch into position. Use rings instead of ties to attach the tieback to the hook.

5

Pencil-pleated Tieback

Made in the faded flower colours of a muted linen, this tieback, a version of the ruffled tieback described previously, is given a slight touch of formality as the ruffles are tamed into a line of narrow pleats.

MAKING UP

❑ Cut the tieback buckram to length.

❑ Cut a strip of fabric to twice the width plus seam allowances and to the same length plus seam allowances.

❑ Fold in half lengthwise, right sides together, and machine-stitch along the side and one end. Trim the corner, turn and press.

❑ Insert the buckram. Turn in the open end and slipstitch.

❑ Run four parallel lines of machine-stitching the length of the tieback.

❑ Form neat pencil pleats and prickstitch firmly into place.

❑ Sew a ring onto each end of the tieback. (**6**)

6
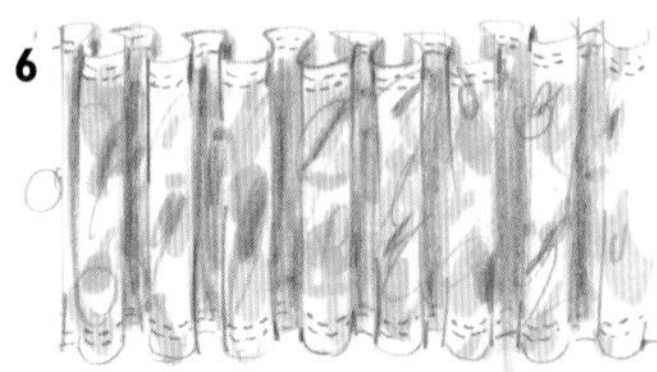

Tieback Shapes

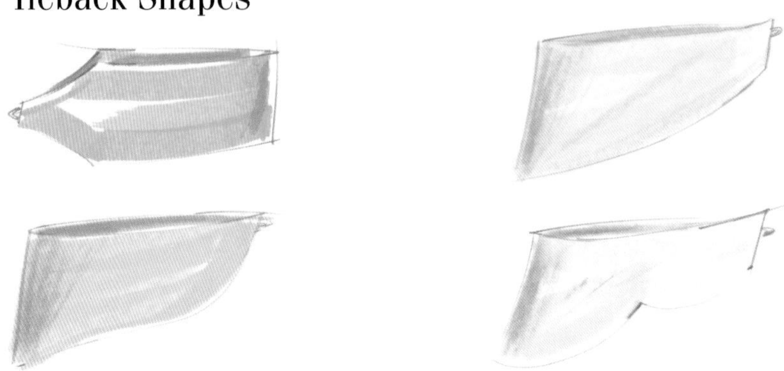

Pocket Tieback

The intricate folded surface of this tieback appears to have been invented either by an origami expert or a napkin folder from an expensive French restaurant. The result is both original and charming, the crisp pleats a perfect foil to the flat surfaces of the curtain beneath.

MAKING UP

❑ Cut out a strip of face fabric and one of lining to the width of the tieback plus two seam allowances by three times the finished length.
❑ With right sides together, stitch around three sides, leaving one end open. Clip the corners and turn. Press, turn in the open end and slipstitch across.
❑ Form into regular box pleats (see page 183). Machine-stitch down the back of each pleat. (**7**)
❑ Attach the edges of the box pleats to one another with a stitch one-third in from the top (*a*) and another the same distance from the base (*b*). (**8**)
❑ Fold back the centre of the top and base edge of each pleat and secure with a few small stitches (c). (**9**)
❑ Stitch a ring to each end.

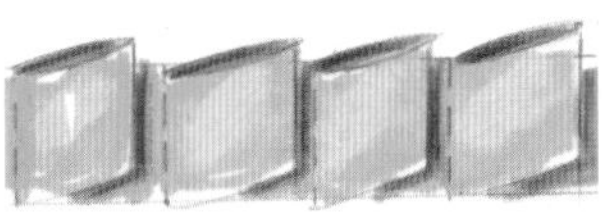
7

8
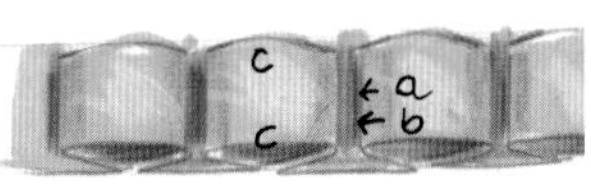

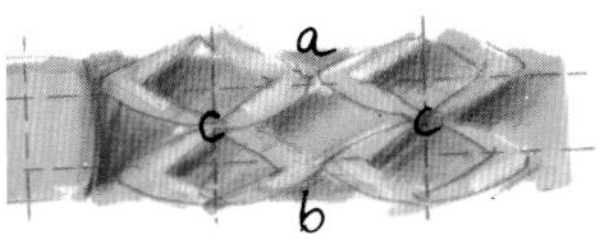

9

Roses Tieback

Yellow velvet roses and green velvet leaves, set against a printed velvet curtain, provide an irresistible combination of colours and texture. Made with a simple tieback as its base, the skill in this project lies in fashioning the roses and, to a lesser extent, the leaves.

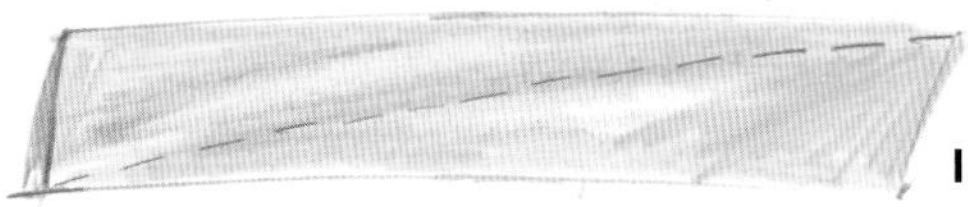
10

MAKING UP

❑ Take a strip of fabric about 20cm (8in) wide and 86cm (34in) long, preferably of velvet or velveteen. Fold in half lengthwise. Cut a wedge from the raw edge so that the fabric measures 2.5cm (1in) wide at one end and 20cm (8in) at the other. (**10** above)
❑ Starting at the narrow end of the folded fabric, which forms the centre of the rose, make a cartwheel spiral, twisting and bunching the fabric to achieve natural looking 'petals'. (**11**)

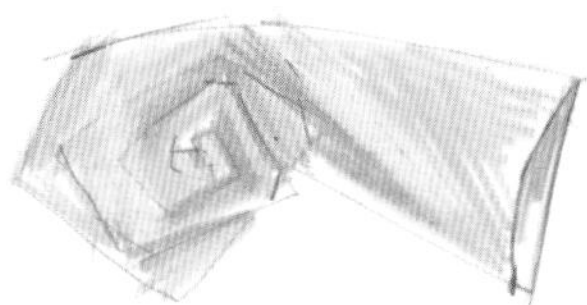
11

❑ Tuck the raw end behind the rose and hand-stitch the spiral into place.
❑ Repeat to make the smaller roses, using strips of fabric one-third to one-half the size of the principal rose.

❑ Cut out leaf-shaped pieces of fabric measuring about 7.5 x 5cm (3 x 2in). Place right sides together and stitch around two-thirds of the edge, close to the raw edge. (**12**)

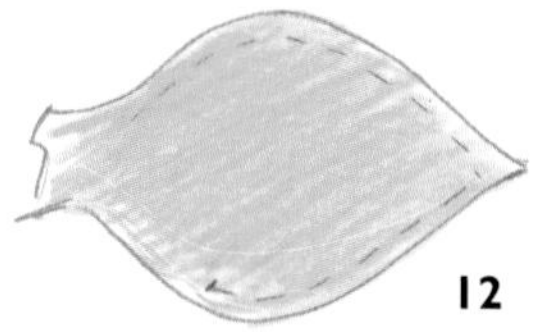
12

❑ Trim the seams and turn. Insert pliable wire into the seamline around the outer edge. Tack wire into place.
❑ Using the zig-zag stitch on the sewing machine, stitch along the edges and up the middle of the leaves. Using a straight stitch, run fanning lines of stitches in imitation of the leaves' natural veins. (**13**)

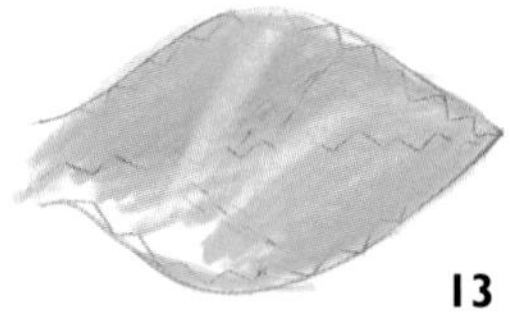
13

❑ Gently form the leaves into natural-looking shapes.
❑ The roses and leaves are attached to a crescent tieback (see page 139) before the lining is sewn to the back. The tieback should, however, be made unusually narrow. Stitch the roses and the leaves to the front and side of each tieback.

Blinds

A blind is a single piece of fabric, raised by means of a spring mechanism or cording system. It can be ruched into festoons, like old-fashioned cinema curtains, it can be gathered into a pull-up blind, or it can be flat to the window, either rolling up or rising into a series of horizontal pleats.

Blinds are wonderfully versatile – they can block out all light or operate as filters of daylight. They can be hidden away beneath a pelmet or pair of curtains, or serve as the decorative focus themselves. They can be plain and unobtrusive or show a bold design.

As a blind need only cover the window itself, it is often a useful treatment where there is insufficient room for a curtain to stack back to either side. Similarly, if small children with dirty fingers or splashes from a sink are likely to cause problems, a blind will pull up out of the way. If a radiator or window seat causes an obstruction, one or more blinds, ending at the level of the window sill, will cover the window most effectively.

Blinds exclude light to varying degrees. A pull-up blind and, to a lesser extent, a Roman blind will always obscure a window's top section – this is a problem that can be partially overcome by raising the pelmet board slightly (care should be taken not to make the blind look detached from the window, however). A roller blind is the only type of blind that clears the window entirely.

Aesthetically, blinds can be adapted to any setting. Sleek Roman blinds complement the clean lines of a modern apartment, a pull-up curtain (a floor-length version of the pull-up blind) would be an authentic choice for a Georgian panelled drawing room and a reverse roller, made of checked cotton, would find a perfect setting in a Scandinavian farmhouse.

INSPIRATION *17, 21, 32-3, 42-3, 59*
MEASURING *87*
MATCHING PATTERNS *89*
TOOLS AND ACCESSORIES *166*
FITTING *176*
HERRINGBONE STITCH *179*
SLIPSTITCH *180*
PRICKSTITCH *180*
FLAT-FELL SEAMS *181*
CUTTING BIAS STRIP *182*

PROJECT

Roller Blinds

Roller blinds offer a wide range of possibilities, from the purely functional to the highly decorative. By varying the shape of the lower edge, using large designs or geometric patterns, painting or stencilling, the common-or-garden roller blind can be adapted to suit a multitude of settings. In its simplest form it screens or filters light, rolling up when not needed.

Close-weave fabrics such as cotton are suitable for roller blinds when used with a stiffening spray, (loose-weave fabrics tend to lose their shape). Ready-stiffened fabric is also available.

If you are thinking of a shaped lower edge, bear in mind that it will only be completely functional if hung outside the reveal, clearing the ledge.

MATERIALS

- ❏ Fabric and stiffening spray or ready-stiffened blind fabric
- ❏ Bias binding or contrast fabric
- ❏ Lath
- ❏ Stiff brown paper or newspaper (template)

FITTINGS

- ❏ Roller blind kit

TOOLS

- ❏ Spirit level

FITTING

❏ Screw the brackets supplied with the kit into position, making sure that they are perfectly aligned. This is one of the few fittings that requires a spirit level to ensure a perfect horizontal.

MAKING UP

Ready-stiffened fabric

❏ This will not fray when cut. Make sure to cut precise right-angled corners.

Unstiffened fabric

❏ Cut to size, allowing an extra 30cm (12in) in width and 46cm (18in) in length (the stiffening agent will cause shrinkage). The fabric should be sufficient for the main panel and the base to be cut from it.

❏ Hang the fabric in a well-ventilated place, and spray both sides evenly. Leave to dry thoroughly.

❏ Cut to size. Allow an extra 2.5cm (1in) for side turnings and add 30cm (12in) to the finished length.

Shaped base

❏ Make a template (see page 115). Cut out the shaped base, matching any pattern with the top section and allowing for the same side turnings. Allow for a generous overlap with the main section. This will form the slot for the lath.

❏ Cut a bias strip in the unstiffened contrast fabric or bias binding to the width of the blind plus turnings.

❏ Glue or stitch the bias strip or binding to the base shape.

❏ Make side turnings in both sections and zig-zag-stitch into position.

❏ Overlap the top and base sections. Run two horizontal lines of machine stitching close to the overlap edges, forming a slot to accommodate the lath. (**1**)

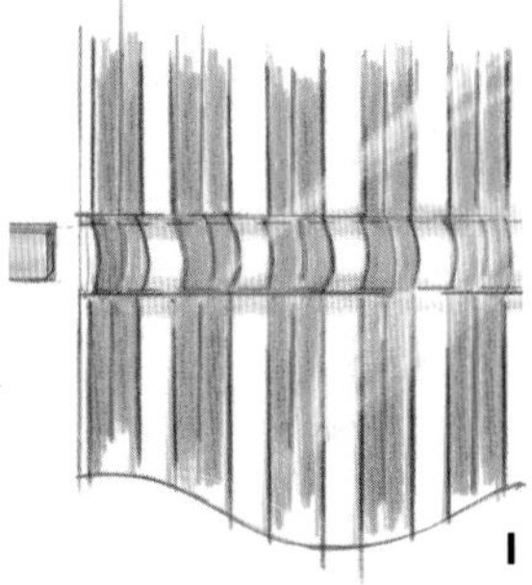

1

❏ Cut the lath 2.5cm (1in) shorter than the finished width and insert. Slipstitch across the ends of the slot.

❏ Screw the acorn fitting to the centre point of the lath through the fabric. (**2**)

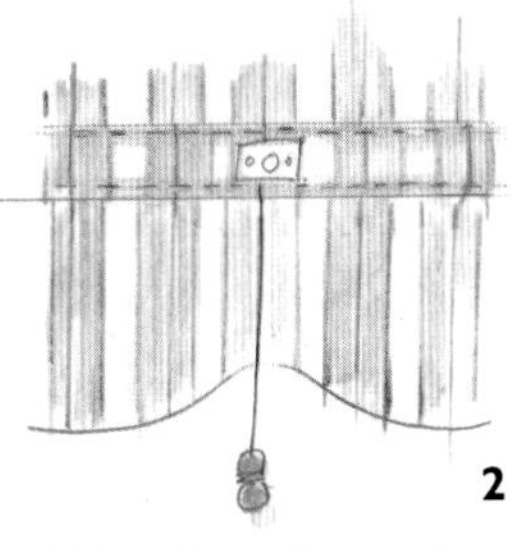

2

❏ Lay the roller on the right side of the blind's top edge. A guide line will help to achieve a straight line. Tack the top edge of the blind to the roller. (**3**)

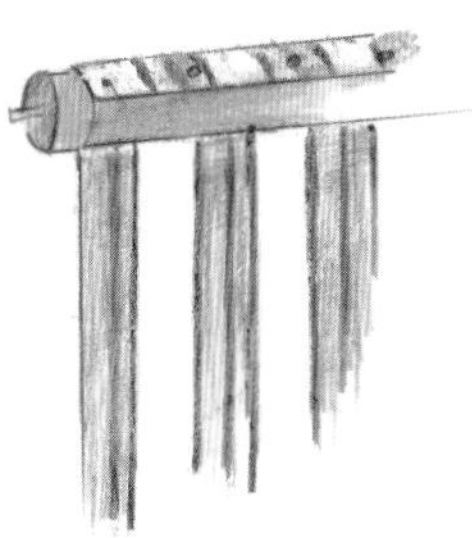

3

Straight base

❏ Make a double hem turning large enough to accommodate the lath. Insert the lath and slipstitch across the ends of the slot. (**4**)

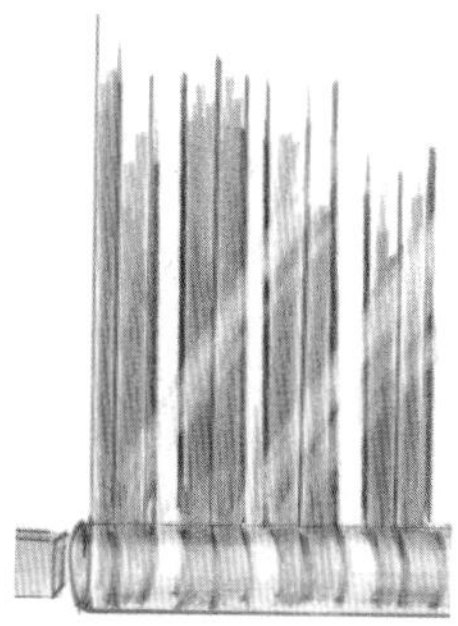

4

❏ Screw the acorn fitting to the centre point of the lath through the fabric.

HANGING

❏ Roll the blind on to the roller. Insert the roller into the brackets.

Alternative Shapes

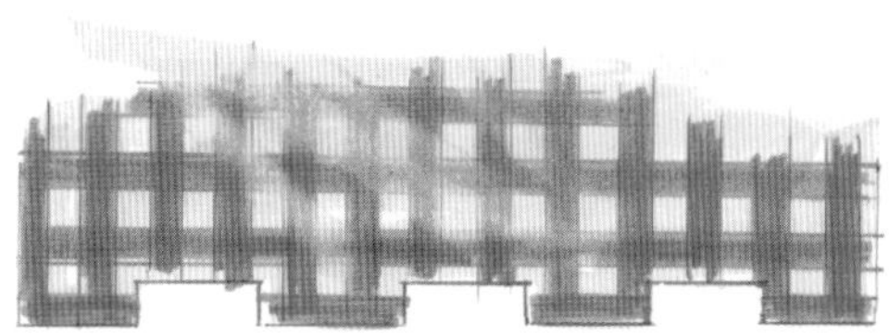

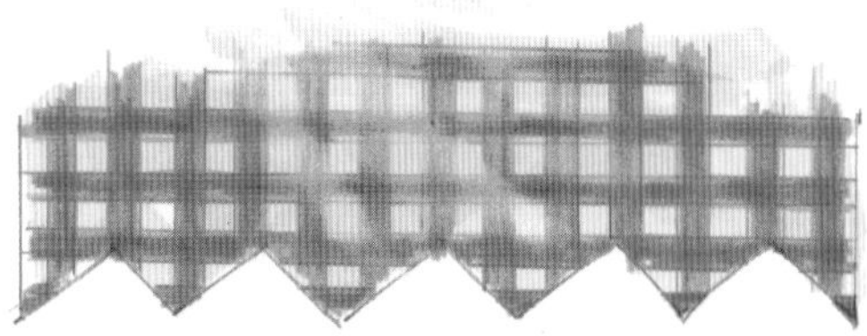

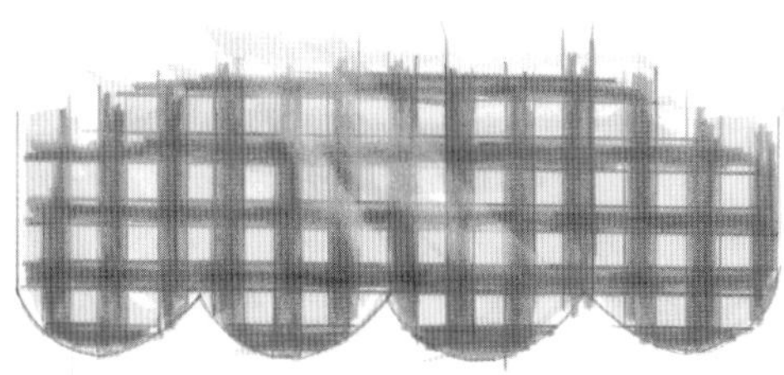

VARIATION

Reverse Roller Blind

This blind is made from an unlined cotton check material, and is lowered or raised by means of screw eyes and cording. With its painted panelling and graceful swag of white cotton, the room has the tranquil atmosphere of a Scandinavian farmhouse, and such a simple, unsophisticated blind seems entirely at one with its surroundings. A single cloak hook anchors the cords.

It is best to use lightweight fabrics for this project – anything heavier would prove too cumbersome. Keeping a small roll of material at the base of the blind facilitates the rolling process.

MATERIALS

- ❑ Fabric
- ❑ 19mm (¾in) dowel
- ❑ Blind cord
- ❑ Touch-and-close fastening

FITTINGS

- ❑ Pelmet board
- ❑ Brackets
- ❑ Screw eyes
- ❑ Cloak hook
- ❑ Brass or wooden acorn
- ❑ S-ring

MEASURING

❑ Width: the finished width should be equal to that of the window. Add 5cm (2in) for the side turnings.

❑ Length: the finished length should be 10cm (4in) longer than the space itself (even in its lowered position, the blind retains a base roll). Add 9.5cm (3¾in) for the hem and top turnings.

FITTING

❑ Staple a line of touch-and-close fastening along the top of the pelmet board, close to the front edge.

❑ Fix screw eyes to the base of the pelmet board at the points where the cords will attach.

❑ Using a bradawl, prepare the holes for the screw eyes in the front of the board. Two should be in line with the screw eyes below. The third should be on the pull-up side of the blind, above the anchor point. (**1** below)

❑ Fit the pelmet board on to the brackets. Fix the cloak hook to the anchor point.

1

MAKING UP

❑ Cut the required number of drops and join using flat fell seams. If more than one drop is involved, make sure to have a central panel.

❑ Turn in double 12mm (½in) side turnings and machine-stitch close to the fold.

❑ Make a single 7cm (2¾in) bottom turning and fold the turning in half to form the dowel pocket. Machine-stitch close to the fold. (**2**)

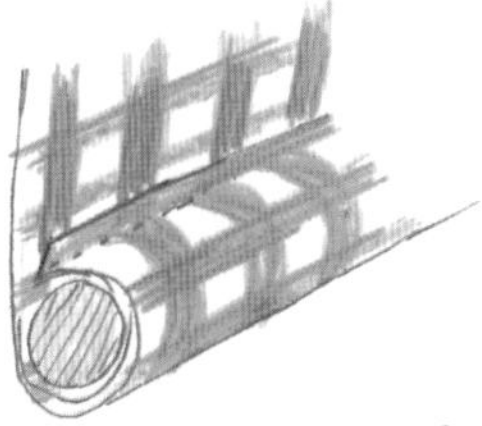

2

❑ Make a double 12mm (½in) top turning and machine-stitch close to the fold.

❑ Machine-stitch a line of touch-and-close fastening to the back of the heading.

❑ Cut the dowel to length, 19mm (¾in) short of the finished width of the blind. Insert the dowel into the pocket and slipstitch across either end.

HANGING

❑ Join the lines of touch-and-close fastening.

❑ Knot each cord to the appropriate screw eyes on the base of the pelmet board (see page 149).

❑ Pierce the fabric with the bradawl at the three screw eye positions on the front of the pelmet board, taking care not to break the fibres but instead pushing the weave apart, so that the screw eyes will not twist the fabric.

❑ Insert the three screw eyes into the front of the pelmet board, through the blind, using the prepared bradawl holes. Slot the cords through the frontal screw eyes. (**3**)

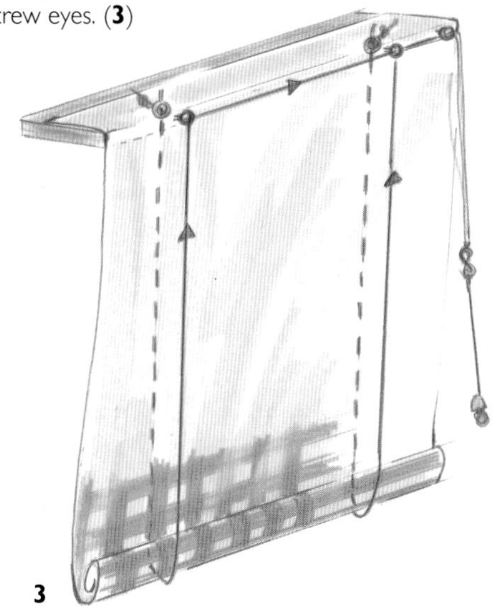

3

❑ Roll the base section of the blind.

❑ Holding the blind in a perfect horizontal, trim and knot the cords and attach them to an S-ring (see page 151).

❑ Thread the single cord coming out of the base of the S-ring cord through a brass or wooden acorn and knot the end.

Blinds
Roman Blinds

MATERIALS
❑ Face fabric
❑ Lining
❑ Interlining (domette)
❑ Dowels
❑ Touch-and-close fastening

FITTINGS
❑ Pelmet board or batten
❑ Brackets (optional)
❑ Screw eyes
❑ Cleat
❑ Blind cord
❑ Brass or wooden acorn
❑ S-ring

TOOLS
❑ Drill
❑ Staple gun or hammer and tacks
❑ Bradawl

A Roman blind is basically a flat piece of fabric, backed by a line of parallel, horizontal bars, which pulls up on cords to form neat folds.

These blinds take many forms. When lined and interlined they have all the thermal qualities of curtains. If blackout-lined they will exclude light; if unlined they will filter sunlight, while retaining privacy. When pulled-up during the day, they permit uninterrupted daylight – and keep clear of sleepy cats and children.

Bordered, fringed, painted or plain, Roman blinds can stand on their own or be stacked away behind a pelmet or lambrequin. They can hang inside or outside the architrave, but will become unwieldy if wider than 1.4m (4ft 9in). In such cases, it is as well to increase the number of blinds, using divisions in the window as a guide.

Roman blinds are economical with fabric and will show off any design to best advantage. Once in place, the cording should prove efficient and predictable – unlike some roller-blind mechanisms which can lose their tension. In time, however, the cords will fray and will need to be replaced.

FITTING
❑ The pelmet board or batten from which the blind will hang should be of sufficient depth to allow a line of screw eyes to be inserted between the front surface of the blind and the wall or architrave. However, as a Roman blind has no returns it should also be as shallow as possible. There is a danger that the edge of the pelmet board or batten will be visible and that the blind will hang away from the window, letting in light and draughts around the sides.
❑ The fittings will be taking considerable strain and should therefore be firmly attached to the wall or window. Most blinds will hang from 5 x 5cm (2 x 2in) wooden battens which can be screwed into the wall or ceiling. If greater

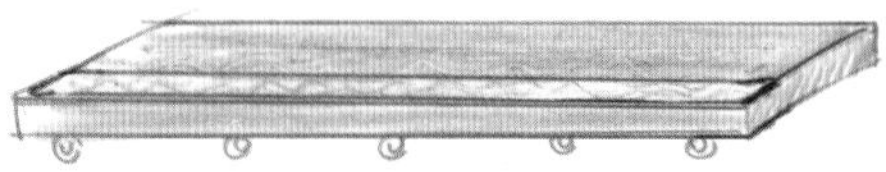

1a

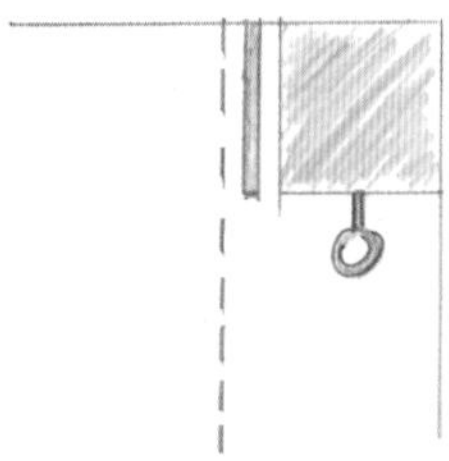

1b

depth is needed, a pelmet board can rest on brackets to either side of the window. The fittings are usually positioned resting on top of the architrave.
❑ Cut the pelmet board or batten to length and prepare it in the usual way.
❑ Run a line of screw eyes along the base of the board or batten. Most Roman blinds have two or three lines of cords running vertically up the back and each line should have a screw eye directly above it.
❑ Staple or tack a line of touch-and-close fastening along the top of the board or batten, slightly behind the front edge. If the batten is fixed to the ceiling, staple the touch-and-close fastening along the front edge. (**1a** & **1b** above)
❑ Fix a cleat into the wall at a point where the cords can conveniently be tied – usually somewhere between waist and chest level.

MEASURING
❑ Width: The finished width should be equal to the width of the window. Add 6cm (2½in) for the side turnings.
❑ Length: extra length is needed for the strip of touch-and-close fastening if it runs along the top of the pelmet board.
❑ For the face fabric and interlining, add 20cm (8in) for turnings.
❑ Allow extra length for the lining, as it will be folded and stitched to form horizontal pockets for the dowels. Multiply the length of each pocket by the number of dowels needed up the back of the blind.
❑ Allow approximately 20cm (8in) between dowels, depending on the size of the window, and calculate how many will run across the back

of the blind. Allow approximately 10cm (4in) between the lowest dowel and the lower edge of the blind. For example, if there are ten dowels with 7.5cm (3in) needed to house each one (they should fit snugly but not tightly), add 70cm (30in) plus two seam allowances to the finished length of the lining.

MAKING UP

❑ Cut out the face fabric and interlining to size.

❑ Use flat-fell seams to join drops of fabric or lining.

❑ Turn in the side edges of the lining twice by 19mm (¾in) – 3.8cm (1½in) in all each side. Machine-stitch along the edge of the turning close to the fold.

❑ Making sure that the seams are strictly parallel and at right angles to the sides, mark the batten pockets on the lining front. (**2** right)

❑ Fold the lining so that the seam lines match, tack and then machine-stitch them together. Press. (**3**)

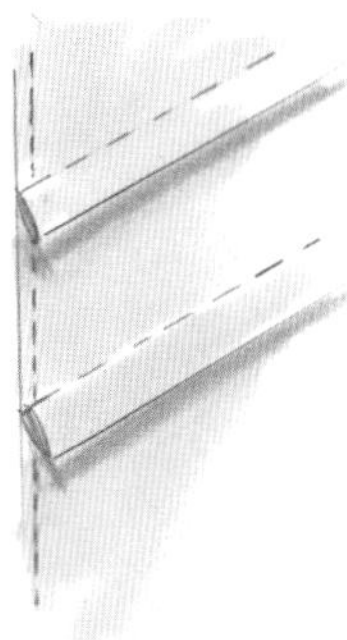

3

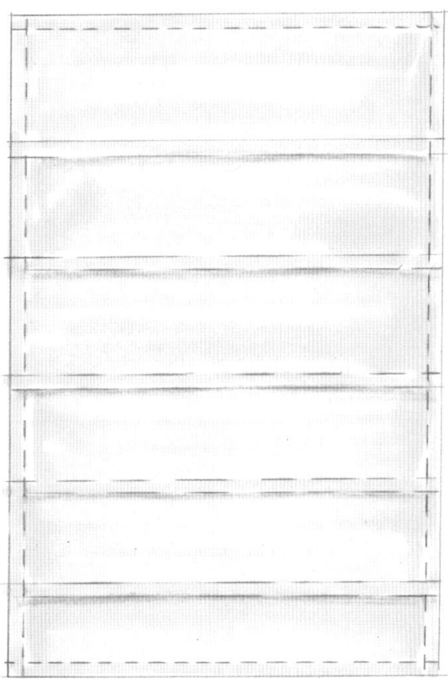

2

❑ Lay down the face fabric and interlining.

❑ Turn up a 10cm (4in) hem in the fabric and interlining (to run in line with the lowest batten). Fold over the side and top turnings and press.

❑ Using the pressing lines as a guide, trim the interlining around the top and sides so that the raw edge fits neatly into the turnings.

❑ Herringbone-stitch the hem and slipstitch the edges (no mitre is needed).

❑ Lay the lining into position on the back of the blind. Turn under at the top and bottom, pin around all four sides and, through all the thicknesses, just above the batten lines. Tack into place. Slipstitch around the edges.

❑ Machine-stitch the batten lines. Make sure that the machine tension is right and that the thread matches the fabric.

❑ Run a line of touch-and-close fastening behind the top of the blind. Machine-stitch into place.

❑ Insert the dowels into the pockets and slipstitch across each end.

❑ Using strong thread, sew brass or plastic rings

to the dowel pockets. Three lines of rings – one up the centre and one 5cm (2in) in from each edge – is normally sufficient; add more if the blind is unusually wide. (**4** below)

5

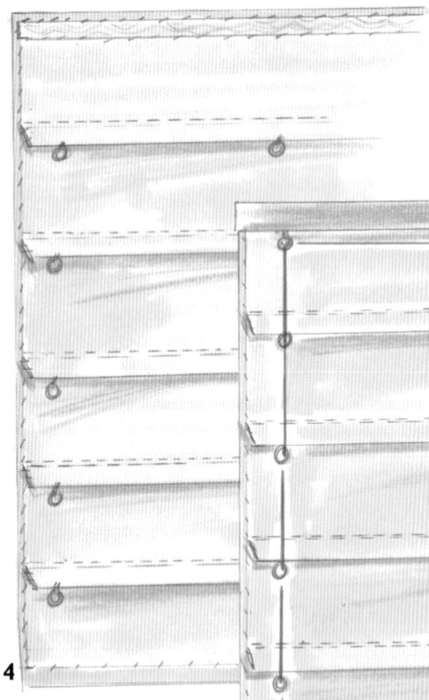

4

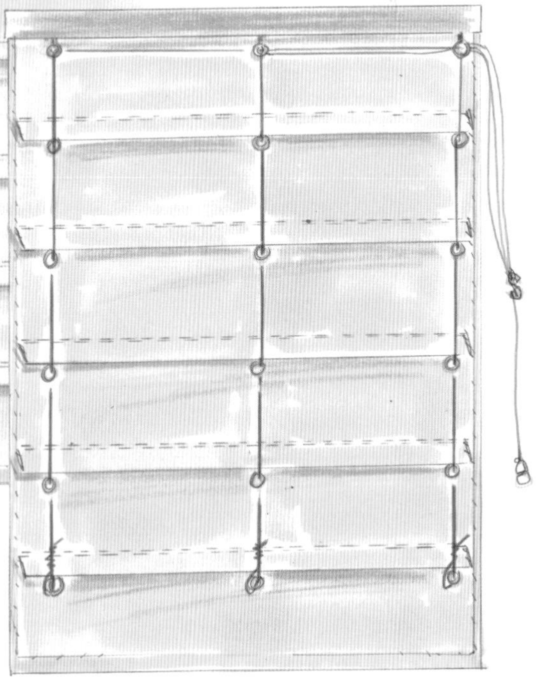

6

CORDING AND HANGING

❑ Lay the blind face down. Decide which side you wish the pull-cord to hang.

❑ Cut the cords to the right length (about one-and-a-half times the length of the blind, plus their individual distances along the top of the blind).

❑ Starting from their respective points on the base of the blind, train the cords through the rings, across the back of the heading and down to the point where they will join the S-ring. Cut each to length. Make a hangman's noose about 19mm (¾in) long in the end of each cord. Insert the first noose through the end ring and slot the other end of the cord through the noose. Pull tight. (**5** right) In this way the cord will be firmly attached and the knot cannot become loose. Repeat the process for the remaining cords.

❑ Join the lines of touch-and-close fastening.

❑ Slot the cords through the screw eyes on the base of the pelmet board.

❑ Holding the cords taut, with perfectly even tension, and making sure that the blind is hanging straight, insert the cords through one half of the S-ring. Stitch into place and disguise the join with a spiral of cord also secured with stitches. Run a single cord off the other part of the S-ring, disguising the join in the same way (see page 151). (**6** above)

❑ Thread the end of the cord through the acorn and knot to secure.

❑ Pull up the blind and secure by wrapping the cord around the cleat.

VARIATION

Zig-zag Roman Blind and Matching Pelmet

A bound zig-zag edge to both blind and pelmet, finished with a row of tiny tassels, gives a dashing finish to an otherwise conventional room. The pelmet is made with a buckram backing; the Roman blind is soft, with only one piece of dowel slotted through above the bottom panel.

MATERIALS

Blind

❑ Face fabric
❑ Lining
❑ Contrast fabric
❑ 19mm (¾in) in cotton tape
❑ Tassels
❑ Touch-and-close fastening
❑ Brass or plastic rings
❑ Lath

Pelmet

❑ Face fabric
❑ Lining
❑ Contrast fabric
❑ Interlining (domette)
❑ Buckram
❑ Touch-and-close fastening

FITTING

❑ Fix a pelmet board on strong brackets above the window. A line of touch-and-close fastening along the front edge will hold the pelmet in place.

❑ To the base of the pelmet board and 3cm (1¼in) behind the front edge, fix a square-section batten. Staple or tack touch-and-close fastening to the front edge. Run a line of screw eyes along the base to accommodate the cording. (**1**)

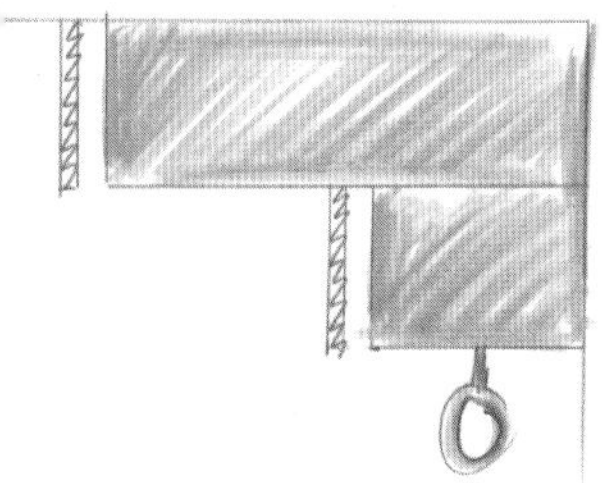

1

❑ Fix a cleat to the wall or window to anchor the cording.

MAKING UP

Blind

❑ Cut the face fabric and lining to the correct length and width of the window plus one seam allowance all round. Allow for the zig-zag shape to hang below the window ledge.

❑ Using a template, cut out a zig-zag shape along the base of the face fabric and lining.

❑ Pin the fabric and lining together along the sides and base. Tack and machine-stitch allowing 19mm (¾in) for seams.

❑ Turn, trimming and clipping as necessary, and press flat.

❑ Cut a bias strip in the contrast fabric (see page 182). Fold in half lengthways, make side turnings and press. Pin and slipstitch the bias strip along the lower edge.

❑ Stitch on the tassels.

❑ Run parallel vertical lines of cotton tape up the back of the blind, from the top of the batten slot to within 19mm (¾in) of the top, raw edge. Prickstitch up the centre of the tapes, penetrating both layers.

❑ Mark the positions of the rings on the tapes. The rings should be in line with each other, at approximately 20-30cm (8-12in) intervals. With the first ring attached to the top of the slot, stitch the rings on to the blind using strong thread. All but the lowest rings should penetrate both layers of fabric.

❑ Make a 19mm (¾in) turning along the top. Cover with a line of touch-and-close fastening, machine-stitched into position.

❑ Cut a strip of lining fabric to accommodate the lath. It should be the necessary width plus two generous seam allowances. Its length is the finished width of the blind plus two seam allowances.

❑ Turn in the ends of the lining strip and machine-stitch close to the raw edge.

❑ Pin into position, turning in the side edges.

❑ Machine-stitch close to the upper, then the lower, folds.

❑ Cut the lath 2.5cm (1in) shorter than the finished width of the blind and insert into the slot. Slipstitch across both ends. (**2** below)

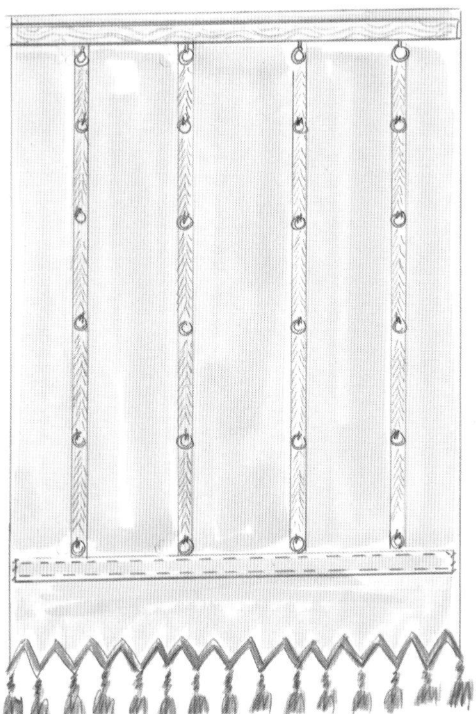

2

HANGING

See page 148.

Pelmet

❑ A matching zig-zag pelmet, backed with plywood or buckram and given coordinating banding, completes the scheme. For making up, see page 120.

VARIATION

Stained-glass Blind

As the daylight penetrates, this paper-thin, translucent blind lights up, rather in the manner of a stained-glass window. The loose weave of the pure white linen and the bands of clear glass-green screen the window without excluding the light. The fabric is shown off to advantage in what is essentially a highly decorative and original alternative to the conventional net curtain. It may either be used for reasons of privacy or simply as adornment.

The basic principle behind the blind's construction is the same as the lining of a normal Roman blind (see page 146). The fabric sections are overlapped and stitched, the blind is then folded and stitched to form the dowel slots.

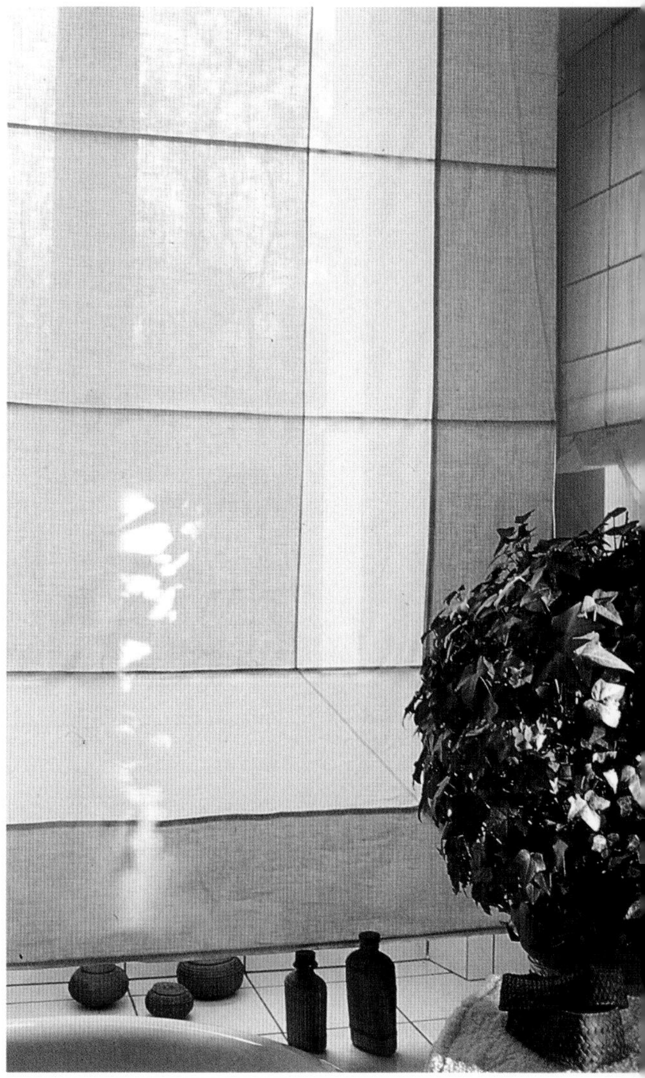

Pull-up Curtains and Blinds

MATERIALS
- ❏ Face fabric
- ❏ Lining
- ❏ Interlining (domette)
- ❏ Fusible heading buckram
- ❏ Weights
- ❏ Narrow cotton tape
- ❏ Fringe
- ❏ Braid
- ❏ Tassel
- ❏ Blind cord
- ❏ Brass or plastic rings
- ❏ Touch-and-close fastening

FITTINGS
- ❏ Pelmet board or batten
- ❏ Brackets
- ❏ Screw eyes
- ❏ Two small brass or wooden knobs or cloak hook
- ❏ S-ring

TOOLS
- ❏ Drill
- ❏ Bradawl
- ❏ Staple gun or hammer and tacks

In recent years the pull-up curtain or 'Austrian blind' has attracted some bad press. In fact, the simple pull-up curtain has been in common use since the 18th century, and was one of the earliest forms of curtaining, used to protect interiors against sunlight.

The example here is a copy of a curtain at Osterley Park, near London, famous for its mid-18th-century interior, re-modelled by Robert Adam. The house illustrated belongs to much the same period, and the curtain provides an ideal solution for its panelled entrance hall.

At night the curtain drops to floor length and loses its billowing festoons. Heavy weights at the base of each line of rings, and figure-of-eight cording finished with a flamboyant tassel, make it extremely simple to operate.

A pull-up curtain is not difficult to make. This facsimile example is raised through an ingenious wheel system and has specially cast pear-shaped lead weights along the lower edge but ordinary screw eyes and standard curtain weights make excellent substitutes, producing an equally successful end result.

Once lowered the blind takes on the appearance of a graceful curtain, grazing the polished wood floor. Pulled up to its daytime position, it forms billowing swags and the decorative purpose of the fringe becomes apparent.

FITTING

❑ Decide on which side of the window the pull cord will hang.
❑ Prepare the pelmet board or batten in the usual way.
❑ Insert screw eyes along the base to carry the cording, one for each vertical line of cord and one slightly in from the edge on the pull-up side.
❑ Staple or tack touch-and-close fastening to the front edge and returns of the board or batten. Fix in place using brackets, or screw it directly into the wall or ceiling.
❑ Fix a pair of small knobs, spaced about 25cm (10in) apart, or cloak hook into the wall at chest height, in line with the pull cord. These will hold the cording in place. A cleat can be used instead, but will not be decorative.

MEASURING

❑ Width: the flat, unpleated width should be two and a half times the finished width. Add 10cm (4in) for turnings.
❑ Length: the fringe should graze the floor and the heading should project 5cm (2in) above the pelmet board or batten. Add 20cm (8in) for turnings.
❑ Fringe and braid: these should extend along the width of the hem and one-quarter of the distance up each side.

MAKING UP

❑ Cut and join the drops of face fabric and lining. Press and trim the seams.
❑ Cut an 8cm (3in) strip of interlining and fusible buckram. Insert into the heading, folding over the top and sides of the face fabric. Tack into place.
❑ Cut a 20cm (8in) strip of interlining and insert into the hem. (**1** below)
❑ Fold in the sides and hem, and secure using a herringbone stitch.
❑ Turn up and stitch the hem of the lining.
❑ Lay the lining over the face fabric, wrong sides together. Leave a 19mm (¾in) gap all round. Pin and stitch around all four sides.
❑ Press the heading with a hot iron to release the glue from the fusible buckram.
❑ Mark the positions of the cotton tape with parallel lines up the central section, placed about 20cm (8in) apart.
❑ Pin and prickstitch the lines of tape through all layers, starting 15cm (6in) from the baseline. To avoid wasting time, make your prickstitches at least 2.5cm (1in) long.
❑ Mark the positions of the rings on the tape lines. They should be in line horizontally, and spaced at approximately 15cm (6in) intervals. Stitch into place.
❑ Stitch several weights into lining bags. Stitch the bags into place at each corner and at the base of each vertical line of rings. (**2** below)
❑ Hand-stitch the fringe and braid into position.
❑ Pleat the heading by hand and tack. Stitch a line of touch-and-close fastening to the back of the heading, 5cm (2in) from the top edge. Remove the tacking stitches. (**3**)

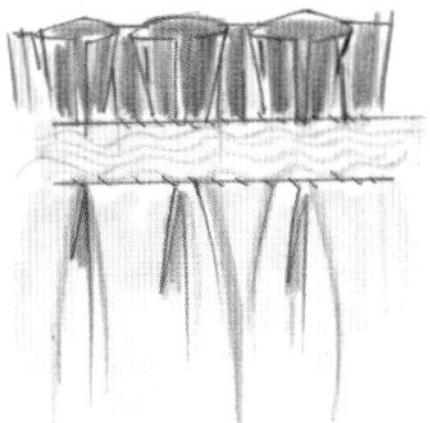

3

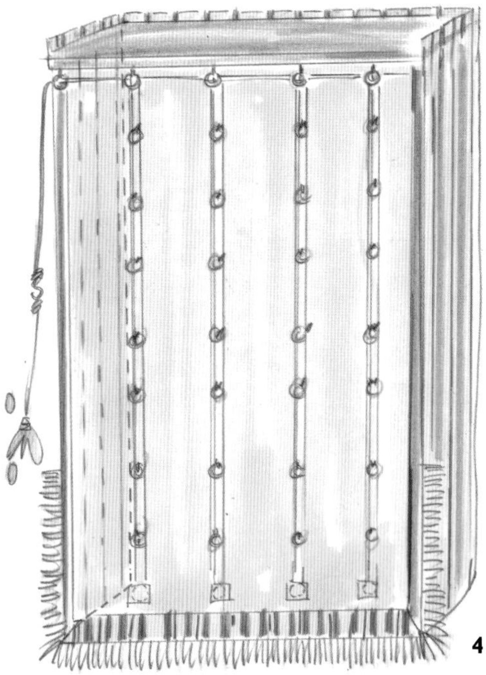

4

HANGING

❑ Cut the cords to length (about one and a half times the length of the curtain, plus their individual distances across the top), tie each to the lowest ring (see page 148) and run them through the lines of rings.
❑ Join the lines of touch-and-close fastening on the curtain and pelmet board or batten. (**4** above)
❑ Feed the cords through the screw eyes.
❑ With the curtain down and equal tension in all the cords, stitch the ends to the S-ring. Neaten by coiling cord around the join and stitching into place.
❑ Cut another piece of cord, attaching the tassel or acorn to one end and the S-ring to the other. Neaten with another coil of cord. (**5**)
❑ To hold the curtain in a raised position, wind the cord around the pair of knobs or cloak hook. (**6**)

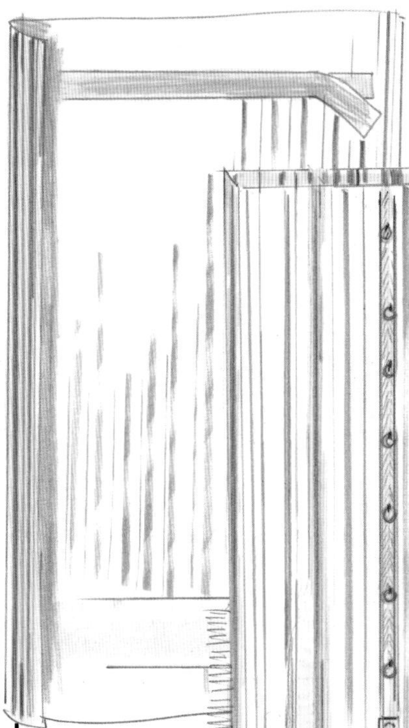

1

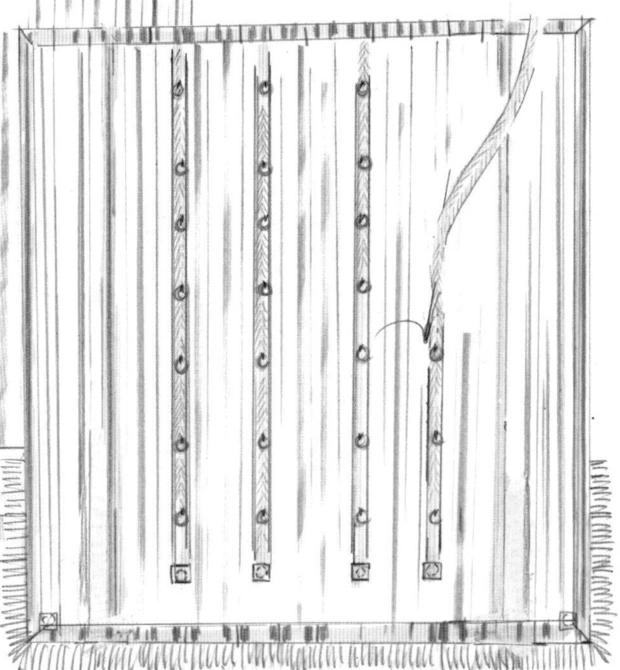

2

5

6

VARIATION

Yellow Silk Blind

This blind is made in much the same way as the pull-up curtain already described. However, instead of the heading being pleated across its width, two large inverted box pleats are placed directly above the lines of cording.

Although the blind is not intended to drop to the floor, in order for it to retain its looped lower edge, even at window-sill level, extra length is needed – about 25cm (10in) below the ledge is usually sufficient.

VARIATION

Child's Blind

A small child lying in bed will take pleasure from any object that moves, reflects light or makes a noise. This blind does all that and more. It is really no more than a simple pull-up blind, but its cording rings carry small bells which chime as the breeze blows through the window or when the blind is raised and lowered. An assortment of seashells sewn to the front jangle and pick up the light, while a row of toy birds stare out from their perches on the top of the pelmet board.

When the child tires of the arrangement, other objects can be substituted. Try, for example, tiny toys, silk flowers or foreign coins. Or how about replacing the birds with a line of brightly coloured paper flags?

MAKING UP

- ❑ Make up in the same way as a pull-up curtain (see page 150), but allow for the blind, when fully extended, to end 25cm (10in) below the sill.
- ❑ Lay the blind flat and work out the positions of the shells. Using the finest drill bit, pierce holes in the shells. Stitch the shells on to the front of the blind, making sure they are firmly attached.
- ❑ Tie bells to the rings up the back of the blind.
- ❑ Pleat up the blind and stitch a line of touch-and-close fastening to the back of the heading.

HANGING

- ❑ Join the line of touch-and-close fastening on the blind to the front edge of the pelmet board.
- ❑ These birds are made of polystyrene, held in position by wooden cocktail sticks stuck into their bases and then inserted between the heading and pelmet board.
- ❑ Take care not to use objects that can be easily pulled off and swallowed by a small child.

VARIATION
Fan Blind

A single line of rings and cord up the centre back of this muslin blind pulls it up to form a pair of fan-shaped tails. The heading is simply gathered.

Paint Effects

Decorating your own fabric is a most satisfactory start to any project, particularly if there is a touch of the frustrated artist in you. Stencilled, printed or painted – you have control over the patterns and the colours, and walls and other surfaces can be matched, imitated or blended with precision.

Inexpensive cottons provide the basis for any number of techniques and the scope for experimentation is without limit – be warned, it can become a passion. Do not be afraid to stray beyond the ready-cut stencil: try a little freehand work, putting together your own designs.

Stencilling

A few simple do-it-yourself paint effects can completely transform a plain piece of natural cloth, be it cotton, linen or silk. The most straightforward of these is probably stencilling and a huge range of stencil shapes is available, in books and ready-cut, for sale or for hire, from the plainest star shapes to amazing willow patterns. Even more intricate, three-dimensional patterns can be built up using one or more stencils, each taking a different colour.

For the more adventurous, stencilling can be used in conjunction with hand painting. This allows you to soften the stencil's hard outline and gives scope for a structured yet hand-crafted finish.

The basic principle of stencilling is simple: a shape is cut in card, the card is laid on the fabric and, by dabbing the card with paint, the design is transferred to the cloth. Alternatively, you can draw around the edge of the stencil shape to give a graphic outline rather than a block of colour.

A stencilled design of a celestial cherub enlivens a plain unlined Roman blind. (LEFT)

INSPIRATION *28, 43, 92*
ITALIAN STRINGING *134*
ROMAN BLIND *146*

PROJECT

Stencilled Cloud Blinds

Yellow cherubs lying across puffy yellow clouds use an unlined Roman blind as their canvas. Stencilled in fabric paint of just one colour – taken from the border fabric – the cherubs lie along the horizontal battens of the blind, lending the design its essential structure.

The stencil can be made by any of the methods described below. To ensure that the cherubs are in perfect line with the batten slots, make up the blind (see page 146) and stencil the design before inserting the battens.

MATERIALS

❑ Fabric
❑ Cloth plus interlining (to protect the worktable)
❑ Fabric paints
❑ Stencil card or equivalent
❑ Glass cutting mat or equivalent (if cutting your own stencil)
❑ Masking tape
❑ Carbon paper

TOOLS

❑ Stencil brush
❑ Ruler
❑ Tape measure
❑ Set square
❑ Craft knife
❑ Palette knife
❑ Dishes for mixing colours
❑ Clamps or covered bricks

TECHNIQUE

Preparation

❑ Cover the worktable with a layer of interlining and plain cloth, pulled tight and secured below with tape or staples.
❑ If you are cutting your own stencil, use a glass-cutting mat or other dense surface on which to cut it out.
❑ Wash and iron the fabric before the paint is applied.
❑ Have some spare fabric to hand for trying out designs and techniques. Paint cannot be removed, so make your mistakes in advance.

Making your own stencil

❑ Stencil shapes can be cut from three different materials:
1. Stencil card: made from oiled manilla. The stencil is drawn on it and cut out.
2. Acetate: this is a transparent sheet, on to which the stencil shape is drawn in permanent ink with a technical drawing pen and then cut out. If you are using several stencils, they can be laid one on top of the other to show the final design.
3. Untreated card or paper: ordinary paper or card can be water-proofed with wax or linseed oil. Thicker card should be painted with vegetable or linseed oil. This is useful if the basis of the design is a photocopy.

Drawing the stencil

❑ If using stencil or other card, trace the design on to tracing paper.
❑ Lay a piece of carbon paper, carbon side down, on the stencil card. Lay the tracing on top and draw around the outline again, thereby transferring the design to the card.
❑ If using acetate lay it on top of the design and trace, using a technical drawing pen and permanent ink.
❑ If the design needs enlarging, mark a grid on the original, draw a larger grid on the card or acetate and copy the design with the aid of the grid.
❑ Alternatively, the design can be enlarged on a photocopier and then traced as above.
❑ Patterns that were not intended as stencil shapes may fall apart if 'bridges' are not introduced to hold the sections together.
❑ Leave at least 2.5-5cm (1-2in) around the shape to make the stencil stable.
❑ Tape the stencil card or acetate to the backing mat and cut out the stencil shape. Make sure that the blade is very sharp. Use a fluid motion, and try to avoid stopping and starting.

Registration marks

❑ To align the pattern correctly, mark the position of the stencil board with small crosses across the fabric, preferably in removable chalk.

Paint

❑ There are many fabric paints – and pens – available, so follow the printed instructions carefully.
❑ The paint is water soluble and so can be diluted. Take care not to make the paint too thin, as this can cause the design to 'bleed'.
❑ Instead of buying ready-mixed colours, you can mix your own using a basic range. Each colour should be mixed with a palette knife (not the brush) in its own dish. The paint pot should then be closed tightly to avoid evaporation. If the paint dries during the work, add a little extra water.
❑ Try not to use too much paint as this may also lead to bleeding at the edges of the design. Test by pressing the brush down on to a cloth or kitchen paper – it should be barely damp.
❑ Allow each application of paint to dry thoroughly before another is applied.

Brush

❑ A stencil brush is squat in shape and should be held like a pen, at right angles to the cloth. The paint is then applied in a stabbing, dabbing motion.
❑ Do not allow the brush to dry out after use, but quickly wash it in mild soap and water. If it has to be left for a while, wrap it in foil to prevent evaporation.

Stencil Shapes

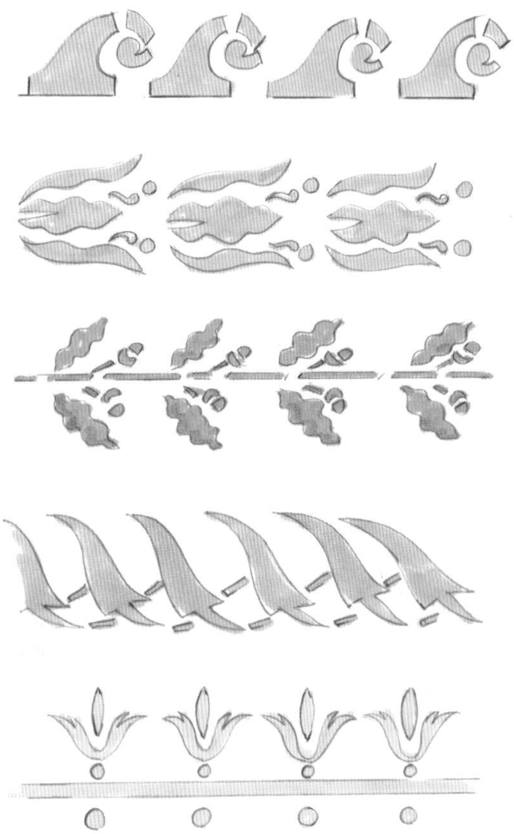

PROJECT

Painted Stripes

One of the quickest and most effective ways of decorating a plain cloth is to paint stripes along the surface. Carried out on this scale it consumes a fair amount of fabric paint, so prepare yourself with plenty of the small pots in which such paint is sold.

Here, a combination of biscuit colours has been used, but if you prefer a more vivid palette each stripe could be picked out in a different colour against a plain white cotton – sea-greens with blues the colour of turquoise, blancmange pinks with brilliant oranges.

These stripes are applied using a crumpled rag, made damp (not wet) with fabric paint, giving them an interesting marbled finish. Masking tape gives the stripes a hard edge.

PROJECT

Block-printed Curtain

Block-printing is one of the simplest ways of decorating cloth. At its most basic, a cut potato can provide a suitable surface for printing. In fact, any raised surface can be dipped in paint and its shape transferred onto cloth by pressure.

Here, a lino cut has been used to create a slightly more taxing two-colour teardrop design and border. Bare floorboards, pale walls and handmade rugs match the rustic feel of the scheme. The curtain is held back by an informal Italian stringing system (see page 134).

MATERIALS

- ❑ Fabric, pre-washed and ironed
- ❑ Two same-size lino blocks for the main design and two for the border
- ❑ Block-printing ink

TOOLS

- ❑ Roller
- ❑ Glass sheet
- ❑ Chalk
- ❑ Clamps or covered bricks
- ❑ 'V' tool
- ❑ Gouge

TECHNIQUE

❑ Four lino boards are needed for this design. One part of each design (teardrop and border) is printed, then the other is superimposed.

❑ Cut the boards as follows:

1. The teardrop shape, with the inner flower shape and the area around the teardrop both cut away.
2. The flower shape, with the rest cut away.
3. The outer border shape, with the inner shape cut away. The board should be the depth of the border. In this way the edges of the board produce sharp upper and lower borders.

1

2

3

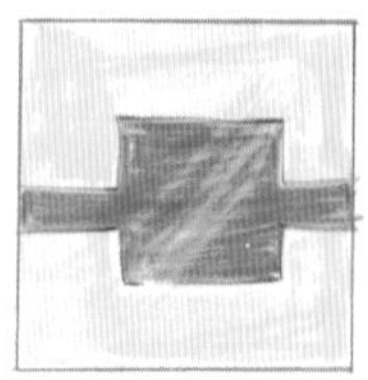

4

4. The inner border shape, with the outer border cut away.

❑ 1 & 2 & 3 & 4 use same-size lino boards. The designs should be placed in matching positions.

❑ The sizes of the board will dictate the pattern repeat. If you want a closely grouped design use a small board; and vice versa.

❑ First warm the lino board by placing it near a radiator or the steam from a kettle. This softens the material and makes it easier to work.

❑ Mark out the design. Cut around it using the 'V' tool, and then cut away the excess using the gouge.

❑ Lay the fabric on the worktable and anchor it with clamps or covered bricks.

❑ Using chalk, make registration marks to guide the positioning of the lino boards. (**5**)

❑ Pour a little block-printing ink on to the glass sheet. If necessary, dilute the colour with some water. Run the roller to and fro to obtain an even coating, and roll over the lino block.

❑ Aligning the corners of the board with the registration marks, press the board firmly down on to the fabric. Repeat the process with each board in turn. (**6**)

❑ To re-use the boards in other colours, wipe them clean with water.

❑ Dry the fabric and fix the colours according to the manufacturer's instructions.

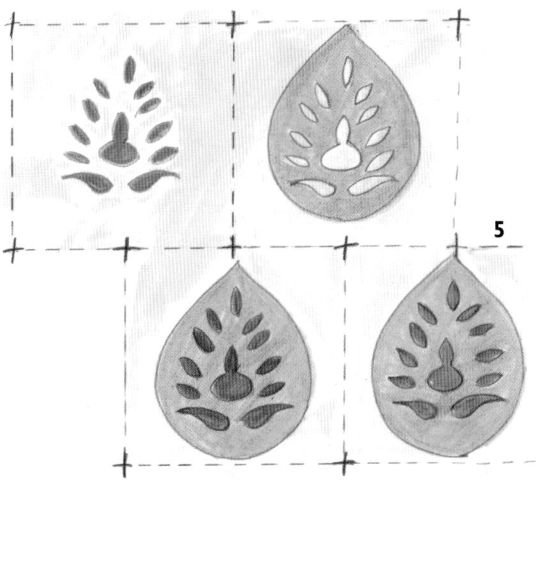

5

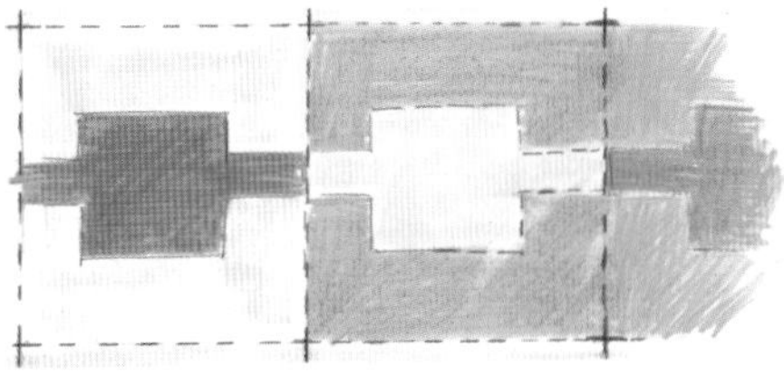

6

Finishing Touches

The judicious use of trimmings or decorative details can enhance any curtain, pelmet or blind. Indeed, the plainer the project, the better the end result. A chou or bow might be buried in a busy print – on a plain cream silk or calico it stands out to great effect. Choux, rosettes, bows and Maltese crosses are not difficult to make and repay any effort handsomely.

There is also scope for enhancing leading edges. A padded edge gives a luxurious and unusual finish, and a wide band can contrast blocks of colour brilliantly. The grander the gesture, the better the effect. Always try to match the scale of the finishing touches to the scale of the project. Big curtains require fat bows and wide edging; small curtains profit from dainty rosettes and narrow banding.

With bows and Maltese crosses an additional layer of dressmaker's interfacing or light interlining (domette) makes for a a fatter, more upholstered finish. If this is required, imitate the fabric pieces in interfacing or domette, stitch and turn with the fabric, treating the two layers as one but trimming the seams carefully to avoid bulk.

Used sparingly and in subtle colours, bows can provide a happy decorative finish in most schemes. (BELOW)

Bows

Bows are among the most traditional of details and have been used for hundreds of years to decorate hats, clothes and furnishings. Although rooms are often stencilled and chintzes garlanded in a riot of ribbons and bows, bows do not necessarily have to be excessively fussy.

Making bows can be almost as simple as tying a shoelace. Make sure that you start with a tube of fabric that is long enough to achieve the right size of bow: it is remarkable how much fabric is needed to achieve one of even modest size. If a hand-tied bow is too bulky in the centre, a false bow is easily made instead. If sewing the tubes that compose false bows is beyond you, try cutting the fabric into a strip using pinking scissors and take it from there. Perched high on the wall, the bow should not fray to any great extent and the pinking provides additional decoration.

Alternatively, invest in some wide grosgrain ribbon – striped or plain – which will look quite charming knotted or sewn into a bow.

INSPIRATION *8, 27, 133*
PADDED EDGE *45, 74, 127*
CONTRAST EDGE *59, 62*
ROSETTES *78*

False Bow

A false bow is made from three sections: the bow, the central knot and the sashes.

MATERIALS

❑ Face fabric
❑ Domette or interfacing (optional)

MAKING UP

Bow

❑ Cut a strip of fabric twice the width of the finished bow plus two seam allowances and twice the depth plus two seam allowances.
❑ With right sides together, fold the strip in half lengthwise. Machine-stitch along the long side.
❑ Turn and press, with the seam running along the centre back.
❑ Form the tube into a loop, overlapping the raw ends across the centre back.
❑ Run a line of vertical running stitches through the centre, passing the needle through to the centre front of the loop. (**1**) Pull up to form a central gather and secure.

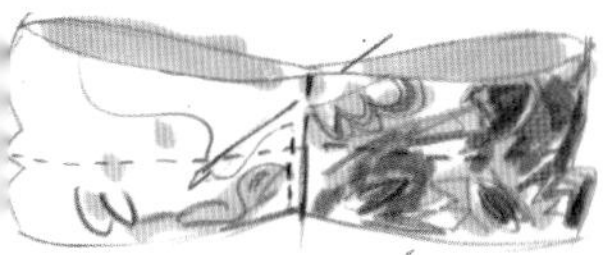

1

Knot

❑ Cut a strip of fabric to cover the centre of the bow. The strip should be twice the width of the 'knot' and sufficiently long to wrap around the centre of the bow and overlap slightly at the back.
❑ Turn in the side edges and wrap around the bow, gathering the strip into informal vertical folds.
❑ Overlap the raw ends behind and stitch them together. (**2**)

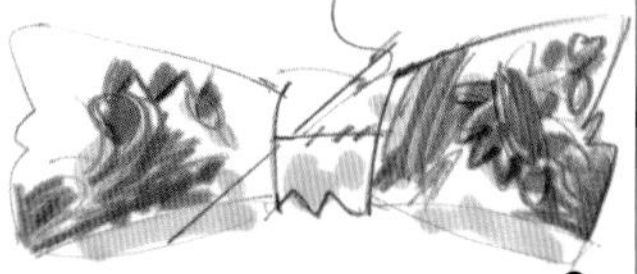

2

Sashes

❑ Cut out one long strip, with diagonal ends. Fold in half lengthways, right sides together, and machine-stitch around the sides and one end. Trim, turn and press.
❑ Turn in the open end and slipstitch closed.
❑ Fold in half and place the folded part over the back of the bow. Stitch into position. (**3**)

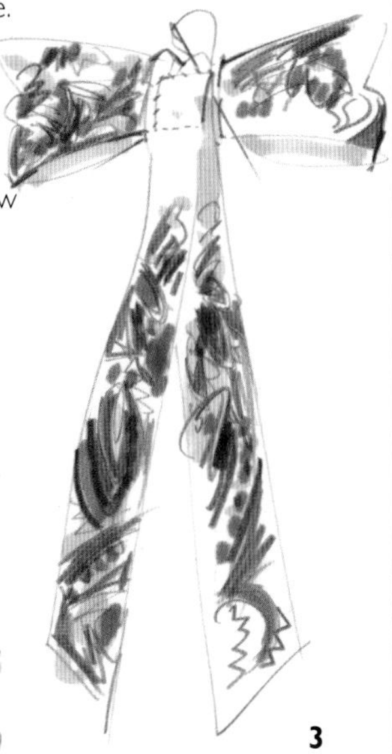

3

Maltese Cross

Maltese crosses sewn to an arrangement of swags and tails, to the overlap of Italian-strung curtains or even across the top of a pull-up blind, lend an air of restrained elegance to a window treatment, neither overtly feminine nor excessively fancy. A contrast edging emphasizes their shape and links them in to the rest of the colour scheme.

MATERIALS

❑ Face fabric
❑ Contrast fabric
❑ Domette or interfacing (optional)

MAKING UP

❑ A Maltese cross is made in much the same way as the main part of a false bow (see left).
❑ Cut the two strips of face fabric that will form the main part of the Maltese cross.
❑ Prepare a bias strip in the contrast fabric (see page 182). Turn in the edges and fold the contrast strip in half lengthways, wrong sides together. Press. In this way the stitching line and central fold will be apparent.
❑ Machine-stitch, turn and press the two tubes of fabric. Pin on the bias strip, aligning the foldlines. (**1**)

1

❑ Slipstitch into place. (**2**)

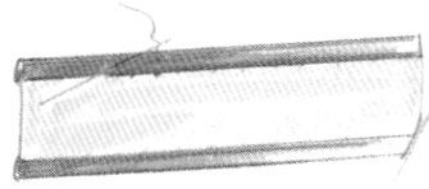

2

❑ Form a loop with each section, overlapping at the back. Place a line of gathering stitches up the centre of each, through all the layers, and pull up.
❑ Place the main sections at right angles to one another and stitch together at the crossing point. (**3**)

3

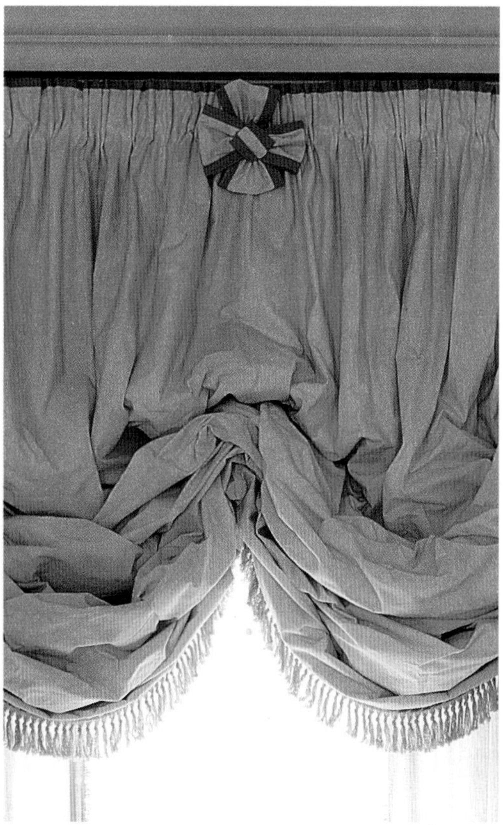

❑ Cut a third piece of face fabric. It is made in just the same way as the main sections but is a quarter of the size, to cover the central section of the cross. Stitch contrast banding to the edges in the same way as before, form into a loop (the raw edges overlapping at the back) and stitch the raw edges together.
❑ Place at a diagonal on the centre of the cross and stitch into place. (**4**)

4

Rosettes

There is something very satisfying about making a rosette. The finished product, with its fanned pleating, is so very regular that one is tempted at once into making others of matching perfection.

Rosettes are used in much the same way as the previous trimmings. They can be placed at the join of a fixed heading or at the top of a pair of tails; they can adorn the front of a tieback or run along the top of a blind. By contrast with the other trimmings, however, they rarely need interfacing or interlining – a rosette should not look bulky.

There are two sorts of rosette: the first has crisp folds and forms a circular fan; the second, described below, is a more formal version of the chou, teased out to form regular, fat folds.

MATERIALS

- ❑ Fabric
- ❑ Contrast fabric
- ❑ Self-covered button

MAKING UP

❑ Cut a circle of fabric twice the diameter of the finished rosette plus 2.5cm (1in).

❑ Run a line of gathering stitches 12mm (½in) from the edge of the circle. (**1**)

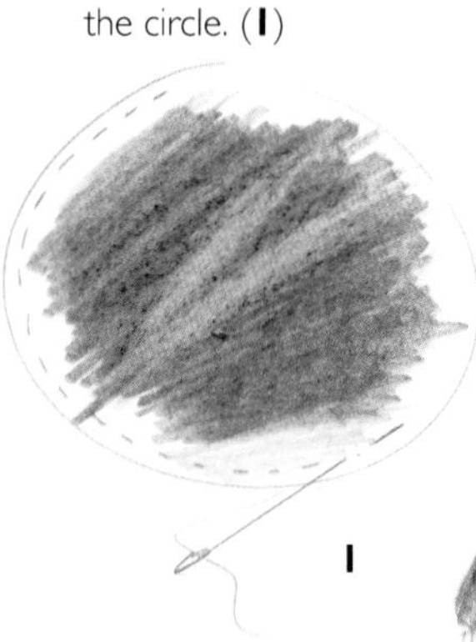

1

❑ Pull the thread up tightly to form the centre point of the rosette. (**2**)

2

❑ Adjust the fanning folds into regular pleats of equal length.

❑ Cover the button in contrast fabric and stitch to the centre of the rosette. (**3**)

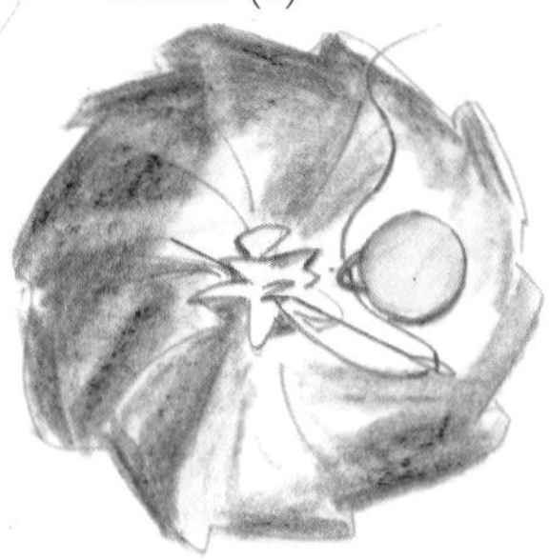

3

Choux

Unlike the other finishing touches in this section, choux should be kept only for projects on the grand scale. They need a certain size to work, usually as the finishing touch to a majestic arrangement of swags and tails. A chou is guaranteed to impress, although the technique is accessible to anyone of average sewing ability.

MATERIALS

- ❑ Face fabric
- ❑ Lining
- ❑ Interlining
- ❑ Fusible buckram

MAKING UP

❑ Cut one circle of fusible buckram and two of domette to the finished diameter of the chou.

❑ Sandwich the buckram ring between the two domette pieces. Press with a hot iron to release the glue and fuse the layers together.

❑ Cut another circle in the face fabric, three times the finished diameter of the chou.

❑ Make chalk marks or cut notches to mark quarter sections in the edge of the buckram and domette fabric circles. (**1**)

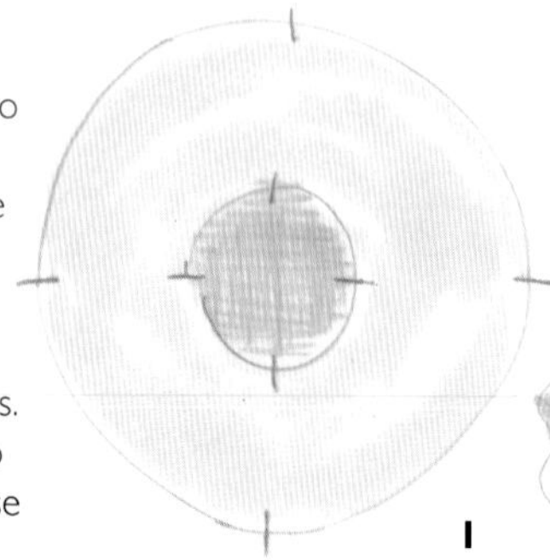

1

❑ Turning the edge of the fabric under that of the buckram ring, pin the quarter marks of the two pieces together. Then pleat up the rest of the fabric around the circumference of the base. Passing the needle from back to front through all the layers and close to the edge, stitch the pleats into position. (**2**)

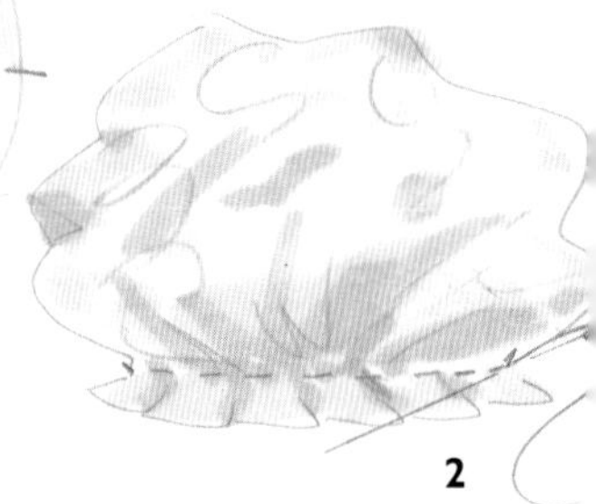

2

❑ Form the balloon of fabric into uneven, random folds and prickstitch into place. (**3**)

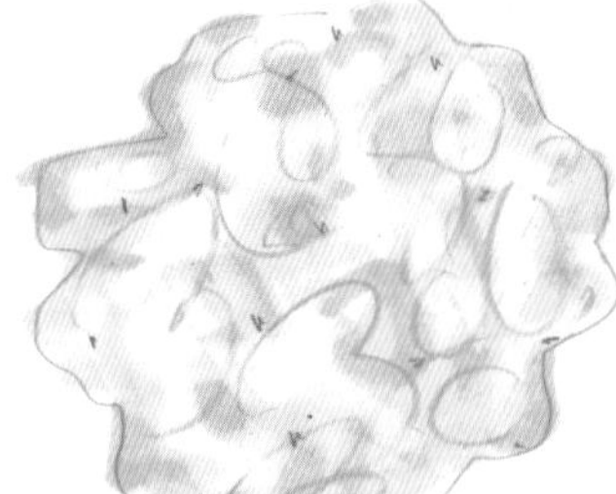

3

❑ Cut another circle in lining fabric, slightly wider than the base. Lay the chou on the lining, turn in the edges and slipstitch into place.

Padded Edge

In the Victorian and Edwardian eras, the trailing hems of heavy velvet curtains would be finished with fat, padded edges. More recently, expensive designers have adapted the technique to lend a look of discreet luxury to leading edges. A padded edge is best used on full-length, interlined curtains (see page 127).

MATERIALS

❑ Interlining or wadding

MAKING UP

❑ The padded edge is formed by a long roll of interlining or wadding, stitched into the leading edge. The dimensions of the padding depend largely on the scale of the curtain. Allow an extra-large side turning in the curtain to enclose the padding.

❑ First experiment with a piece of interlining or wadding, rolling it lengthways to achieve the required circumference.

❑ Cut a strip of interlining or wadding to the length of the leading edge and to the required width.

❑ Roll it up lengthways to form a long sausage and slipstitch along the raw edge to hold it in place (interlining is easier to control than wadding). (**1**)

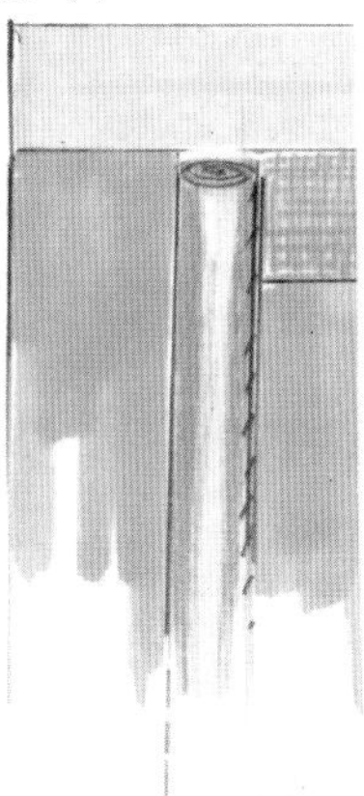

2

❑ With the curtain fabric already locked to the interlining (see page 180) and the heading stiffening in place, position the roll behind the leading edge, from the finished top foldline to the hem fold. (**2** below left)

❑ Smooth the side turning over the roll, trapping it with a line of pins.

❑ Turn up the hem of the curtain and mitre it over the roll. Tack and then prickstitch along the edge of the padding. Match the colour of the thread carefully with that of the face fabric. Small stitches will be visible every 2.5cm (1in) up the front of the curtain. (**3**)

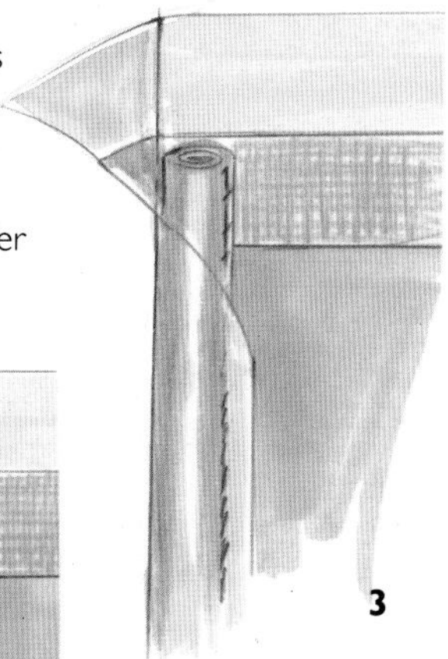

3

❑ Lock in the lining across of the back of the curtain in the usual way.

❑ Turn in along the edge of the padding and slipstitch into place.

Contrast Edge

A generous band of colour down the edge of a curtain will enhance the simplest combination of fabrics. Think about the possibilities, say, of edging a simple cream fabric with a wide stripe of dusty pink or midnight blue. Or, in a modern interior, why not juxtapose vivid colours – purples, oranges and reds – perhaps using whitewashed walls as a foil?

Contrast bands can be run up the leading edge only, or taken all around the curtain or even the pelmet for a more dramatic statement.

MATERIALS

❑ Fabric

❑ Contrast fabric

MAKING UP

❑ The contrast band is treated as an extension of the main fabric.

❑ Decide on the width of the band. Cut a strip on the straight grain of the contrast fabric. It should be twice the width of the finished band plus one seam allowance, and the same length as the fabric drop, including hem and top turning allowances.

❑ With right sides together, raw edges aligned, machine-stitch the contrast band to the leading edge of the curtain fabric. (**1**) Press open seam.

1

❑ Continue making up the curtain in the normal way, turning the contrast edge over the back of the curtain to form the required width. (**2**)

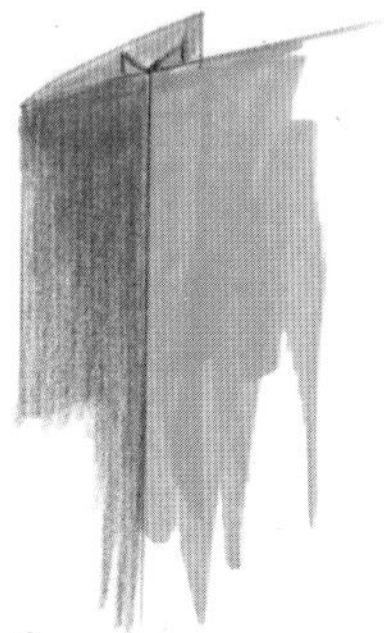

2

Tassel Valance

Many of the most successful decorating projects are based on a high level of improvisation. This is one example. Instead of the usual gathered or stiffened pelmet or valance, a strip of lace is combined with an elaborate fringe, looped cord and tassels, giving a highly original finish to the window. The inspiration came from the mantelpiece of a late 19th-century suburban parlour. A Victorian housewife, wary of bare surfaces, would have used a similar arrangement to grace the front of her black slate fireplace.

Baroque Embroidered Curtains and Pelmet

Swooping baroque curls decorate this pelmet and pair of lightweight curtains. The fabric is neither painted nor printed, but is embroidered with a technique known as couching. The principle is a simple one: wool, narrow cord or embroidery thread is laid over the fabric and secured with tiny stitches along its length. This is undeniably time-consuming but, as can be seen, it is well worth the effort.

MATERIALS
- ❑ Fabric
- ❑ Embroidery thread, wool or light cord

TOOLS
- ❑ Sharp pencil or chalk
- ❑ Needle and thread

MAKING UP
- ❑ Use embroidery thread, wool or cord that is colourfast and pre-shrunk. Do a test on a small piece if you are in any doubt.
- ❑ Mark out your design on the fabric. Lay the cord along the lines of the design, holding it in place with pins placed at right angles.
- ❑ Stitch the cord to the cloth with tiny stitches every 2.5-5cm (1-2in), depending on the scale of the design. **(1a & 1b)**
- ❑ For quicker results use a zig-zag machine-stitch.

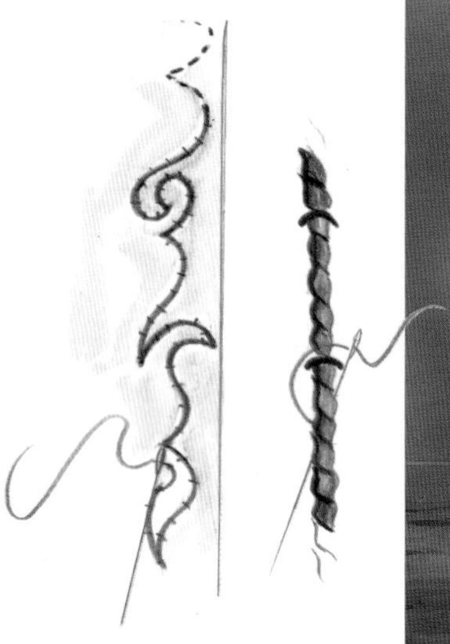

1a **1b**

Drills and bradawls, poles and tracks – a knowledge of the correct tools, together with all the practical information presented here, will guide the curtainmaker, whether beginner or more experienced, through every stage of a project, from conception to completion

fitting

Many curtain or blind projects end in failure when measurements are vague or inadequate, the wrong fittings are chosen or the hanging is incorrect. With a little know-how, thought and effort, however, smooth-running, perfectly fitting curtains and blinds can be achieved. By checking through the materials required and reading the instructions on their applications and fitting, you will learn exactly what to ask for and, just as important, how to use it correctly. Familiarity with the hardware and vocabulary of soft furnishings will allow you access to the multitude of options available. Whether fixing a brass tieback hook to the wall, measuring for a decorative arrangement of swags and tails or drilling into a steel lintel, the detailed instructions in this chapter will put every task within reach.

Who is this beautiful presence who wraps her golden-skinned hand, with bracelets of feathery fringing, around these curtains of the richest crimson velvet?

Tools and Accessories

Standing on top of a wobbly chair, inadequate tape measure in hand, reaching for the inaccessible corner of a high window is an experience guaranteed to put most people off the whole idea of homemade curtains or blinds. Starting with the right equipment eases every task immeasurably and is well worth the initial outlay. Always keep an orderly tool box with a stock of basic materials – staples, screws and wall plugs, for example. Proper labelling will also help to speed operations.

From left to right, top to bottom:

1. Spirit level
2. Hammer
3. Curved fronted pelmet board
4. Staple gun
5. Retractable steel measure
6. Cloth clamp
7. Calculator
8. Notebook
9. 12in perspex ruler
10. Hacksaw
11. Dowel
12. Top-fixing rod socket
13. Face-fixing rod socket
14. Wooden acorn
15. Wax candle
16. Craft knife
17. Bradawl
18. Screwdriver
19. Eyelet punch and eyelets
20. Brackets (pelmet)
21. Brackets (shelf)
22. Wall plugs and galvanized steel screws
23. Thread
24. Tailor's chalk
25. Stitch unpicker
26. Webbing
27. Sewing machine needles
28. Thimble
29. D-ring
30. Sew-on hook
31. Screw eyes
32. Cavity wall/plaster board screws
33. Split rings
34. Brass rings
35. Spacer
36. Pincer rings
37. Heading tapes
38. Pin cushion
39. Set square
40. Embrasures
41. Pole socket
42. Vine eye
43. S-rings
44. Cornice pole bracket
45. Central pole bracket
46. Tie-back hooks
47. Ombras
48. Rings (gilded, plain wood)
49. Penny weights
50. Blind cord
51. Piping cord
52. Roller blind cord fixing
53. Cloak hook
54. Cleat
55. Scissors
56. Pinking shears
57. Pin-on hook
58. Brass hooks
59. Plastic hooks
60. Triple-pronged hook
61. Touch-and-close fastening
62. Leadweight tapes
63. Steam iron

5
6
BRAUN
7
8
9
22
20
21
18
19
25
24
28
27
26
23
35
36
32
33
34
37
38
39
48
47
49
50
51
62
61
59
58
57
63
56
60
55
54
53

Fitting Poles, Pelmet Boards and Tracks

Curtains and blinds can be hung from any number of fittings, from the simplest wooden pole to elaborate patented multi-track arrangements in aluminium. The main options to consider before making your choices are practical and aesthetic. Aim for a system that will operate efficiently while complementing the style of your curtain or blinds. Try to use the best quality track that you can afford – it will pay in the long run – and take special care to give it a firm fixing. If in doubt, make use of your supplier – do not be shy to ask advice when necessary.

POLE

(below left)

❑ If the curtains are to be drawn back, a pole is often the most attractive solution and has the advantage of not blocking the light when the curtains are open.

❑ Poles are unsuitable for blinds, pelmets and valances, although you can have the best of both worlds with an attached valance (see page 118) or a draped pole backed with curtains on a hidden track.

❑ Finials and rings provide additional sources of decoration.

❑ In short, poles are much to be recommended but are impractical on bow windows.

❑ Bay windows can be fitted with a pole but these must be held by special brackets at the internal angles of the window, so the curtains cannot draw all the way around the window – each section of window carries its own pair of curtains. A false pole is another way of using a pole at a bay window.

PELMET BOARD

(1 below)

❑ A pelmet board is a length of ordinary wood, fixed above the window on brackets, rather in the manner of a bookshelf. It will carry a pelmet, valance, swags and tails, Roman or pull-up blind or a pair of fixed-headed curtains, and the base can be fitted with a blind batten or curtain track.

❑ A pelmet board is essential for multiple layers – a pelmet with a Roman blind behind it or a valance supported by a pair of curtains, for example.

❑ When a pair of curtains hangs alone, without a pelmet or valance, the choice is between a pole, an exposed track (often unsightly) and a covered board and fascia.

❑ Do not be confused by the plethora of high-tech, multi-track systems, often tailor-made to your window. These can be very expensive and are often no more effective than a simple wooden board, fitted with the appropriate tracks or blind fittings.

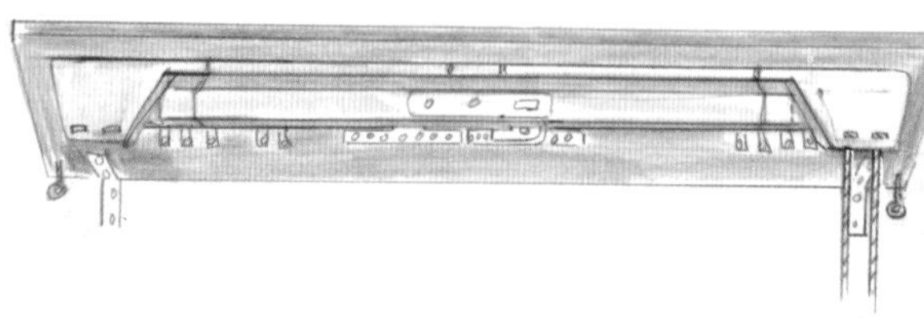

1

COVERED BOARD & FASCIA *28*
TOOLS AND ACCESSORIES *166*

COVERED BOARD AND FASCIA

(**2a** & **2b** below)

❑ A wooden pelmet board, covered in fabric or painted, and fitted with a curtain track, is known as a covered board and fascia. A 5cm (2in) band of buckram or plywood, covered in the curtain fabric, is attached to the front of the board to hide the track. The curtain hooks extend just below the fascia, while the top edge of the curtain heading runs along the front, hiding the fascia when the curtains are closed. This is a useful means of avoiding an exposed track when there is no valance to hide the fittings. The advantages of a covered board and fascia are similar to those of a pole – no loss of light and the decorative possibilities of an exposed heading. When a pole is less practical (in a bay window for example), this type of fitting comes into its own.

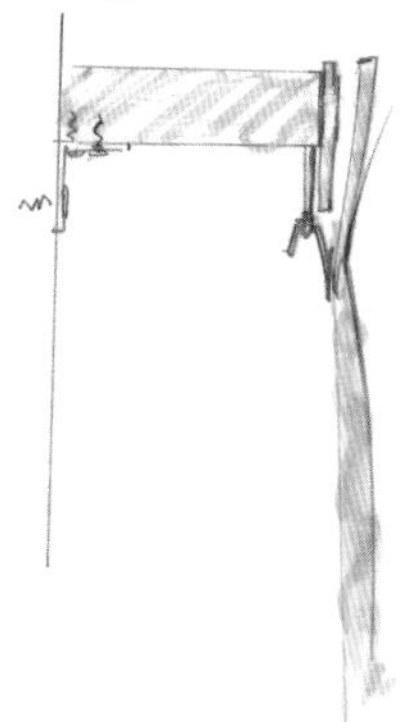

2a

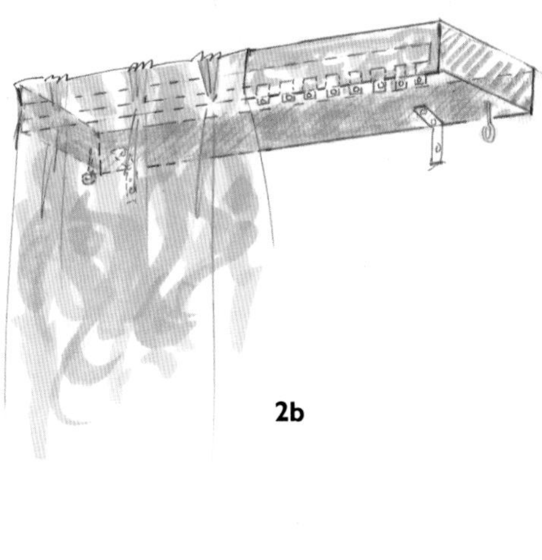

2b

Fixing

Before you begin, examine the surface that you are intending to fix into, and check that you have all the right tools. Ask a second person to help, as single-handed fixing can be very tricky. Also, remember that windows and floors may not be level; unless wildly out of true, place fittings parallel to windows, without using a spirit level. Only roller blinds need perfectly aligned fittings. It is often impossible to know what lies behind a plaster surface, so when fixing tracks, poles and boards in position always proceed with caution. Drill a small exploratory hole to test the depth of the plaster and to see what lies behind it. Then take appropriate action.

WALL AND CEILING SURFACES

Plaster

Most walls, unless of bare concrete, are covered with a layer of plaster of varying thickness.

❑ If the fittings are not destined to take much weight – for example, a light rail or tieback hook – wall plugs into the plaster will be adequate.

❑ Heavier curtains or blinds need deeper fixings into the surface behind the plaster.

Wood

❑ To avoid splits, drill pilot holes with the appropriate drill bit or pierce with a bradawl. Then put in the screw.

❑ Avoid inserting screws close to the edge of the wood, as this may cause it to split.

Concrete

Many windows have concrete lintels, and modern buildings often have concrete ceilings. This is a hard surface to drill, but will provide a firm base.

❑ A hammer-action drill is necessary for drilling into concrete. A pneumatic hammer-action drill is even more effective.

❑ Use 40mm (1½in), No 8, or 40mm (1½in), No 10, galvanized steel screws, with the equivalent wall plugs.

Steel

Steel lintels are sometimes found over windows: the hollow sound of a drill on steel is easily recognizable.

❑ Sometimes the plaster in front may be deep enough to take the fixing. Otherwise change to a drill bit appropriate for metal.

❑ If the screws cannot be 'tapped' in (screwed directly into the metal), drill a slightly larger hole and insert wall plugs.

❑ Do not drill into a steel lintel from below. Move the fitting clear of the lintel, or bring the fitting forwards on brackets.

Brick

❑ Use a masonry drill bit and wall plugs. Screws 50mm (2in) in size are usually strong enough, but screws of up to twice the length and heavy-duty plugs may be needed if the brick has softened with age.

Thermal (breeze) blocks

❑ 50mm (2in) holes and wall plugs will anchor most fittings into thermal blocks.

❑ Avoid using a hammer-action drill, as thermal blocks are soft and need gentle handling. A masonry drill bit is the most suitable.

❑ Leave a gap of at least 5cm (2in) between the edge of the reveal and the drill hole.

❑ Specially ribbed wall plugs for thermal blocks are available.

Cavity walling

Timber-frame walls are constructed of plasterboard fixed to wooden battens, running up either side of the window.

❑ Fixings should be screwed through the plasterboard into the battens.

❑ Special cavity fixings are needed between the battens. Wall plugs are unsuitable.

Ceilings

❑ Ceiling joists run at right-angles to floorboards, usually at 40cm (16in) intervals. To identify their exact position, check the floor above and then run a line of exploratory holes into the ceiling: these can then be filled in afterwards. Screws 50mm (2in) in size will hold most fittings.

❑ Concrete: proceed as for concrete walls.

❑ Plasterboard: use cavity fixings, or screw into the joists.

❑ Lath and plaster: for light curtains, screw into the laths. Try to avoid over-tightening the screws as this may split the laths. Otherwise, screw into the joists.

WIRING

❑ Before starting work, take special care to locate any wiring in the room. Drilling into wires is extremely dangerous.

❑ Electrical wires run directly up or down from a switch or socket. If necessary, you can discover the direction by unscrewing the front plate.

PIPES

❑ Take care, too, to avoid radiator or heating pipes when drilling into ceilings or around windows.

❑ A range of simple gadgetry is available for locating pipes, wires and joists.

Poles

A selection of gilded finials – pineapples, arrow heads and feathers – of a type to be had from a variety of sources. Their deliberately antiqued gilding makes an exquisite contrast to the deep folds of a dark velvet, silk or linen curtain. (BELOW)

A curtain without a pelmet can look starkly utilitarian. If so, a handsome pole can provide a decorative lift. Poles are both functional – the curtains can be drawn right back to let in the daylight – and lend distinctive style. They range from contemporary wrought iron, finished in a shepherd's crook or curl, through shades of stained and varnished wood to thick reeded brass poles and thin brass rods. Every sort of antique model has been sought out and copied: gilded ram's heads, acanthus leaves, painted pineapples and scores of brass arrow heads and feather flights. Modern designers have been at work, too, lending their talents to a previously neglected area of design.

Among the chief charms of the curtain pole is versatility. Not only used to carry a simple pair of curtains, they can also be swathed in Napoleonic swags or encased by a slotted or puffed heading. In fact, poles are hard to beat for showing off a heading, perhaps corded or decorated with choux or Maltese crosses. Be prepared to invest in the best pole available. Often a highly inexpensive fabric will appear the ultimate in luxury, set against a pair of grand gilded finials and a fat mahogany-stained pole.

INSPIRATION *16, 29, 35, 42, 103-4*
DORMER ROD *21*
TOOLS AND ACCESSORIES *166*
FITTING POLES *168*
FIXING/SURFACES *169*

POLES

❑ Brass or wooden curtain poles come in various diameters, from 25mm (1in) to 8cm (3in).
❑ Wooden dowels, available from timber merchants and DIY shops, are less substantial than dedicated curtain poles, up to a diameter of 4cm (1½in), and are used for hanging light curtains and nets. Dowel is generally fixed using rod sockets; curtain poles with cornice brackets or pole sockets.
❑ When buying, check that there is no warp and that the pole or dowel is quite straight.
❑ A pole or piece of dowel can carry wooden, brass or pincer rings.
❑ Pincer rings act like a set of clothes' pegs and can attach to simple squares of cloth – Indian saris or checked tablecloths, for example – for easy, improvised curtains and valances (see below).
❑ Tied, tab, cased or slotted headings will attach to the pole without the use of rings.

BRACKETS AND SOCKETS

❑ Poles rest on brackets (cornice pole fittings) fixed to the wall on either side of the window.
❑ The brackets can either come flush against the edge of the finial (useful for slotted headings that are impeded by the bracket) or, more usually, they are positioned several inches in from the edge of the finial, with one or more rings left outside the bracket.
❑ If each end of the pole is abutting the wall, with no room for finials, the pole will slot into a pole socket.
❑ Brass or chrome-plated rod sockets are best if net or other lightweight curtains are to hang from a piece of dowel.
❑ Poles can be bought with all the parts pre-packed, but finials, brackets and rings, as well as the poles themselves, can also be bought separately.
❑ When purchasing items individually, remember to make sure that finials, rings and brackets fit the diameter of the chosen pole or dowel.

FALSE POLES

❑ Ordinary curtain poles are not always suitable for bay or bow windows so false poles come into use. These give the appearance of a pole, seeming to turn the internal angles of the window, but a hidden track, set into the base of the pole, actually carries the curtain hooks.
❑ To avoid interfering with the track, false poles use overclip brackets that allow the curtains to pass below the fixing.

FINISHES

❑ Pre-packed poles come with an existing

Draping a pole in a length of cream fabric makes for an elaborate effect. The curtains behind the swag hang from a simple track hidden just above the window. (ABOVE)

A more flamboyant antique pole, finished in the grandest of brass finials, shows off an unpleated heading while providing an important element in the room's decorative scheme. (ABOVE)

finish, but unfinished wooden poles can be stained, painted or otherwise treated to suit a particular project.

❑ Whatever the finish, it is a good idea to run a candle or lubricating spray along the top of the pole and inside the rings to make the curtains run smoothly.

Brass poles

❑ Brass poles are usually finished in a clear varnish that will resist tarnishing. The varnish can sometimes be stripped to give an antiqued effect.

❑ Check the type of varnish, and consult an art shop for advice on stripping.

Wrought iron poles

❑ Wrought iron poles give any room an up-to-date air, marrying well with colourful cotton checks and stripes, or bold designs in linen. The scope for twisting and turning each end is infinite – corkscrews or curls to name but two of the more popular shapes.

Wooden poles

❑ Paint or stainer and varnish can be applied to raw wooden poles and rings.

❑ Apply stainer thinly, wiping off any residue. Build up a number of layers, depending on the depth of colour required, and finish with a coat of varnish.

❑ Leave to dry thoroughly before use.

❑ Oil-based eggshell-finish paint is best for painting poles.

❑ Build up the paint in thin layers, allowing each to dry thoroughly.

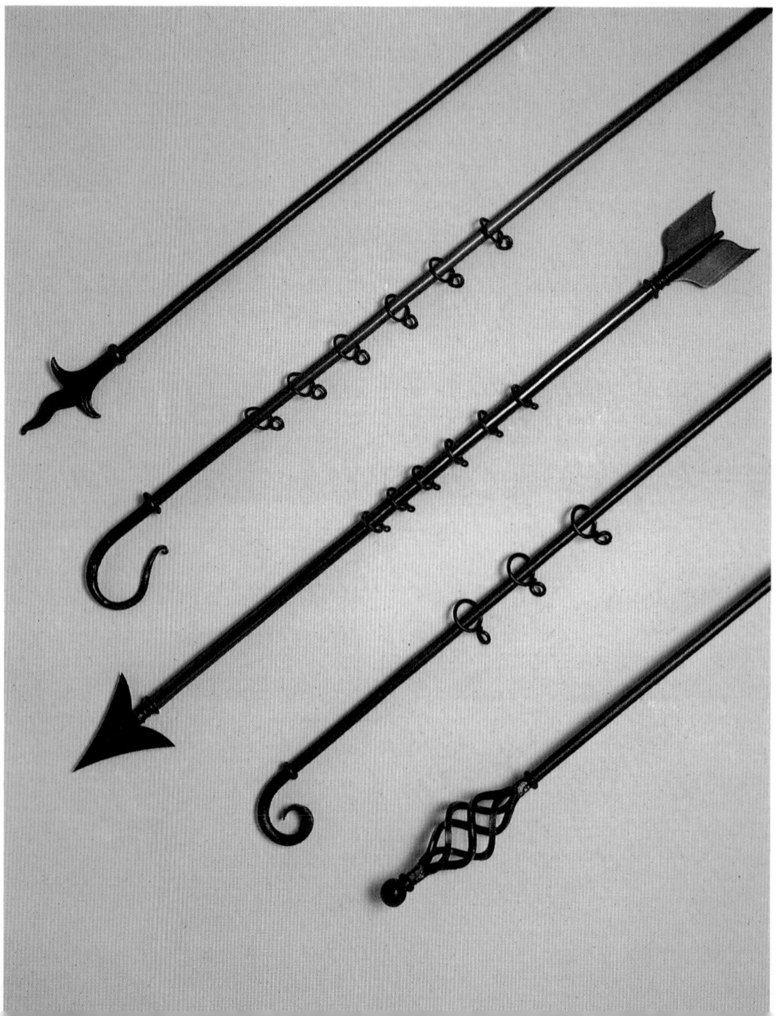

LEFT ABOVE (from top to bottom):
1. Brass rod with fleur-de-lys finial
2. Brass twisted pole with acanthus finial
3. Polished steel pole with copper lily finial
4. Steel rod with tassel finial
5. Steel rod with corkscrew finial
6. Polished steel rod with neo-Baroque glass finial

LEFT BELOW (from top to bottom):
1. Steel pole with fleur-de-lys finial
2. Steel pole with shepherd's crook finial
3. Steel pole with arrow finial
4. Iron pole with ram's horn finial
5. Iron pole with basketwork finial

RIGHT ABOVE (from top to bottom):
1. Reeded mahogany pole with ram's head finial
2. Ebony pole with cherry-wood Biedermeier finial
3. Wooden pole with gilded heraldic finial
4. Stained wooden pole with domed finial
5. Wooden pole with gilded flame finial
6. Reeded gilt pole with pineapple finial

RIGHT BELOW (from top to bottom):
1. Wooden pole with pewter finish and spearhead finial
2. Natural ash pole with pyramid finial
3. Natural beech pole with ball finial
4. Stained wood pole with pineapple finial
5. Wooden pole with verdigris finish and dome finial
6. Stained wooden pole with seahorse finial in verdigris finish

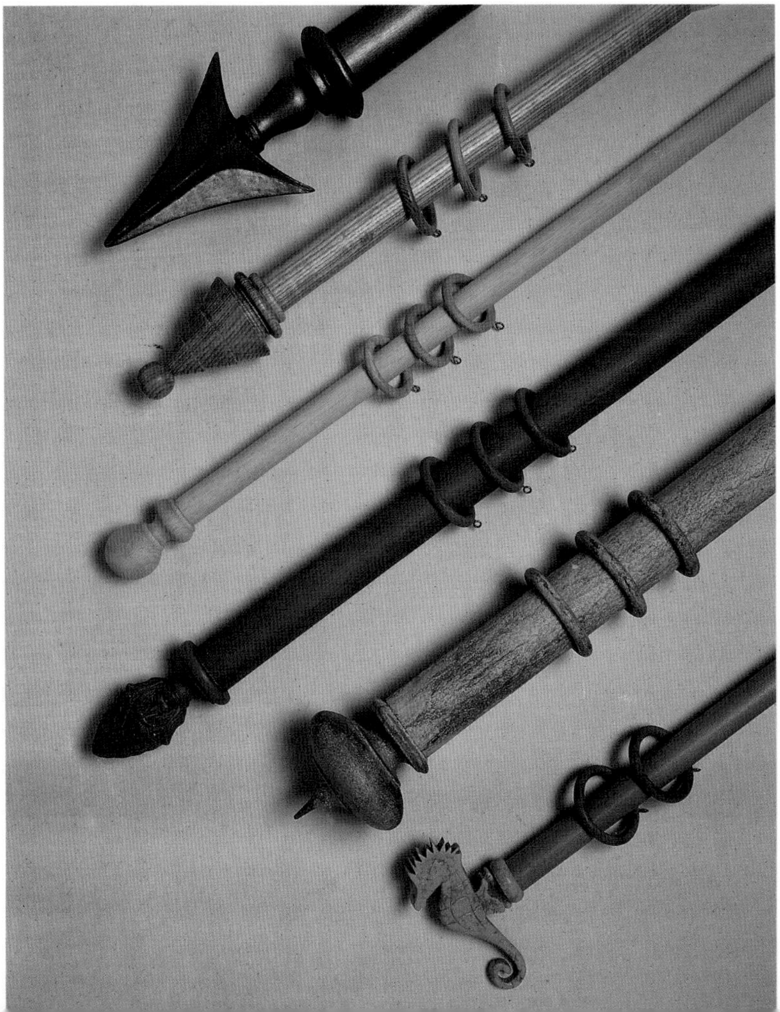

Dormer or portière rods

❑ Both types of rod swing out from the wall. A hinged dormer rod swings back to the side wall, useful with a deeply recessed window. A portière rod moves back with the door as it opens.

FITTING POLES

❑ When fixing a curtain pole, bear in mind that the curtains will hang from the rings, the top edge of each curtain running a few centimetres (about 1in) below the pole.

❑ Place the pole high enough to stop light coming over the top of the curtains, i.e. slightly higher than a pelmet board.

❑ Often the brackets will not project the pole clear of the window architrave. If so, fit the brackets on to blocks of wood screwed into the wall.

❑ The blocks can be painted or covered in wallpaper or fabric. (**3**)

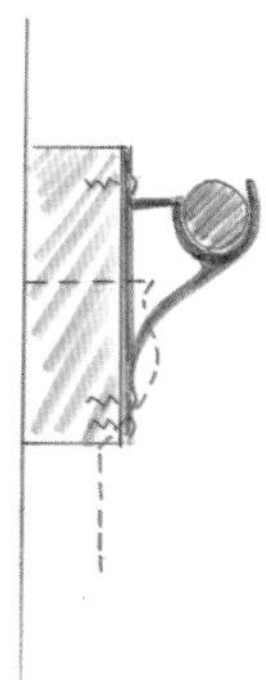

3

❑ Support the centre of long poles with a central bracket. As a rough guide, a 2.5cm (1in) pole carrying interlined curtains will need a central bracket if it is over 1.5m (5ft) in length, as will a 4cm (1½in) pole if over 1.8m (6ft) or a 5cm (2in) pole if over 2.1m (7ft).

Slotted headings

❑ Slotted (or cased) curtains have fixed headings that are never drawn back. A casing in the top of the curtain is gathered on to a pole. There are three options for fixing a slotted heading on to the pole:
1. Slot the curtains onto the pole, mark the positions of the brackets and make two small holes in the back of the casings. The brackets can then pierce the casing and will be hidden behind the casing front. (**4**)

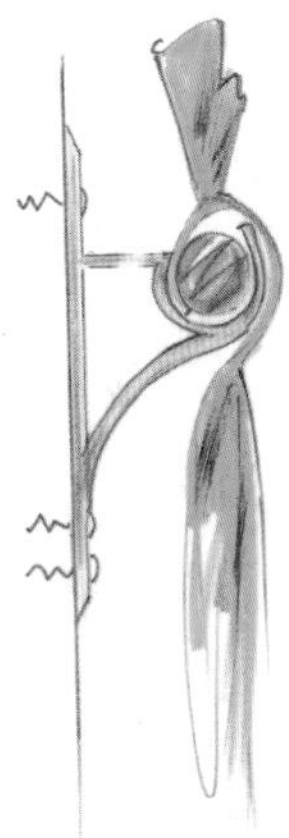

4

2. If no finials are attached to the ends of the pole, slipstitch the ends of the slot or casing and tack to the end surfaces of the pole.
3. Use rod sockets (for narrow-gauge poles/dowels) which, once in place, are covered by either end of the slot or casing. A pole socket will act in the same way for curtains hung inside the reveal or inside two projecting wall surfaces.
4. Place the brackets flush with the insides of the finials and overlap with the edges of the slot or casing.

Tracks

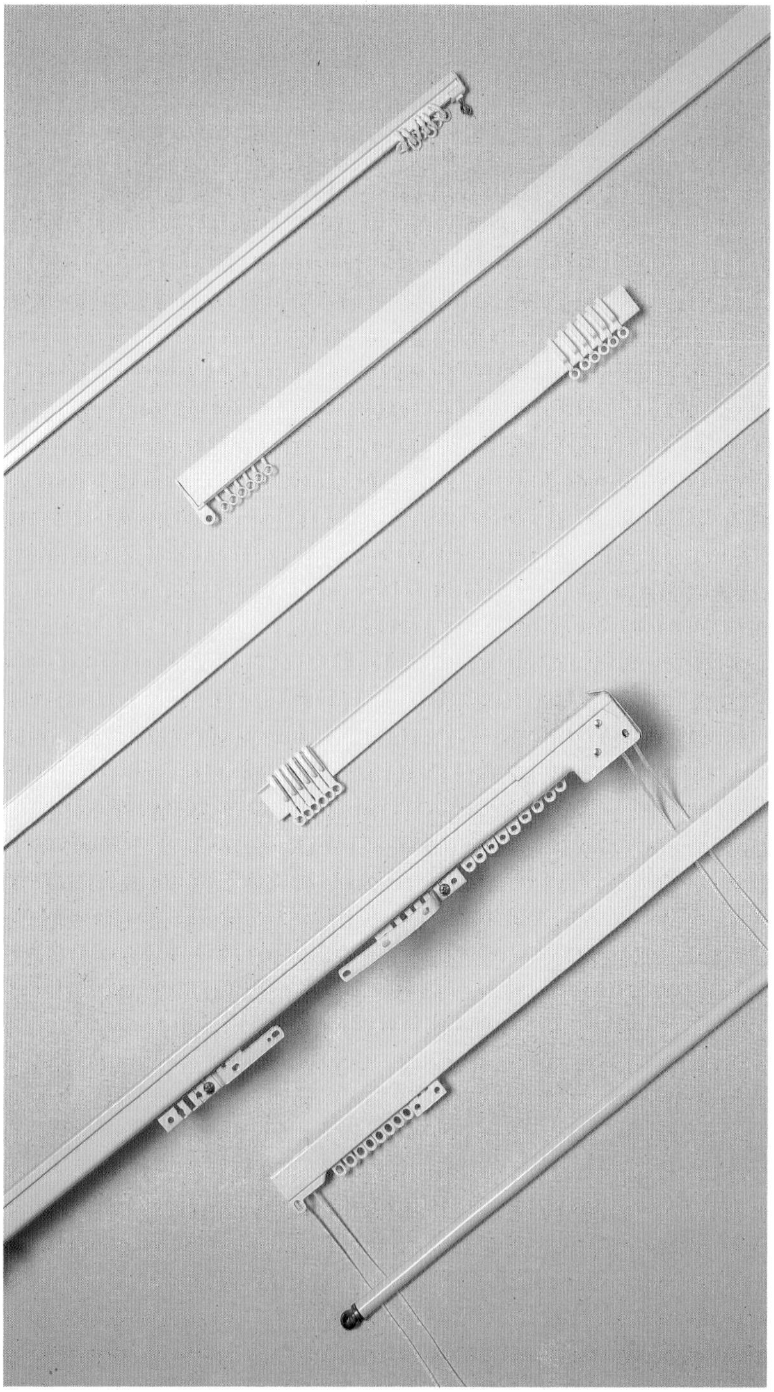

Given all the effort that goes into making curtains or blinds, it is a pity to stint on the fittings. A rail that slides cleanly, with properly adjusted cords, firmly fixed to the wall, will fully repay the investment of time and money.

Numerous tracks and systems are available; they can be motorised or manual, single or multiple, plastic or metal, corded or uncorded, bent or straight. Ask the supplier's advice (small specialist shops often score over the giant superstore in this respect) and consult the instructions carefully: the rail must be the right one for the task.

For most, the choice is between a corded or uncorded track. A corded track has a loop of cord to one side, held taught by a tension pulley. The curtain is never handled, the leading edges of the curtain kept free of dirt and wear. Overlap arms carry the leading edges over one another to minimise light penetration and cold draughts. An uncorded track, of metal or plastic, lacks such sophistications but is easily cut down and fitted – well adapted to simple projects and the inexperienced handyman.

Always choose a rail that is adapted to the weight of the curtain and make sure that it has a good fixing into the wall or window.

LEFT (from top to bottom):
1-4. Lightweight, uncorded plastic tracks
5. Corded metal track with overlap arms
6. Corded plastic track
7. Net drop rod for lightweight curtains and nets

TOOLS AND ACCESSORIES *166*
TRACKS *39, 75*
FIXING/SURFACES *169*

TRACKS

Uncorded

These tracks may be plastic or aluminium. They are designed for nets, light unlined or lightweight curtains.

❑ Buy the right strength for the choice of curtain.

Corded

Internally corded, ready-assembled tracks are suitable for most curtains.

❑ The easiest to fix are telescopic steel tracks.

❑ Otherwise, use a hacksaw to cut the track to length, making sure that the cords do not twist.

❑ The cords can be held around a tension pulley screwed to the skirting board. This means they will remain separate and tight.

❑ Alternatively, the looped cord can be cut and each pulley cord slotted through a brass acorn. The effect will be more decorative, but the cords are more likely to twist.

❑ Corded tracks are designed for two curtains to be drawn back to either side, but it is also possible to adjust the track to carry only one curtain.

Net drop-rods

❑ Hollow plastic drop-rods are ideal for washable nets suspended from the top of the window on cords, which are then fed through screw eyes and secured on one side of the window.

Bay windows

❑ Ideally tracks around bay windows should be suspended from a tailor-made pelmet board, which has been measured and fitted professionally. Problems can arise when DIY flexible tracks are bent around tight corners, as the passage of the curtain is often impeded.

❑ An exposed track can be unsightly and may cause the difficulties described above.

Bow windows

(See bay windows)

❑ Measuring and fixing pelmet boards into the curve of a bow window is even more difficult than for a bay window and a DIY, exposed, plastic track tends to spoil the decorative effect of the curtains.

FITTING TRACKS AND PELMET BOARDS

❑ As a general rule, a board carrying a single track should be 12.5cm (5in) deep, while boards for a double track should measure at least 18cm (7in).

❑ Extend the pelmet board or exposed track for at least 10cm (4in) to either side of the window, to give the appearance of extra width to a narrow window.

❑ Paint the board to match the wall or fabric, or staple curtain or blind fabric to the board, wrapping it like a parcel.

❑ Attach the brackets to the wall about 10cm (4in) above the window. If you want to make the window appear taller, place the brackets nearer the ceiling.

❑ Fix the brackets to the wall; then screw the board to the brackets.

❑ Curtains draped from a fixed heading, with a generous overlap, will disguise a high board, or a pelmet can be used to hide the gap between board and window. Try not to expose any wall space above the window.

❑ Screw the track to the base of the board. Leave a 2.5cm (1in) gap between the end of the track and the edge of the board.

❑ The track should be suspended at least 7cm (2¾in) behind the front edge of the board. For use with covered fascias, the track should be directly behind the back of the buckram or plywood band.

❑ Insert a vine eye (a screw eye on a longer stem) into each rear corner of the base of the board. These will hold the curtain returns in place. The outer left- and right-hand hooks in the curtain headings will be slotted into the vine eyes, holding the outer edges of the curtains flush with the wall.

Multiple tracks

❑ When more than one track is needed, the front track should hang from a pelmet board. The second will either hang behind it from the same board, or be attached to the architrave or wall above the window.

❑ The second track should be placed at least 5cm (2in) behind the first and, if hanging from the same board, at least 4cm (1½in) from the wall.

Pelmets, valances and covered fascias

❑ The front edge of the wooden pelmet board carries either a pelmet, valance or a 5cm (2in) band of buckram or plywood, covered in fabric (known as a covered board and fascia), to hide the track. The track lies directly behind the fascia.

❑ To fit a pelmet board into a bay window, make a paper template of the internal angles. Cut the three pieces of wood to length, angle the ends to fit snugly against one another and fix the three sections using mending plates and screws. (**1** below)

❑ Curve-fronted or D-shaped pelmet boards are most attractive for fixed-headed curtains, pelmets or valances. In the latter case a curtain track, fixed to the base of the board, can be bent slightly to follow the curve of the board. (**2**)

❑ Take care to see that they do not finish at too sharp an angle, as this may cause problems with any track running below, and in positioning the brackets.

Brackets

❑ It is very important to use strong brackets to hold the pelmet board as ordinary right-angled brackets may bend under the strain. Special brackets, designed for use with curtains and blinds, are available.

❑ Strengthened shelf brackets are sufficiently powerful but have a rib that impedes the action of the hooks along the track. With these you will have to use a washer-like spacer to lower the track slightly, clear of the rib. (**3a** & **3b**)

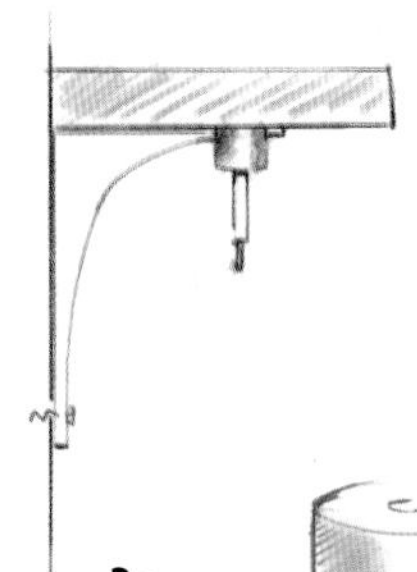

3a

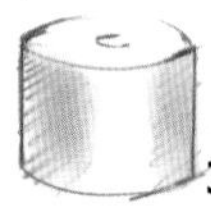

3b

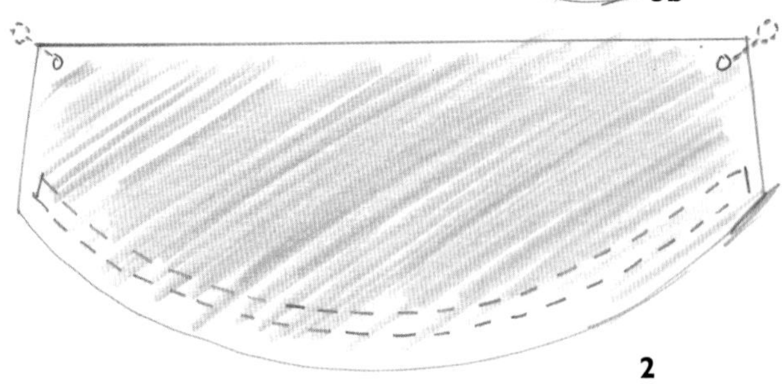

2

1

Fitting Blinds and Italian-Strung Curtains

When fitting blinds or Italian-strung curtains, similar methods are used. First fix a pelmet board above the window using strong brackets. The depth of the board will be dictated by a ledge or radiator that might interfere with the back of the blind or curtain and by the depth of the architrave. The blind should hang as close to the window as possible but there should be sufficient room for the screw eyes in the base of the board to operate effectively. Bear in mind that the returns of the board can be hidden by the returns of fixed-headed curtains, a pelmet, valance or pull-up blind but not by a Roman blind which is, by its nature, flat.

ROMAN AND PULL-UP BLINDS OR CURTAINS

(see page 146 and 150)

❑ Staple touch-and-close fastening along the top of the board just behind the front edge (Roman blinds) or to the front edge and returns of the board (pull-up blinds or fixed-headed curtains).

❑ Position a screw eye in the base of the board or batten, above each line of rings on the back of the blind. Another towards the end of the batten carries the cord to the end of the board on the pull-up side (Roman or pull-up blinds).

❑ Fix a cleat or pair of knobs into the wall between chest and waist height, below the point at which the pull cord emerges. These will hold the cord while the blind is raised (blinds or pull-up curtain).

❑ If a Roman or pull-up blind is to hang behind a pair of ordinary curtains, screw a 3cm (1¼in) square batten to the base of the pelmet board, at least 5cm (2in) behind the front track and at least 4cm (1½in) away from the wall. Insert screw eyes in the base of the batten to carry the blind's cording.

ROLLER BLINDS

(see page 143)

❑ Roller blinds are held in special brackets, usually fixed on to the architrave itself.

❑ The brackets need to be aligned with the help of a spirit level.

❑ If hung inside the reveal make sure that imperfectly straight walls do not interfere with the edges of the blind.

❑ Roller blinds are operated either by a side-winding mechanism or by a sprung roller.

Undertensioned roller blinds:

❑ Roll the blind down.

❑ Take the blind out of the brackets.

❑ Roll it up by hand.

❑ Replace the roller in the brackets.

❑ Pull the blind down.

❑ Repeat a further time if necessary. As the spring is self-winding, the tension will build up.

❑ Avoid over-winding at all costs as this will immobilise the blind completely.

ITALIAN STRINGING

(see page 134)

❑ Italian stringing is based on much the same principle as the pull-up blind, using a pelmet board fitted with screw eyes to carry the cording.

❑ A screw eye should be fitted to the wall or architrave directly below each outer screw eye on either side of the window, behind the curtain's outer edges. These will guide the diagonal cord up the back of the curtain into a vertical line up to the base of the pelmet board.

Hanging Curtains and Blinds

Hanging curtains and blinds is a stressful operation not to be undertaken lightly. Interlined curtains can be very heavy and Roman or pull-up blinds unwieldy so enlist help, holding the stepladder and bearing some of the weight as you slot the hooks or match the lines of touch-and-close fastening. Prepare as much as possible in advance – cording up blinds, pulling up heading tapes and marking centre points on pelmets and boards will save time in the long run.

Points to remember

❑ Always protect curtains and blinds with polythene tubing while in transit.
❑ Wear gloves to avoid marking curtains or blinds.
❑ Pull up the cord in the heading tape evenly to the exact finished width before hanging. Insert the correct number of hooks. If the curtain is very wide, mark the heading tape into sections and pull it up in stages.
❑ Never cut the heading tape cords.
❑ While hooking a curtain onto a track, support the weight by carrying the curtain thrown over one shoulder.
❑ Avoid working with your arms above your head, as this will quickly make you dizzy.
❑ Start to hang the curtains from the centre – the weight is then distributed more evenly and later adjustments are easier. Do not begin by hooking the curtain to the overlap arm, as it will bend under the weight.
❑ Avoid ironing curtains and blinds once they are in place.
❑ When fitting swags and tails or a heavy pelmet, use small-headed nails. To hide the nail, work the head behind the front layer of fabric.

Dressing Curtains

Curtains must be 'dressed' if consistent folds are to form whenever they are drawn or pulled back
❑ With the curtains open, tease the folds into place. Draw the curtains, retaining the folds. (**1**)

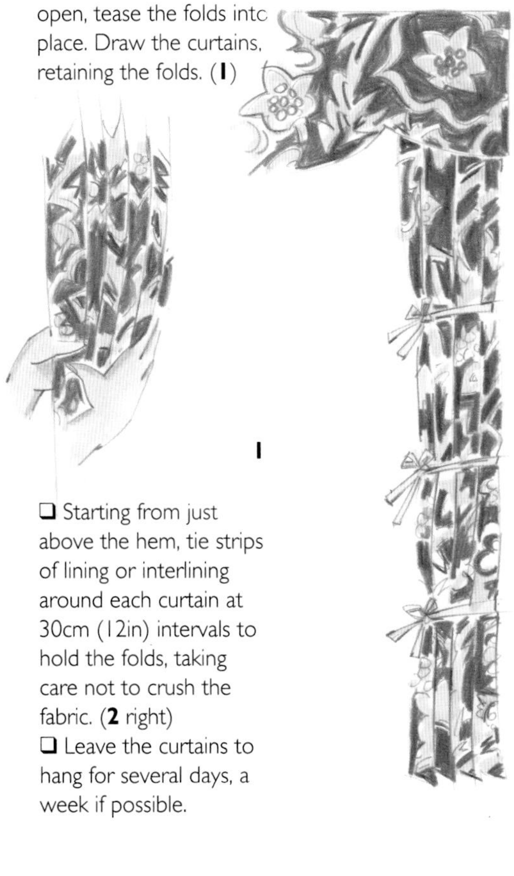

1

❑ Starting from just above the hem, tie strips of lining or interlining around each curtain at 30cm (12in) intervals to hold the folds, taking care not to crush the fabric. (**2** right)
❑ Leave the curtains to hang for several days, a week if possible.
❑ Once the folds are set, the curtains will retain the folds as all the layers will move as one.

2

Sewing Techniques

Using the correct stitches and sewing techniques is the key to making successful curtains or blinds. The layers of a curtain – fabric, interlining and lining – should hang together as if attached by an invisible force. There should be no signs of internal tensions where stitches are too tight; nor should the lining or interlining sag below the fabric. Carefully clipped seams, neatly mitred corners and accurately matched patterns all contribute to curtains, pelmets or blinds that hang well and will last for a lifetime.

Cutting Out

Accurate cutting out is an important part of curtainmaking. Always check your measurements before you begin and use a large, sharp pair of scissors.

Finding the fabric grain

❑ Most fabrics should be cut on the straight grain (unless, like swags, piping and contrast edging, they are deliberately cut on the cross grain).
❑ To find the straight grain on woven fabrics, pull a weft (horizontal) thread from the fabric.
❑ Snip across the selvedge edge close to the end of the fabric and ease out one thread from across the fabric with a pin. Then cut along the channel formed by the withdrawn thread.
❑ Patterns are not always printed on the straight grain. When the pattern has been printed slightly off-grain, cut out following the pattern, not the grain. Patterned fabric can be cut out up to 5cm (2in) out of alignment without causing a problem.
❑ When cutting fabric lengths, snip off a corner at the top of each length. In this way it will always be evident which way the fabric should be joined, so any pile or shading will run in the same direction.

Sewing

Check the following points before you start to stitch:
❑ Use short lengths of thread (except lockstitch) – long ones will snag and knot.
❑ Work with a single thread. For greater strength use a stronger thread.
❑ Secure the stitches firmly at each end.
❑ Wear a comfortable thimble for all handsewing.
❑ Make sure that the stitch is neither too tight nor too loose.
❑ Seam allowance is always 15mm (⅝in), unless otherwise stated.

Stitches

The following stitches are those most commonly used for soft furnishings. The sizes of stitch given in the instructions are for guidance only. Larger scale projects can use equivalently larger stitches – just make sure that the stitches are sufficiently firm to be effective.

Backstitch

Backstitch imitates machine stitching and is the strongest hand stitch. It will hold two fabric pieces firmly together.

❑ Bring the needle through to the upper side of the fabric.

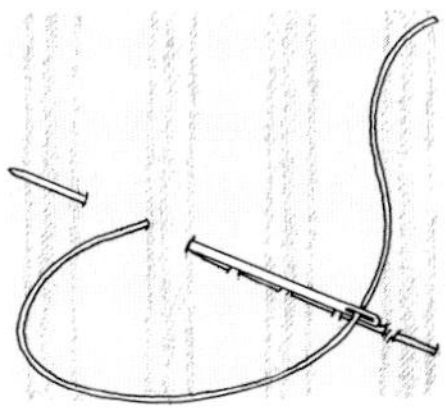

❑ Insert the needle 6mm (¼in) behind the point where the thread emerges, bringing it out the same distance in front.

❑ Continue in this way to the end. Stitches on the underside will be twice as long.

Herringbone stitch

This stitch holds hems on heavier curtains, when it is often worked over a raw edge. Herringbone stitch is also used to join together lengths of interlining and wadding as well as a means of attaching non-fusible buckram.

❑ Work from left to right, with the needle pointing left.

❑ Pick up a few threads in the curtain, then, working diagonally, take a small stitch in from the hem edge, with the needle still pointing left.

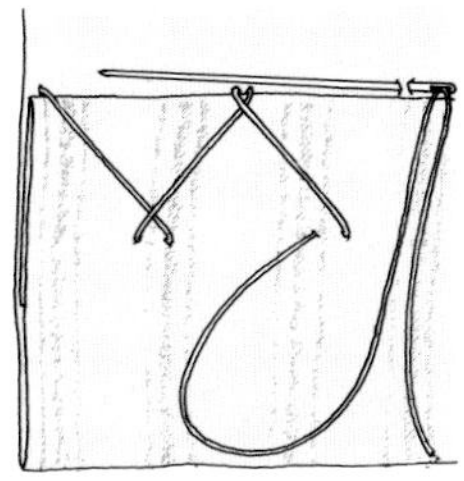

❑ Continue, forming diagonal, crossing stitches.

❑ To join wadding, place two pieces with edges butting together but not overlapping, and herringbone-stitch across the join.

❑ Herringbone stitch can also be used to join overlapping widths of interlining in the same way.

❑ Non-fusible heading or tieback buckram is secured to the face fabric or interlining using a herringbone stitch.

Ladderstitch (slip-hemming)

This form of tacking allows a pattern to be matched accurately before the seam is stitched. The stitching is worked from the right side (front) of the fabric.

❑ Turn under and press one seam allowance on the first piece of fabric.

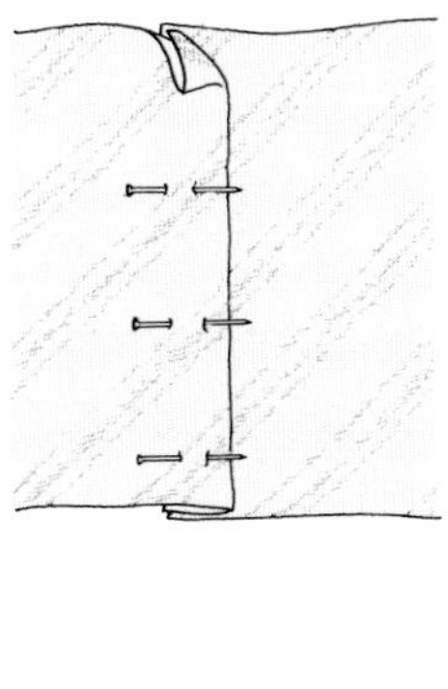

❑ With right sides up, place the first piece overlapping the second piece. Manoeuvre the pieces so that the pattern matches horizontally.
❑ With a knotted thread starting under the fold, take equal, alternating stitches down through the fold and then just to one side of it, forming tiny, horizontal 'ladder' stitches across the join.

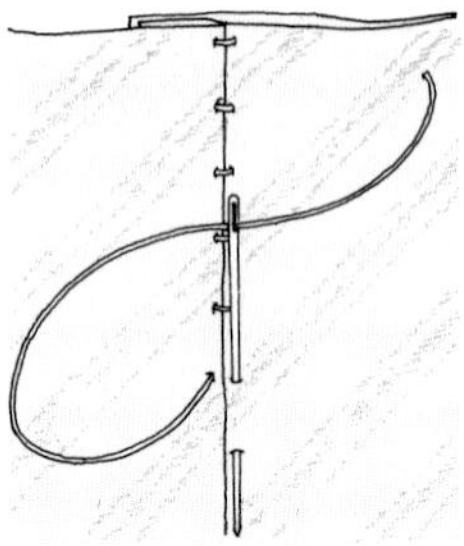

❑ When the ladderstitching is complete, the fabric pieces can be folded with right sides together and the seam stitched in the usual way.

Lockstitch

This stitch is used for linking interlining to the main fabric, and lining to the interlining, so that all layers will move as one. Use a thread which exactly matches the fabric, and position vertical lines of lockstitching every half fabric width for interlining and every fabric width for lining.
❑ Place the fabric right side down. Position the interlining over the wrong side of the fabric and smooth the interlining flat.
❑ Turn the interlining back on itself to form a vertical fold up the centre of the first width.
❑ With the thread secured to the interlining back, pass the needle through the interlining fold close to the edge, then pick up a few threads of fabric. The two stitches are made in one movement.
.❑ Do not pull the stitch tight, but leave a loop. Pass the needle through the loop and take a second stitch, 10-15cm (4-6in) below the first.

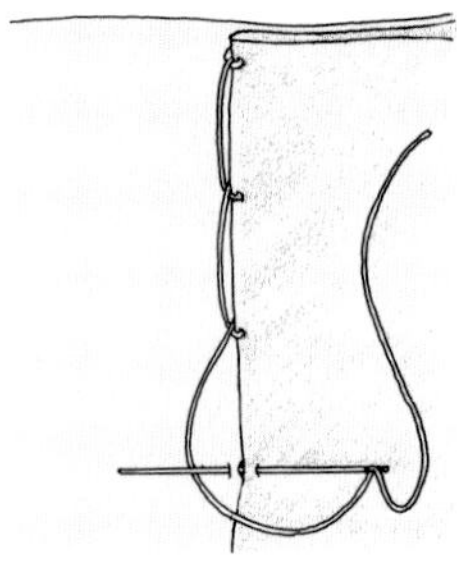

❑ Use the same technique to lock the lining to the back of the curtain, folding the lining back over the interlining.
❑ Unlike other techniques, lockstitch requires long lengths of thread to avoid the tension created by securing the thread in a line of stitches.

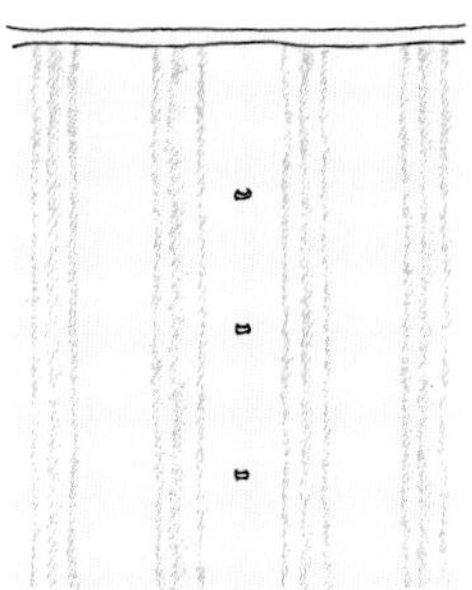

Oversewing

This stitch will neaten the raw fabric edge by hand.
❑ Secure the knotted thread on the wrong side.
❑ Working from right to left, take the thread diagonally over the raw edge, placing stitches about 6-12mm (¼-½in) down from the raw edge. Do not pull the stitches too tight.
❑ Use deeper stitches on fabrics that fray badly.

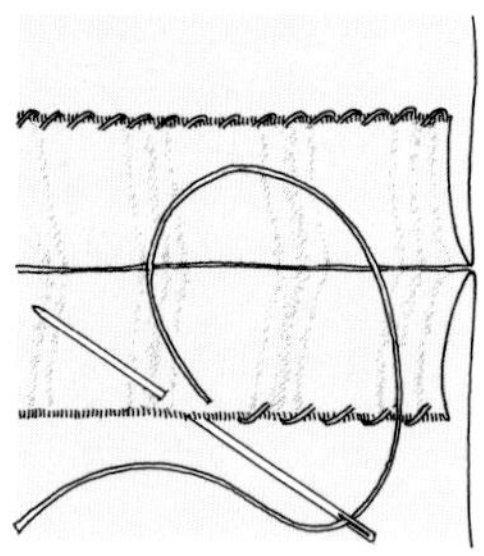

Prickstitch

This is a strong stitch, like backstitch, but is less visible.
❑ Work from the right side of the fabric and from right to left.
❑ Fasten the thread on the wrong side and pass the needle vertically through the fabric.
❑ Make a small reverse stitch, then bring the needle to the right side 12mm (½ in) further on.

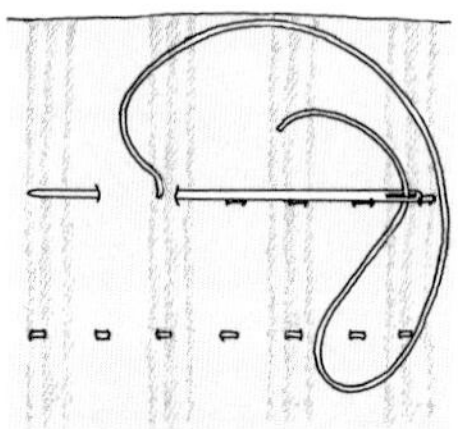

❑ Small stitches will show on the right side, with long, overlapping stitches on the wrong side.

Gathering stitch

This stitch is used for gathering fabric by hand.
❑ Begin with a small backstitch to hold the line of stitching in place; then work in and out of the fabric, taking even stitches and spaces. The size of the stitches depends on the fullness of gathering required. Use a single thread and leave a generous length of thread unsecured at the end.
❑ Work a second line of identical stitches above the first, starting from the same side. Match the stitch positions in the two lines precisely and check that the stitching lines are parallel. Leave the end of the second thread unsecured.

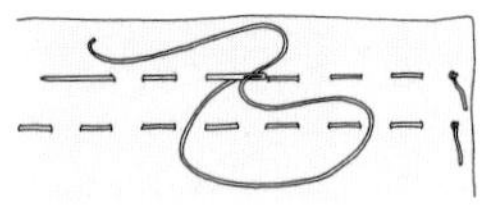

❑ To gather, pull up the loose ends together to form evenly spaced gathers.
❑ To hold the gathers in place, wrap the threads together in a figure-of-eight around a pin placed vertically through the fabric at the end of the stitching.

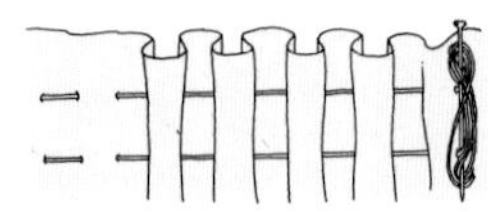

❑ On very long lengths of gathering, divide the fabric into equal sections and gather up each one separately.

Slipstitch

Use this stitch for hems on lightweight fabrics. and for holding down turnings of all sorts.
❑ Work with a long, fine needle, almost parallel to the stitching line and from right to left.
❑ Pick up a few threads of the flat fabric, then pass the needle through the folded hem, close to the edge. It is important to pick up the minimum number of threads with each stitch.

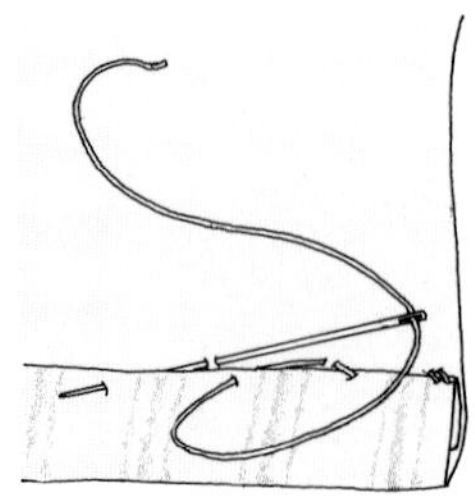

❑ Pull the stitch firm, but not tight.

Tacking

Tacking will hold two pieces of fabric together temporarily.
❑ Secure the thread with a knot on the wrong side.
❑ Working from the right side, just inside the seamline, pass the needle in and out through all the layers at approximately 19mm (¾in) intervals.

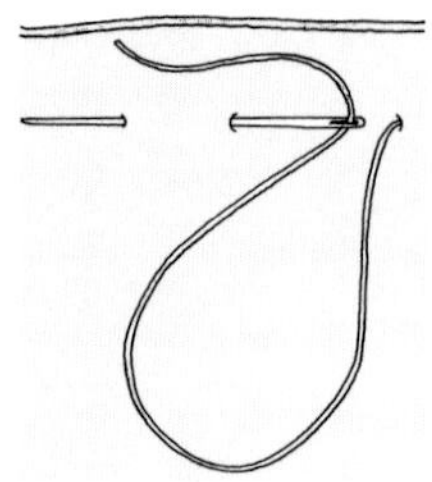

❑ Try to avoid machine-stitching over tacking, as caught threads are difficult to remove.

Seams

When choosing the correct seam for your project, take into account the weight of the fabric and the position of the seam.

Plain seam

This is the most usual seam used when joining any two pieces of fabric.

❑ With right sides together, raw edges matching, run a line of tacking stitches just outside the seamline. Machine-stitch 15mm (⅝in) in from the raw edge.

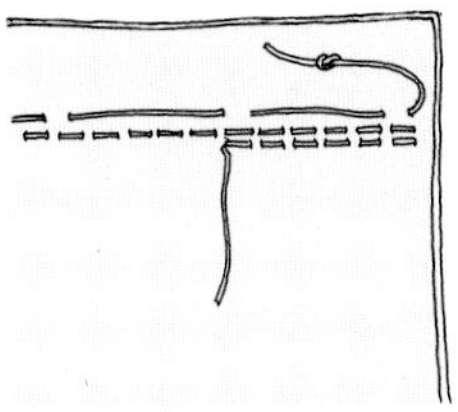

❑ Work a few stitches in reverse at each end of the seam to prevent it separating. Remove the tacking stitches. Press seam open.

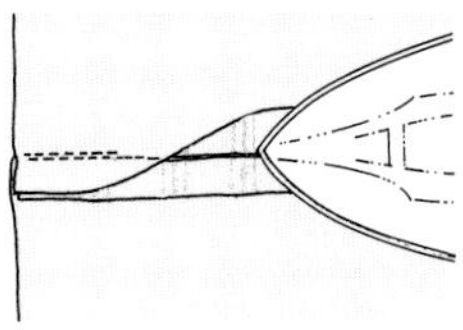

❑ To avoid tacking, pin the seams at right angles to the seamline. Stitch, using chalk line as a guide.

❑ Machine slowly over the pins, as the needle can snap if it hits one.

Square corners

❑ To avoid bulk, cut diagonally across the corners, close to the stitching line.

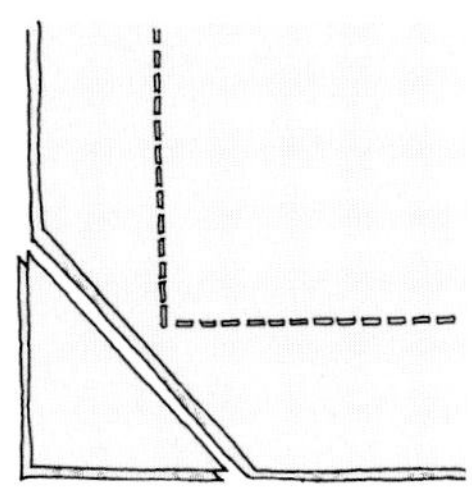

Acute-angle corners

❑ Give acute-angle corners a slightly blunt end by working a few stitches across the corner.

❑ If necessary, reinforce with reverse stitching.

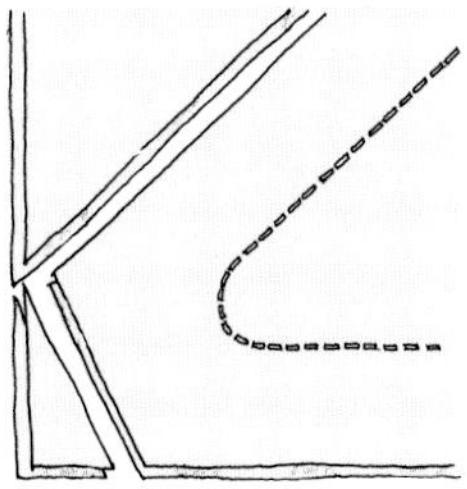

❑ Cut the seam allowance across the corner, trimming until all bulk is removed.

Clipping straight seams

❑ To ease tight selvedges, cut into the seam allowance at 5cm (2in) intervals. The cut is diagonal to the seamline, pointing downwards.

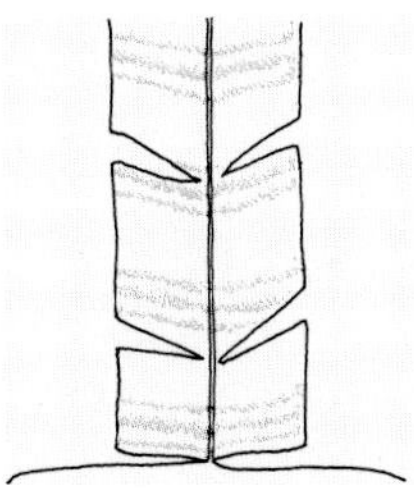

❑ Clipping should be avoided if there is light behind the curtain or blind, when it will show through to the right side. In this case, trim the selvedges generously to release all tension.

Clipping curved seams

❑ To avoid tension, clip notches into the seam allowance at right angles to the seamline on the inner curves.

❑ On outward curves, cut at right angles to the seamline.

❑ Tight bends require closer-spaced clipping.

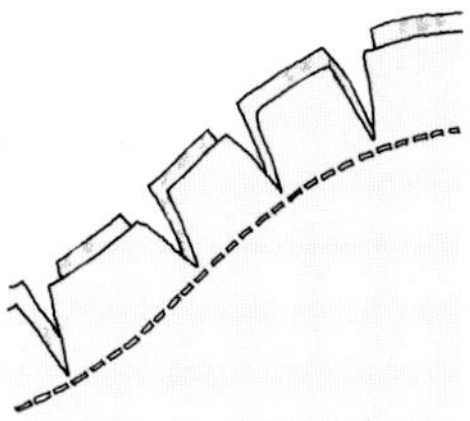

Neatening raw edges

❑ If a raw edge is visible or likely to fray, oversew either by hand or with a machined zig-zag stitch worked 6mm (¼ in) in from the raw edge.

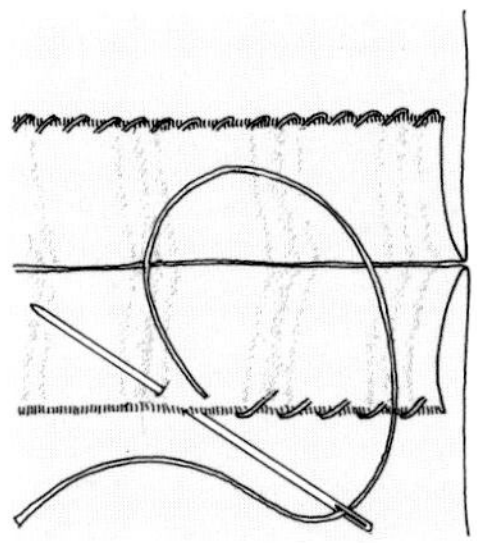

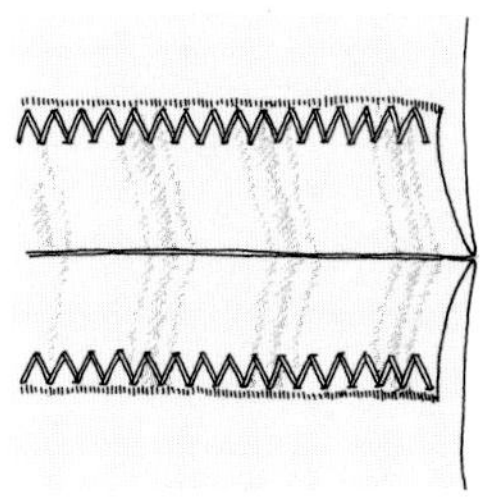

French seam

If a seam is visible from the back or tends to fray badly, a French seam will hide the raw edge. For lightweight fabrics only.

❑ Proceed as for a plain seam (see above), but with wrong sides together.

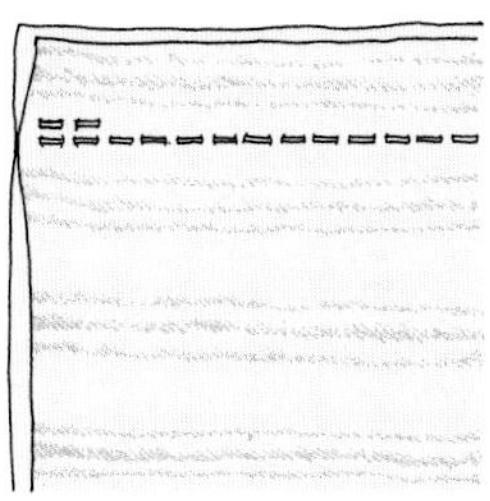

❑ Press open and trim the seam allowance to half its original width.

❑ Turn, with right sides together, encasing the raw edges.

❑ Stitch a plain seam 15mm (⅝ in) from the edge.

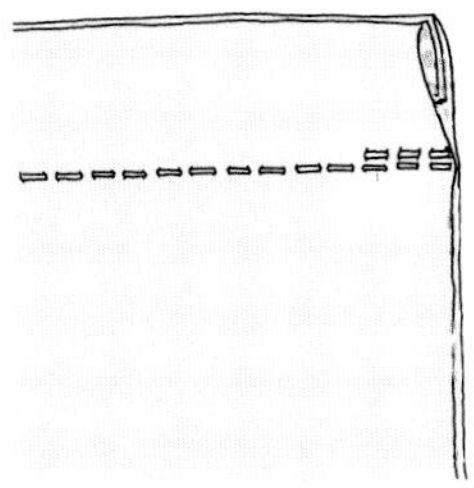

Flat-fell seam

This is a self-neatening seam, stronger than a French seam.

❑ With right sides together, stitch a plain seam.

❑ Press both seam allowances to one side of the seamline.

❑ Trim the lower seam allowance to half the original width.

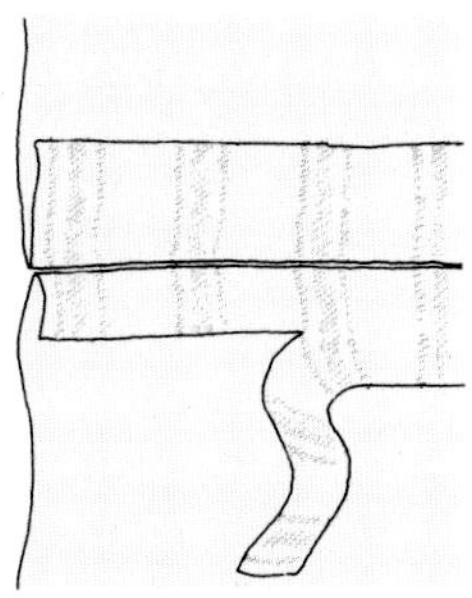

❑ Fold the edge of the upper seam allowance over the raw edge of the lower. Pin at right angles to the seam.

❑ Stitch down the seam again just inside the folded edge.

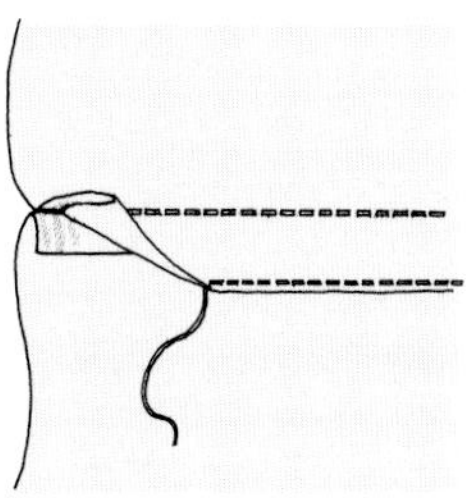

Hems

Mitred corners

Mitres make for crisp corners and help to remove bulk.

❑ Turn in the sides, then the hem and press. Open out again.

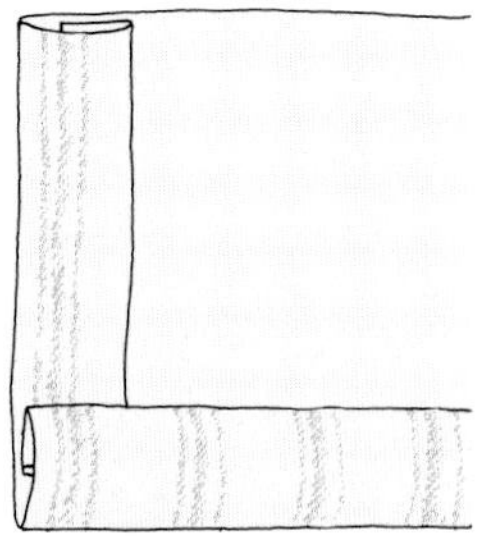

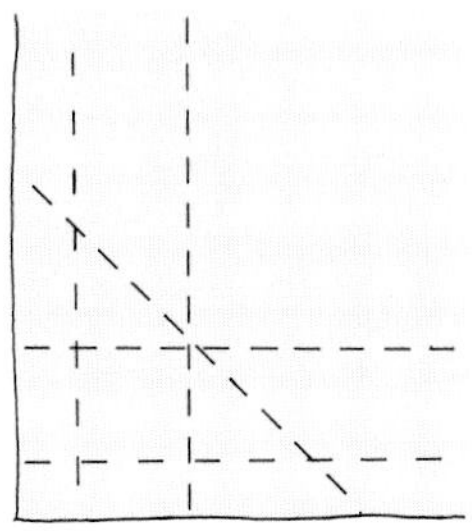

❑ Turn the triangular corner over, using the finished corner point of the fabric as the pivot, matching the foldlines.

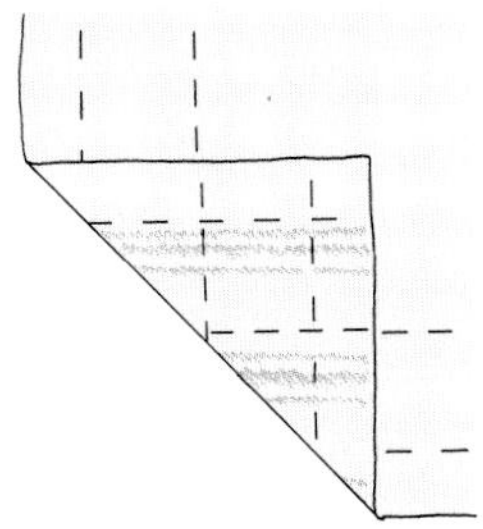

❑ Turn up the single or double hem and side turnings to form the mitre. Slipstitch.

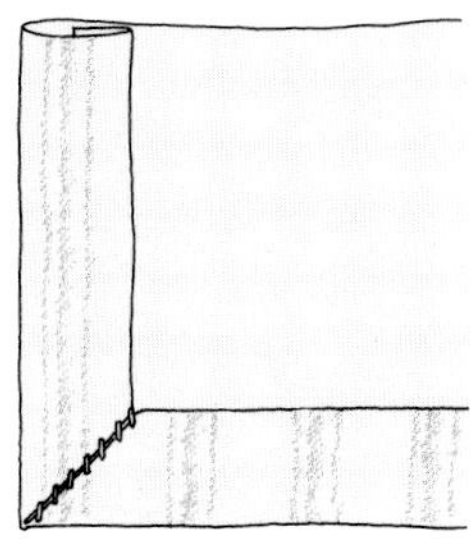

❑ If the mitred corner remains bulky, trim excess fabric but follow the same instructions. Trim excess interlining if necessary but beware if you are ever likely to let the hem down again.

Machine-stitched mitres

These are suitable for a single hem in lightweight fabric.

❑ To machine-stitch a mitred corner, fold the fabric at the corner, matching selvedges.

❑ From the corner point, run a line of stitching at right angles to the fold. Trim close to the seamline.

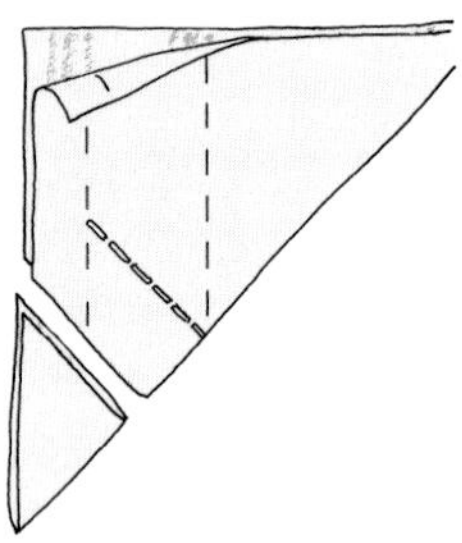

❑ Turn out the corner and press open.

Decorative trimming

Edges can be trimmed with piping, frills, fringing, braid or ribbon.

Cutting a bias strip

Bias strips are used for contrast edging or as casing for piping cord.

❑ Cut off one corner along the bias. Mark the fabric with parallel cutting lines from this edge. Use both edges of a ruler as your guide.

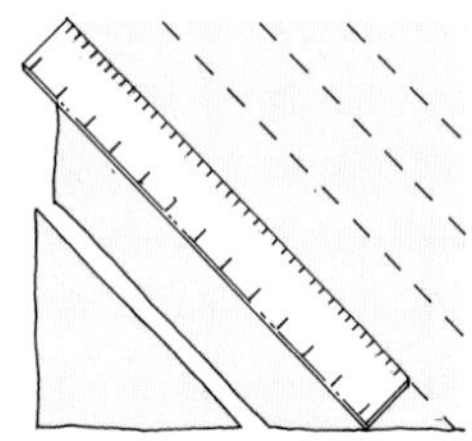

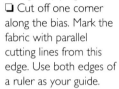

❑ When stitching two bias strips together, follow the straight grain.

❑ With right sides together, match the diagonal seamlines, thereby slightly overlapping the raw edges, and stitch. Press open.

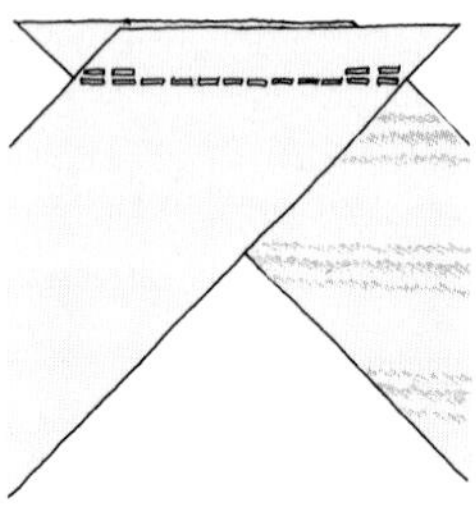

Cutting a continuous bias strip

❑ To cut a continuous length, first cut out a rectangle of fabric. The length of the rectangle must be more than twice the width.

❑ Fold the fabric diagonally from the top corner so that the cut edge lies along the selvedge edge. Press along the fold.

❑ Unfold and cut along the creased line. Stitch to the opposite end.

❑ Mark off the strip width in chalk lines parallel to the cut ends.

❑ Mark the 6mm (¼in) seam allowance down both side edges.

❑ Mark points *A* and *B* on the seamline – *A* is two strips down, *B* is one strip down.

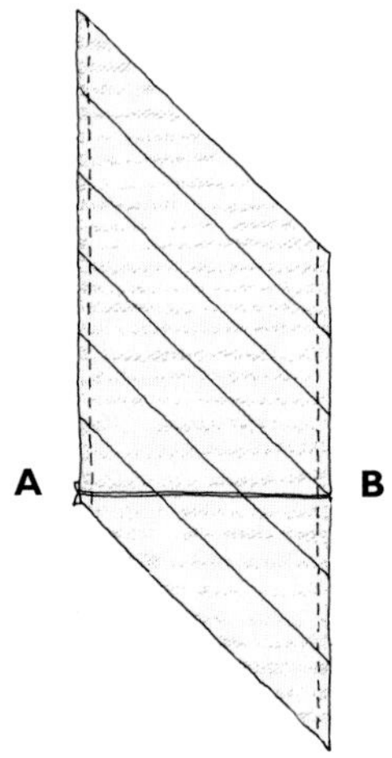

❑ Fold the fabric with right sides together, matching A and B together. Stitch down the seam and press open.

❑ Cut round the spiral, beginning with the overlapping end at the top and following the marked lines.

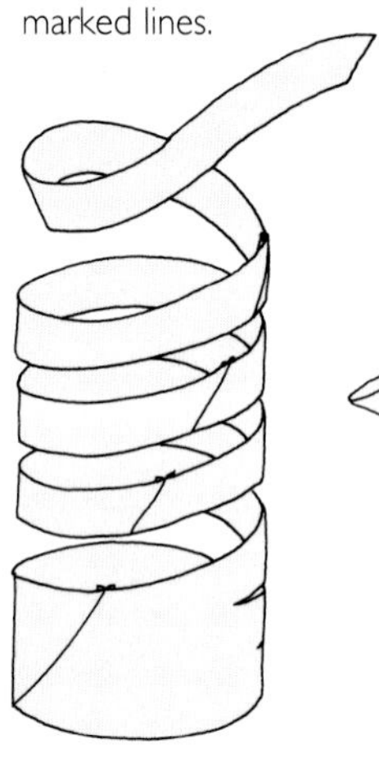

Piping

Piping cord should be pre-shrunk and of a size suitable for the scale of the project.

❑ Measure the edge to be piped, allowing extra for the corners and for joining.

❑ To calculate the width of encasing fabric strips, allow the circumference of the piping cord plus twice the seam allowance.

❑ Cut strips on the bias and join them together until they are the same length as the cord. Press seams open.

❑ Place the cord on the wrong side of the strip. Fold the strip in half, enclosing the cord and matching raw edges.

❑ Tack and stitch close to the edge of the piping cord, using a special piping foot on the machine.

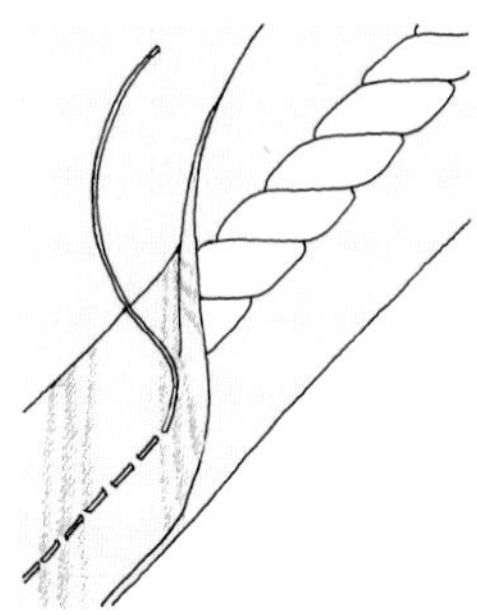

❑ Joining piping

To join two ends of piping, cut the fabric and cord to length, allowing 12mm (½in) for the overlap. Fold in one raw edge. The edges are diagonal, following the cross grain.

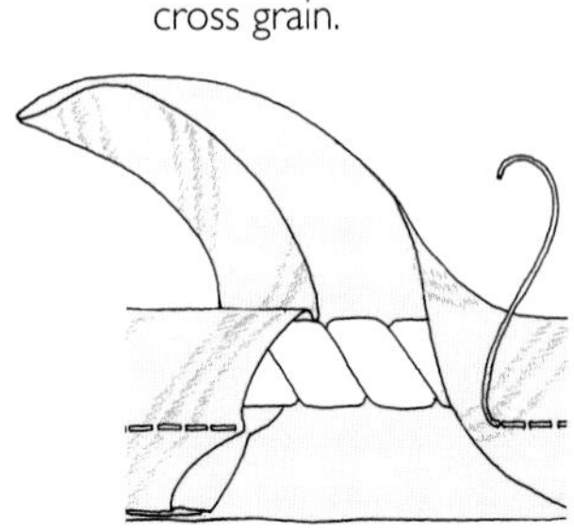

❑ Undo the ends of the cord and twist loosely together. Wind sewing thread round the join to hold.

❑ Overlap the folded and raw edges. Using tiny stitches, join the two ends of casing.

❑ To neaten the raw end of the piping, trim and turn the casing's edge to the inside. Slipstitch the edges together, encasing the cord.

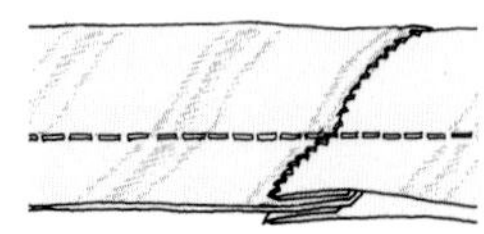

❑ Inserting piping

Place the piping between the two layers of fabric with all four raw edges aligned. Pin, tack and stitch into position, using the piping foot on the machine.

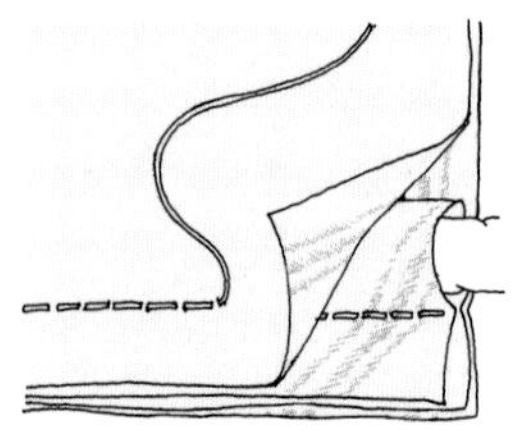

❑ Turning corners

When piping turns a corner, cut a section out or clip into the seam allowance.

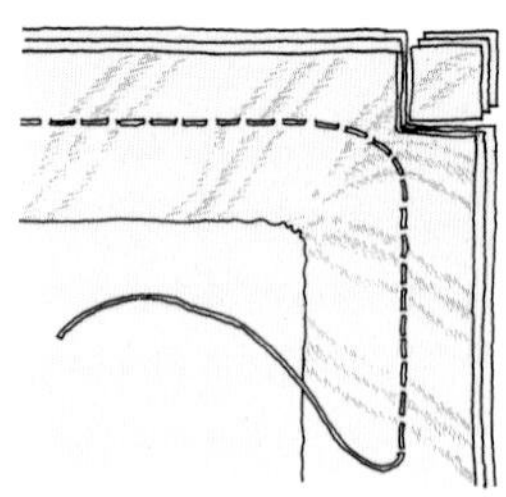

Fringe

❑ Pin the solid part of the fringe to the turned-up edges.

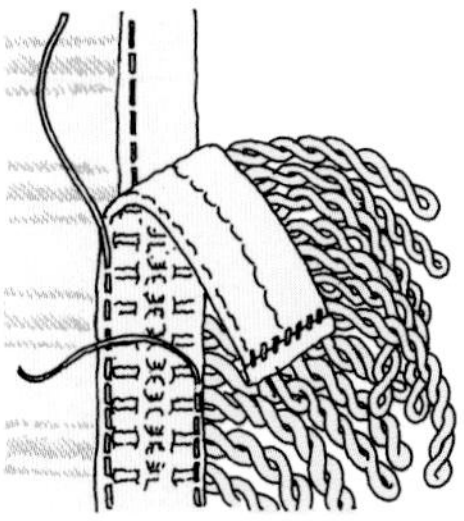

❏ A light fringe can be held with two parallel lines of running stitch; a heavier fringe needs two rows of prickstitch.

Frills

❏ Allow for the flat, ungathered frill to be one and a half to two and a half times the finished, gathered width.
❏ Cut the fabric strips twice the finished depth of the frill plus twice the seam allowance.
❏ Mark out the frill strips across the straight grain. Cut and join the strips with plain seams.
❏ Fold in half lengthwise and turn in the ends.

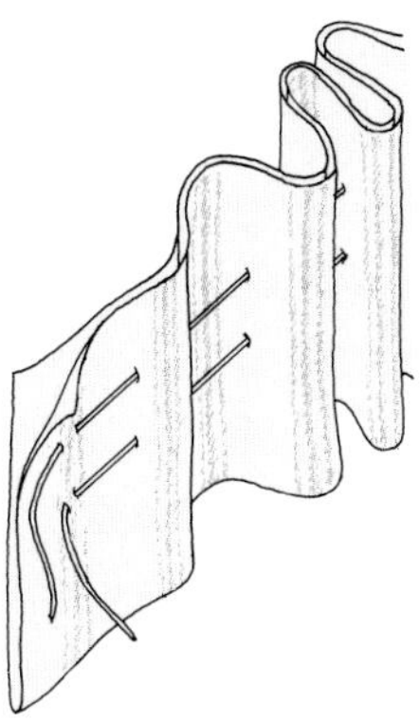

❏ Gather with two lines of stitches. Place one line just outside the seamline, another half-way between the raw edge and the seamline.
❏ Pull up to the required length.
❏ To insert a frill between two layers of fabric, match the raw edges and stitch along the seamline.

Pleats

Pleats are often used for pelmets. Generous-sized pleats give a professional finish, but they must be carefully measured out to achieve a regular and even result. The width of the flat, ungathered fabric should be approximately three times the finished, pleated width for either box pleats or knife pleats.
❏ It is important to trim away excess fabric, particularly when interlining is being used, to avoid bulky seams. Choose domette for interlining as bump is too heavy for pleating.
❏ Cut out the fabric on the straight grain, making sure to match any pattern.
❏ Calculate where box pleats will fall (see page 112) and allow for a size that will exactly cover the front of the pelmet board, ending neatly just short of the corners. The size of the box pleats can be altered by increasing or decreasing the space between the pleats.
❏ Divide the finished pleat length of the pelmet by the pleat width to work out how many pleats will be needed.
❏ Multiply the number of pleats by the amount of fabric needed for each pleat to find the ungathered width of the fabric.
❏ Using pins, mark out the pleat sections on the back of the pelmet, using a set square to mark parallel pleat lines.
❏ Any seamlines should be made to fall behind a pleat on a foldline.

❏ **Knife pleats** Mark the fold lines. Make parallel pleats all folding to the same side.

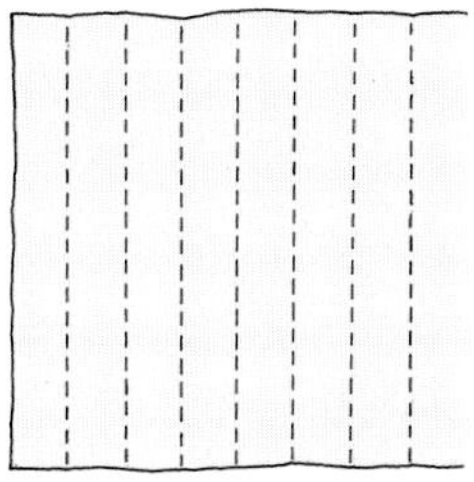

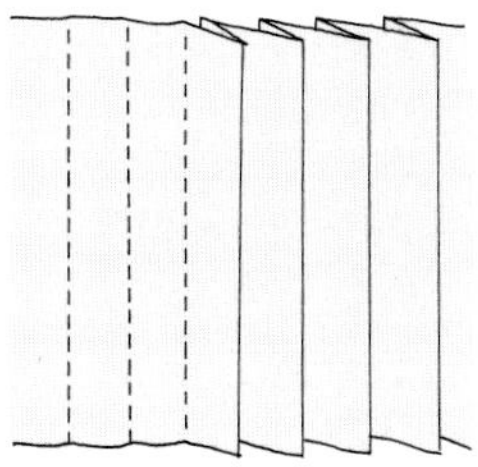

❏ **Box pleats** Measure out the fabric in the same way as for knife pleats. The pleats point in alternating directions to form box pleats. Do not press the pleats too flat: the folds should retain some elasticity.

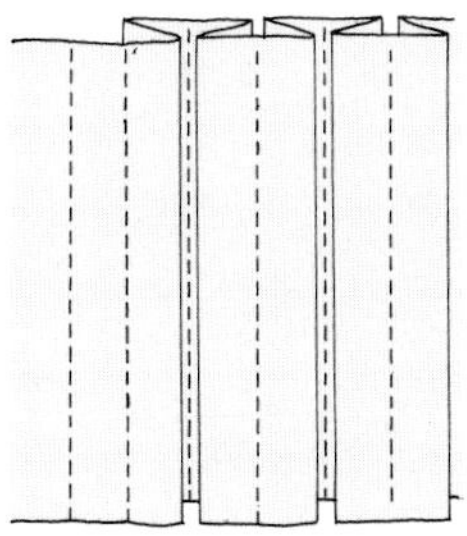

Mitring braids and ribbons

❏ Tack the trimming along the first side, then stitch it along the top of the inner edge only up to the first corner.
❏ At the first corner, fold the trimming back on to itself, right sides together.
❏ Sew a diagonal line of stitching at precisely 45° between inner and outer corners. Trim seam allowance and press open to form mitre.

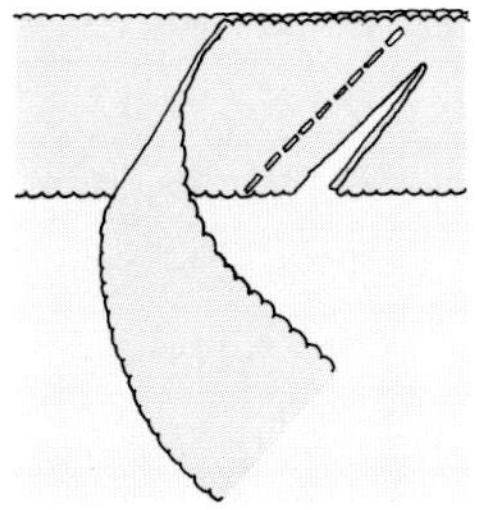

❏ Repeat at each corner, then complete by stitching round the top of the outer edge.

Binding edges

❏ The depth of a binding strip should be twice the finished depth plus twice the seam allowance.
❏ Cut the binding strip on the fabric bias. Fold the strip and make turnings. Press the folds.

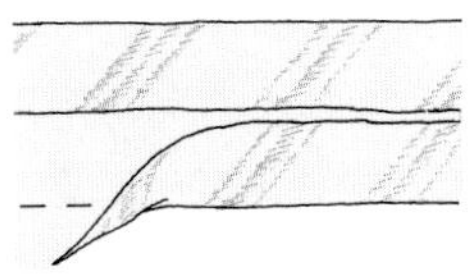

❏ To bind a fabric edge, place the raw edge inside the folded strip.
❏ Hand-stitch into position or machine-stitch close to the edge of the fold.

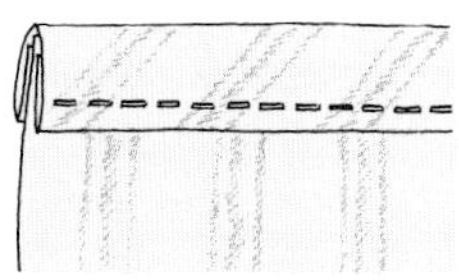

❏ Alternatively, unfold one edge of the bias strip and place it along the fabric edge, raw edges aligned and right sides together.
❏ Machine-stitch along the seamline, 15mm (⅝ in) from the edge.
❏ Turn and press, pushing both seam allowances to the same side. Trim and fold the bias strip over the raw edges.

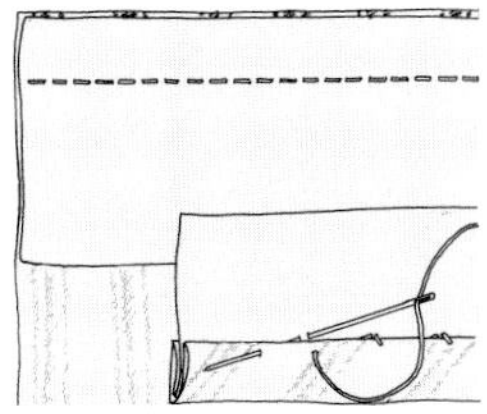

❏ Turn under the edge in line with the previous stitching. Pin and slipstitch into position.
❏ An equal band of binding should show to either side of the main fabric.

❏ **Mitring binding** Stitch the first side up to the corner point.
❏ Fold the binding back over the stitched side, so that the fold is in line with the edge.
❏ Stitch the next side from the corner point.
❏ When the binding has been stitched all round, turn it over the raw fabric edge, pressing the corners into the mitres on both sides.

Calculating fabric quantities

The charts that follow provide a quick method of estimating the metreage for a pair of curtains in plain fabric. They allow for 2.5 x fullness, an 8cm return, 15mm seams and 30cm for headings and hems. Note: extra fabric must be allowed for pattern repeats, tie-backs, valances etc.

- Establish the number of drops required by using Chart One.
- Secondly, establish the total metreage by using Chart Two.
- Here is a worked example for estimating for a pair of curtains with the following measurements:
- fabric width 137cm
- length of track 150cm
- finished length of curtains 215cm
- For a fabric width of 137cm and a track length of 150cm the number of drops of fabric required falls between 3 and 4 drops on Chart One. However, 150cm is only 12cm larger than 138cm (3 drops) whereas it is 43cm smaller than 193cm (4 drops); therefore the number of drops required for a 150cm length of track is 3.
- Now moving on to Chart Two, the finished length of 215cm is rounded up to 220cm (the finished length must not be rounded down as this will result in insufficient fabric). Reading down the 3-drop column, the metreage required is shown as 7.5 m.
- For curtains, gathered valances and pull-up blinds, the flat, ungathered width measurement (the distance along the hem) should be two and a half times the finished width measurement (the distance along the heading).
- For a less voluminous effect, the ratio can be reduced, to a minimum of one and a half.
- Most curtain projects that use plain or small-patterned fabrics require the same amount of lining and interlining as face fabric. Large repeats often require less (see Matching Patterns, page 89).

CHART ONE: CALCULATION OF NUMBER OF DROPS

Number of drops		**2**	**3**	**4**	**5**	**6**	**7**	**8**	**9**	**10**
Fabric 120cm wide	Length of track or pole (cm)	74	118	166	209	257	300	348	391	439
Fabric 137cm wide	Length of track or pole (cm)	88	138	193	243	298	348	402	452	507
Fabric 150cm wide	Length of track or pole (cm)	98	154	214	269	329	384	444	499	559

CHART TWO: CALCULATION OF TOTAL METREAGE

Number of drops		**2**	**3**	**4**	**5**	**6**	**7**	**8**	**9**	**10**
Finished length	100cm	2.6	3.9	5.2	6.5	7.8	9.1	10.4	11.7	13.0
	110cm	2.8	4.2	5.6	7.0	8.4	9.8	11.2	12.6	14.0
	120cm	3.0	4.5	6.0	7.5	9.0	10.5	12.0	13.5	15.0
	130cm	3.2	4.8	6.4	8.0	9.6	11.2	12.8	14.4	16.0
	140cm	3.4	5.1	6.8	8.5	10.2	11.9	13.6	15.3	17.0
	150cm	3.6	5.4	7.2	9.0	10.8	12.6	14.4	16.2	18.0
	160cm	3.8	5.7	7.6	9.5	11.4	13.3	15.2	17.1	19.0
	170cm	4.0	6.0	8.0	10.0	12.0	14.0	16.0	18.0	20.0
	180cm	4.2	6.3	8.4	10.5	12.6	14.7	16.8	18.9	21.0
	190cm	4.4	6.6	8.8	11.0	13.2	15.4	17.6	19.8	22.0
	200cm	4.6	6.9	9.2	11.5	13.8	16.1	18.4	20.7	23.0
	210cm	4.8	7.2	9.6	12.0	14.4	16.8	19.2	21.6	24.0
	220cm	5.0	7.5	10.0	12.5	15.0	17.5	20.0	22.5	25.0
	230cm	5.2	7.8	10.4	13.0	15.6	18.2	20.8	23.4	26.0
	240cm	5.4	8.1	10.8	13.5	16.2	18.9	21.6	24.3	27.0
	250cm	5.6	8.4	11.2	14.0	16.8	19.6	22.4	25.2	28.0
	260cm	5.8	8.7	11.6	14.5	17.4	20.3	23.2	26.1	29.0
	270cm	6.0	9.0	12.0	15.0	18.0	21.0	24.0	27.0	30.0
	280cm	6.2	9.3	12.4	15.5	18.6	21.7	24.8	27.9	31.0
	290cm	6.4	9.6	12.8	16.0	19.2	22.4	25.6	28.8	32.0
	300cm	6.6	9.9	13.2	16.5	19.8	23.1	26.4	29.7	33.0
	310cm	6.8	10.2	13.6	17.0	20.4	23.8	27.2	30.6	34.0
	320cm	7.0	10.5	14.0	17.5	21.0	24.5	28.0	31.5	35.0
	330cm	7.2	10.8	14.4	18.0	21.6	25.2	28.8	32.4	36.0
	340cm	7.4	11.1	14.8	18.5	22.2	25.9	29.6	33.3	37.0
	350cm	7.6	11.4	15.2	19.0	22.8	26.6	30.4	34.2	38.0

Care and Maintenance

Curtainmaking is a time-consuming and sometimes expensive business. A little care will preserve your investment. Foresight, too, is vital. For example, avoid pale and delicate fabrics in a room where children or dogs roam free. A sensible choice of fabric and treatment will allow your curtains and blinds a long life and spare you constant anxiety.

DRY CLEANING

❑ Few curtains or blinds can be washed. Linings and face fabrics, as well as tapes and other trimmings, may shrink, lose body, colour and finish. Check the selvedge of your fabric for cleaning instructions. Always use the best specialist dry cleaner available. Many offer a comprehensive service which involves removing, cleaning, mending if necessary, re-hanging and redressing.

❑ Fabric protectors are available to treat material before or after making up. The process renders the surface less prone to absorb liquids. Some fabrics are already treated in this way – check the selvedge for information.

❑ If you are considering a costly fabric or a non-furnishings fabric (e.g. green baize), first buy a small length and ask a specialist cleaner to test.

❑ Always use pre-shrunk piping cord.

WASHING

❑ Most fabrics, including linings, are liable to shrink. Before making up any project:

1. Leave a large hem for turning down later.
2. Check that the fabric is pre-shrunk, testing a small piece if necessary.
3. If not, wash the fabric before making up. Iron while still damp.

❑ Some specialist dry cleaners will pre-shrink the material for you by passing it over steam. This is the best method. Washing can cause loss of body and will remove any finish, e.g. a glaze.

❑ Muslins and nets will yellow or turn grey with age: only washing will restore brilliance. Muslin, however, will lose body and shrink.

Stains

❑ It is vital to act fast. Scrape off any excess – do not rub in. Blot up wet marks and dust powdery stains. Test a discreet corner before treating a stain. Use water at room temperature; hot water may set a stain. Water should not be used on silk or wool and may cause shrinkage and colour loss.

❑ Take care to use the correct solvent for the fabric and the stain.

PROBLEMS

Fabric glue

❑ Fabric glue can be re-mobilised in the dry cleaning process. Be sure to check the cleaning instructions on the bottle. If necessary, the glue can be replaced after cleaning. Sew trimmings into place rather than use glue.

Finishes

❑ Glazes on chintzes are easily damaged, both on the worktable and in the cleaning process. Try to avoid creasing and handling. Don't fold the fabric; roll it back onto the tube.

❑ Fabric with a watered effect, e.g. moiré, is easily removed if splashed with water and cannot be replaced. But some man-made moirés are unaffected by water.

❑ Use a corded track or special ring-pulls with a pole, to keep handling of the leading edges to a minimum. To extend the life of a pair of curtains, swap them over occasionally to alternate leading edges.

Fusible buckrams

❑ Fusible buckrams are impregnated with glue that is released with ironing. The dry cleaning process causes the glue to be re-mobilised so headings, tiebacks or pelmets, stiffened with a fusible buckram, tend to crinkle and lose body. Washing such materials will have a still more disastrous effect. Sew-in, non-fusible buckrams *can* be cleaned.

Interlinings

❑ Cotton interlinings can be dry cleaned without problem; synthetic interlinings sometimes lose their shape. Neither should ever be washed.

Linings

❑ Cotton linings can be dry cleaned and, if they are detachable, washed, but they will lose body.

❑ Blackout and milium linings can be dry cleaned but not washed. If worn, they may lose opacity.

Roller blinds

❑ The stiffener used in roller blinds makes them unsuitable for either washing or dry cleaning.

Roman blinds

❑ Only attempt washing if the blind is made from pre-washed, pre-shrunk fabric. Be careful to remove any brass rings or lead weights that might cause rust marks.

Care of Fabrics

Washing symbols

Always use the recommended care label advice to achieve the best results. Note that many detergents now contain Optical Whiteners. These have the effect of making pastel shades appear paler after washing, and should not be confused with fading.

Wash in cotton cycle Machine wash: very hot 95° C. Hand wash: hand hot 50° C. Normal action, rinse and spin

Wash in cotton cycle Machine wash: hot 60° C. Handwash: hand hot 50° C. Normal action, rinse and spin Wash in synthetics cycle

Machine wash: hand hot 50° C. Hand wash: hand hot 50° C. Reduced action, cold rinse, reduced spin or drip dry

Wash in cotton cycle Machine wash: warm 40° C. Hand wash: warm 40° C. Normal action, rinse and spin Wash in synthetics cycle

Machine wash: warm 40° C. Hand wash: warm 40° C. Reduced action, cold rinse, reduced spin

Wash in wool cycle Machine wash: warm 40° C. Hand wash: warm 40° C. Much reduced action, normal rinse and spin (do not hand wring)

Hand wash

Do not wash

Care labels

May be treated with chlorine bleach

Do not use chlorine bleach

Hot iron (maximum 200° C), for cottons, linen

Warm iron (maximum 150° C), for polyester mixtures and wool

Cool iron (maximum 110° C), for synthetics

Do not iron

Dry clean. Suitable for dry cleaning in all normal solvents

Dry clean. Suitable for dry cleaning in tetrachloroethylene (perchlorethylene), Solvent R113, Solvent R11 or hydrocarbons

Dry clean. Suitable for dry cleaning in above solvents but sensitive to some dry cleaning procedures with strict limitations on addition of water, mechanical action and drying temperatures

Dry clean. Suitable for dry cleaning in Solvent 113 and hydro-carbons using normal dry cleaning procedures without restrictions

Dry clean. Suitable for dry cleaning but with strict limitations on addition of water and/or mechanical action and drying temperatures

Do not dry clean

Tumble dry

Do not tumble dry

Sources / Britain

A selective listing of suppliers of fabrics and fittings, tools and equipment (principal branch details given: please contact for stockists in your area); specialist cleaners; public collections to visit for inspiration.

FABRICS

Trade:

These establishments will only sell through interior decorators or decorating shops. To obtain access to such fabrics:

1. Look at pattern books in decorating shops and order through them.
2. Telephone the company and ask for the name of an account holder in your area.

Some trade-only firms will allow the public to view their showrooms. Some have no retail prices – the price charged to the customer depends on the decorator's mark up.

The larger fabric companies sell through main department stores.

G.P. & J. Baker
274 Brompton Road
London SW3
Tel: (0171) 589 4778
(printed cottons and chintzes, plain cottons)

Bennison
16 Holbein Place
London SW1W 8NL
Tel: (0171) 730 8076
(up-market printed linens)

Brooke London
5 Sleaford Street
London SW8 5AB
Tel: (0171) 622 9372
(silks and crewel work)

Manuel Canovas
2 North Terrace
Brompton Road
London SW3 2BA
Tel: (0171) 225 2298
(bold contemporary designs)

Claremont Furnishing Fabrics
29 Elystan Street
London SW3
Tel: (0171) 581 9575

Guy Evans Ltd
96 Great Titchfield Street
London W1
Tel: (0171) 352 7118
(reproductions of historic French fabrics)

Mary Fox Linton
1-8 Chlesea Harbour
Design Centre
London SW10
Tel: (0171) 351 9908
(glorious coloured silks)

The Gainsborough Silk Weaving Company Ltd
Alexandra Road
Chilton Sudbury
Suffolk CO10 6XH
Tel: (01787) 372081
(silk damasks)

Hodsoll McKenzie
52 Pimlico Road
London SW1W 8LP
Tel: (0171) 730 2877
(English country house style)

Lelievre
101 Cleveland Street
London W1
Tel: (0171) 636 3461
(up-market French fabrics, unusual weaves and finishes)

Percheron
G6 Chelsea Harbour
Design Centre
London SW10
Tel: (0171) 349 1590

Ramm, Son & Crocker
M28 Chelsea Garden Market
Chelsea Harbour
London SW10 0XE
Tel: (0171) 352 0931
(general collection including floral chintzes)

Arthur Sanderson and Sons Ltd
112 Brompton Road
London SW3
Tel: (0171) 584 3344
(general range of mid-market fabrics)

Turnell & Gigon Ltd
M20 Chelsea Garden Market
Chelsea Harbour
London SW10 0XE
Tel: (0171) 351 5142
(French company with general range including trimmings)

Warner Fabrics
Bradbourne Drive
Tilbrook
Milton Keynes
MN7 8BE
Tel: (01908) 366 900
(general collection specializing in chintzes)

Retail

Anta Scotland Ltd
Fearn
Tain
Ross-shire
Scotland
Tel: (01862) 832 4777
(traditional tartans in new colourways)

Laura Ashley
Tel: (0990) 622116
for branches nationwide
(inexpensive traditional cottons, plain and printed)

Celia Birtwell
71 Westbourne Park Road
London W2 5QH
Tel: (0171) 221 0877
(contemporary designs, silk-screened sheers)

The Blue Door
77 Church Road
Barnes
London SW13
Tel: (0181) 748 9785

Campbell & Co
Highland Tweed House
Beauly
Invernesshire
IV4 7BU
Tel: (01463) 782239
(best-quality tartan)

Rupert Cavendish
610 King's Road
London SW6 2DX
Tel: (0171) 731 7041
(Empire/Bierdemeier reproductions and voiles)

Jane Churchill
151 Sloane Street
London SW1X 9LP
Tel: (0171) 730 9847
(English country house style)

Cole & Son Ltd
Chelsea Harbour
Design Centre
Chelsea Harbour
London SW10
Tel: (0171) 376 4628
(country chintzes)

Colefax & Fowler
110 Fulham Road
London SW3 6HU
Tel: (0171) 244 7427
(English country house style)

The Conran Shop
81 Fulham Road
London SW3 6RD
Tel: (0171) 589 7401
(contemporary designs)

Anna French Ltd
343 King's Road
London SW3 5ES
Tel: (0171) 351 1126
(laces and voiles)

Designer's Guild
277 King's Road
London SW3 5EN
Tel: (0171) 351 5775
(brightly coloured cottons)

Pierre Frey
251 Fulham Road
London SW3 6HY
Tel: (0171) 376 5599
(imaginatively printed cottons, up-market)

Habitat
Branches nationwide
(inexpensive contemporary and traditional designs)
Head Office
Tel: (0171) 255 2545

Ikea
Tel: (0181) 208 5600
for branches
(cheerful fabrics, many natural fibres)

Peter Jones
Sloane Square
London SW1
Tel: (0171) 730 3434
(the best comprehensive range of fabrics, linings and trimmings)

Cath Kidston
8 Clarendon Cross
London W11
Tel: (0171) 221 4000
(retro cottons)

John Lewis
278-306 Oxford Street
London W1A 1EX
Tel: (0171) 629 7711
(enormous range, own brand and leading fabric companies)

Liberty
210-20 Regent Street
London W1R 6AH
Tel: (0171) 734 1234
(wide selection, own brand)

Ian Mankin
109 Regent's Park Road
London NW1 8UR
Tel: (0171) 722 0997
&
271 Wandsworth Bridge Road
London SW6 6AH
Tel: (0171) 371 8825
(striped and checked cottons)

McCulloch and Wallis
25-26 Dering Street
London W1R 0BH
Tel: (0171) 629 0311
(cottons and natural fibres)

Mrs Monro Ltd
16 Motcomb Street
London SW1X 8LB
Tel: (0171) 235 0326
(English country house chintzes)

Nursery Window
81 Walton Street
London SW3 2HP
Tel: (0171) 581 3358
(children's fabrics)

Osborne & Little
304 King's Road
London SW3 5UH
Tel: (0181) 675 2255 for nationwide stockists
(wide selection, many comtemporary designs)

Pongees
184-186 Old Street
London EC1
Tel: (0171) 253 0428
(silks)

Russell and Chapple
23 Monmouth Street
London WC2H 9DE
Tel: (0171) 836 7521
(cotton duck, baize and other cloths useful for improvisation)

Bernard Thorp
53 Chelsea Manor Street
London SW3 5RZ
Tel: (0171) 352 5457
(traditional designs printed in client's colourways)

Timney Fowler
388 King's Road
London SW3 5UZ
Tel: (0171) 352 2263
(antique-inspired cottons)

Watts of Westminster
2nd Floor
Chelsea Harbour
London SW10
Tel: (0171) 376 4486
(ecclesiastical silk damasks, many Victorian designs)

Factory Shops

Shops attached to textile mills often sell seconds or discontinued fabrics at discount prices.
See: The Factory Shop Guides Gillian Cutress (mail order)
Tel: (0181) 678 0593

TRIMMINGS

Trade

Henry Newbery & Co. Ltd
18 Newman Street
London W1P 4AB
Tel: (0171) 636 5970

G. J. Turner Ltd
Fitzroy House
Abbott Street
London E8 3DP
Tel: (0171) 254 8187

Wemyss Houles
40 Newman Street
London W1P 3PA
Tel: (0171) 225 3305

Retail

Colefax and Fowler (see above)

Wendy A. Cushing
Tel: (0181) 556 3555

Peter Jones (see above)

John Lewis (see above)

Liberty (see above)

Osborne & Little (see above)

V. V. Rouleaux
10 Symons Street
London SW3
Tel: (0171) 730 3125
(ribbons)

LININGS AND INTERLININGS

Peter Jones (see above)

John Lewis (see above)

F. R. Street Ltd
Frederick House,
Hurricane Way
Wickford Business Park,
Wickford,
Essex SS11 8YB
Tel: (01268) 7666777

FITTINGS

Basic

Habitat (see above)

Ikea (see above)

Peter Jones (see above)

Sainsbury's Homebase
Branches nationwide

Texas Homecare
Branches nationwide

Decorative

Antiques and Things
91 Eccles Road
London SW11
Tel: (0171) 350 0597
(French antique curtains and fittings)

Artisan
Union Court
Union Road
London SW4
Tel: (0171) 498 6974

The Blacksmith's Shop
The Forge,
Stane Street
Halnaker
West Sussex
Tel: (01243) 773 431

The Bradley Collection
Lion Barn
Maitland Road
Needham Market
IPS 4LJ
Tel: (01449) 722 724

Hang Ups Accessories Ltd
7 Lyncroft Farm Workshops
Perrott's Brook
Cirencester
Gloucestershire
GL7 7BW
Tel: (01285) 831 771

McKinney
The Old Imperial Laundry
71 Warriner Gardens
London SW11
Tel: (0171) 627 5077

Oakleaf Reproductions Ltd
Ling Bob Mill
Main Street
Wilsden
Bradford BD15 0JP
Tel: (01535) 272878
(moulded pelmets)

Tempus Stet Ltd
15 Cranmer Road
London SW9
Tel: (0171) 820 8666
(small retail showroom, telephone first)

TOOLS AND EQUIPMENT

John Lewis (see above)

Morplan
56 Great Titchfield Street
London W1P 8DX
Tel: (0171) 636 1887
(clamps and rulers)

Sainsbury's Homebase (see above)

Texas Homecare (see above)

FABRIC DECORATION

L. Cornelissen & Son Ltd
105 Great Russell Street
London WC1B 3LA
Tel: (0171) 636 1045

John T. Keep & Sons
15 Theobald's Road
London WC1X 8SL
Tel: (0171) 242 7578

The Reeves Art Shop
178 High Street Kensington
London W8
Tel: (0171) 937 5370

The Stencil Store
89 Lower Sloane Street
London SW1V 4EX
Tel: (0171) 730 0728

George Weil and Son
35 Riding House Street
London W11
Tel: (0171) 580 3763

SPECIALIST CLEANERS

Hamlyns Dry Cleaning
197 Upper Richmond Road
London SW14
Tel: (0181) 878 0175

Pilgrim Payne & Co Ltd
Latimer Place
London W10 6QU
Tel: (0181) 960 5656

SOFT-FURNISHER DESIGNER

Sally Anne Sturt
Designing Movement
Flat 2,
2 York Road, Acton
London W3 6TP

PUBLIC COLLECTIONS

The American Museum in Britain
Claverton Manor
Nr Bath, Avon

Belton House
Nr Grantham, Lincolnshire

Clandon Park
Nr Guildford, Surrey

Calke Abbey
Nr Derby, Derbyshire

Castle Coole
Co. Fermanagh, N. Ireland

Cothele House
Calstock Cornwall

Frogmore House
Windsor Great Park
Berkshire

Ickworth
Nr Bury St Edmunds, Suffolk

Linley Sambourne House
18 Stafford Terrace
London W8

Osterley Park House
Osterley Middlesex

Sir John Soane's Museum
13 Lincoln's Inn Fields
London WC2

Spencer House
27 St James's Place
London SW1A 1NR

Victoria & Albert Museum
Cromwell Road
London SW7

Australia

FABRICS

As in the UK the larger companies sell through main department stores (see RETAIL). Trade only establishments allow customers to visit their showrooms and will supply information on major retail outlets.

Major fabric suppliers

Wardlaw Pty Ltd
Head Office
230-232 Auburn Road
Hawthorn VIC 3122
Tel: 03 9819 4233
Fax: 03 9819 5083
email:
jmarks@wardlaw.com.au

Wardlaw Pty Ltd
100 Harris Street
Pyrmont NSW 2009
Tel: 02 9660 6266
Fax: 02 9552 1571

Wardlaw Pty Ltd
36 Vernon Terrace
Newstead QLD 4006
Tel: 07 5257 1642
Fax: 07 3854 1801

Wardlaw Pty Ltd
2A Charles Street
Norwood 5067
Tel: 08 8363 5455
Fax: 08 8363 5466

Wardlaw Pty Ltd
256 Stirling Highway
Claremont WA 6010
Tel: 08 9383 4833
Fax: 08 9383 4648

I. Redelman & Son Pty Ltd
Sydney Showroon
37 Ocean Street
Woollhara NSW 2025
Tel: 02 9328 6413
Fax: 02 9328 6801

I. Redelman & Son Pty Ltd
Sydney Showroom
96 Pacific Highway
St Leonards NSW 2025
Tel: 02 9906 6566
Fax: 02 9436 2102

I. Redelman & Son Pty Ltd
456 High Street
Prahran VIC 3181
Tel: 03 9525 1040
Fax: 03 9521 1935

I. Redelman & Son Pty Ltd
49A-51 George Street
Parkside, SA 5063
Tel: 08 8373 1500
Fax: 08 8373 2808

I. Redelman & Son Pty Ltd
42 Berwick Street
Fortitude Valley
Queensland 4006
Tel: 07 3252 2866
Fax: 07 3252 3289

I. Redelman & Son Pty Ltd
Pegasus Centre
42 Bundall Road
Surfers Paradise QLD 4217
Tel: 07 5538 6555
Fax: 07 5638 9300

I. Redelman & Son Pty Ltd
Suite 2
187 Stirling Highway
Nedlends WA 6009
Tel: 08 9386 9311
Fax: 08 9386 9322

John Kaldor Fabricmaker
Pty Ltd
Showroom
110 McEvoy Street
Alexandria NSW 2065
Postal : PO Box 395
Alexandria NSW 2015
Tel: 02 9318 7777
Fax: 02 319 3490

Wilson Fabrics and
Wallcoverings
Head Office 1st Floor
10 – 14 Waterloo Street
Surry Hills
NSW 2010
Tel: 02 9321 6000
Fax: 02 9321 6052

Wilson Fabrics and
Wallcoverings
Showroom
82– 90 Cooper Street
Surry Hills NSW 2010
Tel: 02 9321 6000

Wilson Fabrics and
Wallcoverings
Showroom
37 Seymour Avenue
Armidale
Victoria 3143
Tel: 03 9509 0237

Wilson Fabrics and
Wallcoverings
Showroom
12 Cordelia Street
Brisbane QLD 4101
Tel: 07 3255 0237

Wilson Fabrics and
Wallcoverings
Showroom
15 Cypress Street
Adelaide SA 5000
Tel: 08 8223 4238

Wilson Fabrics and
Wallcoverings
Showroom
2 Hector Street
Osbourne Park WA 6017
08 9445 2933

Charles Parsons and
Co Pty Ltd
Furnishings Division
27 Brunswick Road
Brunswick VIC 3056
Tel: 03 9261 2766
Sales: 03 9261 2777
Fax: 03 9388 0502

Charles Parsons and
Co Pty Ltd
67 Nicholson Street
Brunswick VIC 3052

The Conran Shop
Georges Pty Ltd
162 Collins Street
Melbourne VIC 3000
Tel: 03 9929 9999
Fax: 03 9929 9998

Calico House
521 Chapel Street
South Yarra CIV 3141
Tel: 03 9826 9957
Fax: 03 9827 2613
(Calico also provide a curtain-making service – please call for details.)

Calico House
Christies Homemaker
Centre
34 Goggs Road
Jindalee QLD 4074
Tel: 07 3279 0800

Calico House
32 Florence Street
Teneriffe QLD 4005
Tel: 07 3279 0800

Hoad Home Fashion Pty Ltd
25 Trent Street
Burwood 3125 VIC
Tel: 03 9805 2800
Fax: 03 9889 7377
Email: sales@hoad.com.au
admin@hoad.com.au

FITTINGS

Suppliers of curtain poles, tracks and finials

Major suppliers

Geraldine Cooper Pty Ltd
46 Queen Street
Woollahra NSW 2041
Tel: 02 9327 3566
Fax: 02 9327 7993

Geraldine Cooper Pty Ltd
255 Burwood Road
Hawthorn VIC 3122
Tel: 03 9818 3122
Fax: 03 9819 6789

Curtrax Pty Ltd
90 Oxford Street
Paddington NSW 2021
Tel: 02 9666 3252
Fax: 02 9666 3257
Freephone: 1800 62 32 52

Lincraft
31-33 Alfred Street
Blackburn VIC 3140
Tel: 03 9875 7575
Fax: 03 9875 7500

Klockner Agencies
35 Jikara Drive
Glen Osmond SA 5064
Tel: 08 8373 0055
Fax: 08 8272 2300
After hours: 08 8379 8087

SPECIALIST CLEANING

Lawrence Dry Cleaners
77 Allingham Street
Bankstown NSW 2200
Tel: 02 9791 0977

Karl Chehade Dry Cleaning
410 Unley Road
Unley Park SA 5061
Tel: 08 8271 4666
Fax: 08 8373 3533

PUBLIC COLLECTIONS

Victoria

National Gallery of Victoria
180 St Kilda Road
Melbourne VIC 3004
Tel: 03 9208 0222
Fax: 03 9208 0245
website: www.ngv.vic.gov.au
email: info@ngv.vic.gov.au

Tasma Terrace
The National Trust of
Australia (Victoria)
4 Parliament Place
Melboune VIC 3000
Tel: 03 9654 4711
(Victorian Reproductions)

Mulberry Hill
The National Trust
of Australia
Golf Links Road
Baxter VIC 3911
Tel: 03 5971 4138
(1920s originals and reproductions)

La Trobe Cottage
The National Trust
of Australia
The Domain
South Yarra VIC 3141
Tel: 03 9654 4711

Rippon Lea
The National Trust
of Australia
192 Hotham Street
Elsternwick VIC 3185
Tel: 03 9523 6095
Fax: 03 9523 6921
(Victorian reproductions; 1930s and 1950s originals)

Como House
The National Trust of
Australia (Victoria)
Corner Williams Road and
Lechlade Avenue
South Yarra VIC 3141
(Victorian Reproductions)
Tel: 03 9827 2500

The Johnston Collection
and Historic House
152 Hotham Street
East Melbourne VIC 3002
(by appointment: 18th and
19th century reproductions)
Tel: 03 9416 2515

Powerhouse Museum
Call for details.
Tel: 02 9217 0369
Fax: 02 9217 0462

Elizabeth Farm
70 Alice Street
Rosehill NSW 2142
Tel: 02 9635 9488
Fax: 02 9891 3740
(colonial reproductions)

The Historic Houses Trust
of NSW Conservation
Resource Centre
Lyndhurst
61 Darghan Street
Glebe NSW 2037
For information on
collections contact the
librarian on:
meganm@ho.hht.nsw.gov.au

Useful Books

Authentic Decor
Peter Thornton
Weidenfield & Nicholson,
1984

Barbara Johnson's Album of Fashions and Fabrics
Ed. Natalie Rothstein
Thames & Hudson, 1987

The Cabinet-Maker and Upholsterer's Guide
George Hepplewhite
Dover 1969

The Conran Book of Soft Furnishings
Terence Conran
Conran Octopus, 1992

The Curtain Design Sourcebook
Carol Clifton-Mogg
Ryland, Peters & Small
1996

Curtains and Drapes
Jenny Gibbs
Cassell, 1994

The Curtain-Maker's Handbook
(facsimile)
F.A.Moreland
Potterton Books, 1979

The Curtain Design Directory
Merrick & Day,
Redbourne, Gainsborough,
Lincolnshire, 1991
Tel: (01652) 648814
(a comprehensive directory
written by professionals)

Decorating with Pattern
Katrin Cargill
Ryland, Peters & Small 1997

Drapery Cutting and Making
John W. Stephenson
Potterton Books, 1988

Early American Stencils
Janet Waring
Dover, 1968

The Elements of Style
Gen. ed. Stephen Calloway
Mitchell Beazley, 1991

English Decoration in the 18th Century
John Fowler and
John Cornforth
Barrie and Jenkins, 1974

Grand Illusions
Nick Ronald &
David Roberts
Ebury Press, 1996

How to Decorate
Martha Stewart
Crown, 1998

Kevin McCloud's
Decorating Book
Dorling Kindersley, 1990

Laura Ashley Complete Guide to Home Decorating
Ed. Charyn Jones
Weidenfeld & Nicolson,
1988

Natural Fabrics
Ian Mankin
Ebury Press, 1997

Natural Style
Tessa Eveleigh
Lorenz Books, 1998

The New Fabric Magic
Melanie Paine
Frances Lincoln, 1995

Pure Style
Jane Cumberbatch
Ryland, Peter & Small, 1996

Reader's Digest Complete Guide to Sewing
Hodder & Stoughton, 1978

The Swag and Tail Design and Pattern Book
Merrick & Day, 1993

Terence Conran's New House Book
Conran Octopus, 1991

Tricia Guild on Colour
Conran Octopus, 1992

Twentieth-CenturyDecoration
Stephen Calloway
Weidenfeld & Nicolson,
1988

The Ultimate Interior Designer
Ruth Pretty
Ward Lock, 1997

Vital Colour
Joanna Copestick &
Mary Lloyd
Ryland Peters & Small, 1998

Index

Page numbers given in *italic* refer to picture captions

Acknowledgments

AUTHOR'S ACKNOWLEDGMENTS
I should like to express my deepest gratitude to the following people for their invaluable professional help or personal support: my editor, Denny Hemming – without whom this book would never have been written; Rosalie Beaumont; Elizabeth Forbes; Christophe and Fanny Forbes; Justine Ford; Brigid Juhanson; Di Morley; John Hardy; Anita Hildreth; Ruth White; Nadine Bazar; Nick Protts of L & S Services; Tony Helyer; May Povey; Alan Wharton and Paul Battle of F. R. Street Ltd; Graham Doyle of Pilgrim Payne; David Richardson of The Blinds Company; Francesca Scoones of The National Trust; Catherine Merrick and Rebecca Day, authors of *The Curtain Design Directory*; and Paul Semple, Librarian of the London School of Furniture. I reserve special thanks for my husband, William, who provided unfailing support throughout the project.
I am also grateful to the numerous firms that have lent material for photography:
FABRICS: 52-3, 64-5, 72-3 Laura Ashley; 52-3, 56-7 Bennison; 64-5, 68-9 Celia Birtwell; 52-3 Nina Campbell; 48-9, 52-3, 56-7, 68-9 Manuel Canovas; 68-9 Rupert Cavendish; 48-9 Jane Churchill; 48-9, 52-3, 56-7 Colefax & Fowler; 56-7, 60-1 Collier Campbell; 48-9, 60-1, 64-5, 72-3 The Conran Shop; 48-9, 52-3, 60-1, 78 Designer's Guild; 56-7 Christian Fischbacher; 52-3, 56-7, 64-5 Anna French; 68-9, 72-3 Guy Evans Ltd; 60-1 Pierre Frey; 48-9, 52-3, 60-1 Habitat; 48-9, 52-3, 56-7, 60-1, 64-5, 66-7, 68-9, 78, 166-7 John Lewis; 52-3, 60-1, 72-3 Liberty; 48-9 Ian Mankin; 76, 78 Henry Newbery & Co. Ltd; 48-9, 52-3, 56-7, 68-9, 76, 78 Osborne and Little; 64-5, 72-3 Percheron; 68-9 Sacho Hesslein; 52-3, 60-1 Souleiado; 64-5 John Stephanides; 83, 166-7 F.R. Street Ltd; 60-1, 72-3 Timney Fowler; 68-9, 72-3 Watts & Co.; 76 Wemyss Houles Ltd
POLES & TRACKS: 172-3 Artisan; 172-3 The Bradley Collection; 137 Byron & Byron; 172-3 Hang-Ups Accessories Ltd; 172-3 McKinney Kidston; 174 Swish Products Ltd; 174 Cope and Timmings Ltd
TAPES: 166-7 Rufflette Ltd

THE PUBLISHER WOULD LIKE TO THANK THE FOLLOWING PHOTOGRAPHERS AND ORGANIZATIONS FOR THEIR KIND PERMISSION TO REPRODUCE PHOTOGRAPHS IN THIS BOOK:
1 Ingalill Snitt; 3 IPC Magazines Ltd/Robert Harding Syndication; 4 centre Marie Claire Maison/ Dugied/ Postic; 5 above Courtesy of Designers Guild, photograph by David Montgomery; 5 below Deidi von Schaewen; 6 above left Paul Ryan/International Interiors; 6 below right IPC Magazines Ltd/Robert Harding Syndication; 10-11 Jean-Pierre Godeaut; 12-13 Fritz von der Schulenburg (Jill Barnes-Dacey); 14 Julie Phipps/Arcaid (Antony Sheppard); 15 Nadia Mackenzie; 16 and 17 above left Christian Sarramon; 17 below Simon Brown; 19 Spike Powell/Elizabeth Whiting and Associates; 20 Marie Claire Maison/ Dugied/Postic; 21 below left Derry Moore; 21 below right Osborne & Little; 22 Marie Claire Maison/ Dugied/Postic; 24 Simon Butcher/Houses & Interiors; 25 above Tim Street-Porter (Designer and owner: Kathryn Ireland); 25 below left Paul Ryan/ International Interiors; 25 below right Simon Brown; 26 left Camera Press; 26-7 Geoffrey Frosh (Designed by Stephen Calloway and Oriel Harwood); 27 right Elle Decoration/ Dan Lepard; 29 above Michael Dunne/Elizabeth Whiting and Associates; 29 below Paul Ryan/International Interiors; 30 below left Christian Sarramon; 31 Deidi von Schaewen (Designers: Paul Mathieu & Michael Ray); 32 above Trevor Richards (Timney Fowler); 32-3 above Paul Ryan/International Interiors; 32 below Tim Beddow/ Elizabeth Whiting and Associates; 34 above left IPC Magazines Ltd/Robert Harding Syndication; 34-5 Deidi von Schaewen (Designer: Sylvie Blanchet); 36 above Paul Ryan/International Interiors; 36 below Fritz von der Schulenburg (Julia Boston); 37 Paul Ryan/Internartional Interiors; 38 below left Derry Moore; 38-9 above Agence Top/Roland Beaufre (Chez Gerard Dalmon et Pierre Staudenmeyer – Galerie Neotu, Paris); 39 below left Derry Moore; 40 above David Parmiter/Abode; 40 below left Jerome Darblay; 40 below right Fritz von der Schulenburg (Stephanie Hoppen); 41 Paul Ryan/ International Interiors; 42 above Laura Ashley Ltd; 42-3 below Deidi von Schaewen (Designer: Sylvie Blanchet); 43 above Laura Ashley Ltd; 43 below right Jerome Darblay; 44-5 Christian Sarramon; 45 above right Paul Ryan/ International Interiors; 45 below right Simon Brown; 50 above Simon McBride; 50 below left Stylograph/ Cote Sud/Ingalill Snitt; 50 below right Jean-Pierre Godeaut; 51 Courtesy of Designers Guild, photograph David Montgomery; 54 Fritz von der Schulenburg (Monika Apponyi); 55 above Simon Upton/Elizabeth Whiting and Associates; 55 below left Fritz von der Schulenburg (Lars Bolander); 55 below right Tom Leighton/ Elizabeth Whiting and Associates; 58 left Courtesy of Designers Guild, photograph by David Montgomery; 59 above right Fritz von der Schulenburg (George Spencer); 59 below left Fritz von der Schulenburg (Stephen Ryan); 59 below right Jean-Pierre Godeaut; 62 above Trevor Richards (Timney Fowler); 62 below left Marie Claire Maison/Dugied/ Bayle; 62 below right Marie Claire Maison/Dugied/ Postic; 63 above Camera Press; 63 below Agence Top/ Pascal Chevallier (Decoration: Christian Badin); 66 left Simon McBride; 66 above right Marie Claire Maison/Bailhache/Ardouin; 66 below right Marie Claire Maison/Bailhache/Rozensztroch; 67 above Stylograph/Maison Francaise/Beaud-Cartier; 67 below Camera Press;70 above Fritz von der Schulenburg (Elgahammar, Sweden); 70 below right Stylograph/ Primois; 71 above left Collection La Passementerie Nouvelle, France; 71 below left Jerome Darblay; 71 right Derry Moore; 74 above Fritz von der Schulenburg (Laura Ashley); 74 below left Derry Moore; 74 below right Derry Moore (Nicholas Haslam); 75 above Agence Top/Roland Beaufre (Decoration: Yves Taralon); 75 below Andreas von Einsiedel/Elizabeth Whiting and Associates; 76 Fritz von der Schulenburg (Colefax & Fowler); 77 below left Paul Ryan/International Interiors; 77 below right Collection La Passementerie Nouvelle, France; 78 below left Courtesy of Designers Guild, photograph by David Montgomery; 78 below right Osborne & Little; 79 above Elle Decoration/ James Merrell; 79 below Marie Claire Maison/ Limbourg/Billaud; 84 Courtesy of Designers Guild, photograph by David Montgomery; 90 Stylograph/ Cote Sud/G.de Laubier; 92 Arthur Sanderson and Sons Ltd; 96 above Paul Ryan/International Interiors; 97 Belle; 98 Michael Dunne/Elizabeth Whiting and Associates; 100 Fritz von der Schulenburg (Laura Ashley); 101 Camera Press; 102 left Agence Top/Pascal Chevallier (Decoration; Francoise Dorget, Paris); 102 right Maire Claire Maison/Dugied/Bayle; 103 Jean-Paul Bonhommet; 104 Fritz von der Schulenburg (Mimmi O'Connell); 105 Derry Moore; 106 Derry Moore; 110 Belle; 113 Laura Ashley Ltd;114-5 Lars Hallen/ Design Press; 116 Walter Smalling Jr; 118 Debi Trelor/Anna Owen/Elizabeth Whiting and Associates; 123 above IPC Magazines Ltd/Robert Harding Syndication; 123 below Trevor Richards (Timney Fowler); 125 below Peter Woloszynski; 130 Spike Powell/ Elizabeth Whiting and Associates; 131 Deidi von Schaewen (Designer: Andrée Putman); 133 Agence Top/Pascal Chevallier(Decoration: Henri Garnelli, Paris); 138 Laura Ashley Ltd; 139 Jean-Paul Bonhommet; 140 left Agence Top/Pascal Chevallier (Chez l'antiquaire Catherine Arigoni, Paris); 140 right IPC Magazines Ltd/Robert Harding Syndication; 141 left Jean-Paul Bomhommet; 144 Ingalill Snitt; 148 Vogue Living/ Anthony Amos; 149 Marie Claire Maison/Dugied/ Bayle; 152 left Belle; 153 Christian Sarramon; 154 Marie Claire Maison/Dugied/Bayle (Designer: Danie Postel-Vinay); 156 Deidi von Schaewen (curtains hand-painted by Claudie & Carine Mandel); 157 Paul Ryan/ International Interiors; 158 Fritz von der Schulenburg; 159 Fritz von der Schulenburg (Graham Rust);160 John Hall; 161 Fritz von der Schulenburg (Barbara Thornhill); 162 Elle Decoration/James Wedge; 163 Vogue Living/Geoff Lung; 164 Deidi von Schaewen (Designer: Fabricio Bruschi; 170 Nadia Mackenzie (Clare Moseley); 171 above Paul Ryan/International Interiors; 171 below left Fritz von der Schulenburg (Andrew Wadsworth); 175 Colefax & Fowler; 176 Laura Ashley Ltd; 178-9 Jean-Paul Bonhommet.

THE FOLLOWING PHOTOGRAPHS WERE SPECIALLY TAKEN FOR HOMES & GARDENS: 4 below Robin Matthews; 6 below left Jan Baldwin; 6 centre right David Parmiter; 17 above right Jan Baldwin; 18 Trevor Richards; 21 above Michael Dunne; 28 above James Merrell; 28 below Henry Bourne; 30 above James Merrell; 30 below right James Merrell; 33 above right James Merrell; 33 below right David Parmiter; 34 below left Trevor Richards; 39 above right Kudos; 46 Robin Matthews; 58-9 above Trevor Richards; 96 below James Merrell; 98-9 Michael Dunne;120-1 Jan Baldwin; 122 Trevor Richards; 134 James Merrell; 135 Trevor Richards; 141 right James Merrell (Designer: Sally Anne Sturt); 142 Simon Brown; 147 Trevor Richards; 168 James Merrell; 171 below right Jan Baldwin. With thanks to Robert Harding Syndication.

THE FOLLOWING PHOTOGRAPHS WERE SPECIALLY TAKEN FOR CONRAN OCTOPUS: 70 below left, 150 Jan Baldwin (courtesy John Hardy): 4 above, 6, 8, 127 Nadia Mackenzie (courtesy: Anita Hildreth of George Spencer Decorations): 48-9, 52-3, 56-7, 60-1, 64-5, 68-9, 72-3.76, 78, 166, 172-4, Michael Newton (styled by Ruth Prentice and Camilla Bambrough); 124, 127, 129, 137 Shona Wood (courtesy of Ruth White and Jeffrey Leff); 125 above, 152 right (courtesy of Nadine Bazar).